DETERMINED

Cindi Hart

You never know where the road through life will take you.

Enjoy the ride!

Cindi Hart

First published by Dog Ear Publishing
4010 W. 86th Street, Ste H
Indianapolis, IN 46268
www.dogearpublishing.net

ISBN: 978-1-4575-3061-6

Library of Congress Control Number: has been applied for

This book is printed on acid-free paper.

Printed in the United States of America

My life is dedicated, as well as this book, to:

My parents, Sydney and Herb Pfaff, who not only gave me life,
but gave me the strength to persevere.

Ken, my loving husband who has put up with all of my wild ideas
and continues to love me, hair or no hair, breasts or no breast,
bike or no bike.

And to my beautiful daughter Madison, who inspires me daily and gives
me comfort in knowing that there is hope for the future.

Mike Walden, who helped shape who I am today.

This book is also dedicated to the many lives I have met who have been
impacted by cancer and in memory of those we have lost.

INTRODUCTION

You never know who might be standing next to you in line at the grocery store or perhaps sitting nearby at a restaurant. The world they have seen may be far from what you would ever imagine; their life experience could hold hidden scars and triumphs we might never guess from their outward appearance.

When we meet people for the first time we tend to sum up everything in the first seven seconds: How old do they appear? Are they married or single? Could they have children or grandkids? Are they educated, working, going to school or retired? By looking in their eyes one might get a glimpse of their life through those small windows into the soul.

Each life encountered has a unique story. When most people first meet me they are likely to see just another middle-aged woman living a normal middle-class life. However, friends who really know me will tell you there is nothing normal about my life. While I am not a secret agent, tightrope walker, or big game hunter, I have had some extraordinary adventures.

When I meet someone new, I'm never quite certain how much I should reveal about myself. Should I keep things light by sharing only partial information? Or do I go into some of the deeper levels of my life? Usually, I find out about the other person first and wonder if they might benefit from what I have to share or if they would even care or believe what I could tell them.

I live my life to the best of my ability and feel compelled to share it at times—perhaps this is my way of processing some of the things I have been through. If my experience could help just one person, then it would add meaning to some of the challenges I have faced.

I invite you to read and judge for yourself. Did my life and adventures happen accidentally or did they truly happen for a reason? Perhaps, after reading my story, you will view life a bit differently than before. Maybe YOU are a part of my purpose. Perhaps you will be *determined* to find your purpose.

* * *

PART I – The Road Traveled

My heavy eyelids lifted sluggishly to reveal blurry gray and white shapes around me. As I struggled to open them, I could barely make out the shape of a clock on the wall across the room. I was on my back in an unfamiliar bed and did not recognize anything around me. Confused, I thought to myself, "I must have been really tired last night because I don't remember going to sleep here."

A soft hand touched my arm and I turned my head to the right in response. A kind face leaned into my view. Familiar red hair came into focus accompanied by my mother's voice speaking in quiet comforting tones. "Cindi, can you hear me? You're in the hospital," she said while stroking my hair.

The hospital bed was in an alcove with dividers on each side of the bed which were open to observation by the nurses stationed nearby. Colorful cards and signs of good wishes from friends and family covered the walls that surrounded me. "What happened?" I asked with a weak dry voice. My mother replied, "You were hit by a car. You were in an accident." "Car? I don't remember a car." I responded with a giggle. There was no reason behind my giggle, it just happened. Moments later I asked again, "What happened?" This was not the first time, nor the last that she would answer that same question in the days to come. She patiently repeated, "You were in an accident. You were hit by a car."

A nurse came in and pulled back the white sheet. I looked down at my legs. My right leg was entirely encased in a large plaster cast from my foot all the way up to my hip. Something wasn't right. Pain shot into my consciousness when I tried to move the heavy plaster sculpted leg. Regaining some of my focus, I could see the legs that had been hidden under the sheet did not look like MY legs. I remembered that I had strong muscles and the legs I saw did not match what I recalled.

Another face came into view. "Good morning Cindi. I'm going to shine a light in your eyes," she announced. Suddenly a bright painful light obscured everything from sight. I closed my eyes and turned my head away. "Can you squeeze my fingers?" she asked as she picked up both my hands in hers. I blinked and then giggled. "Do you know what day it is?" she asked. I winced in pain as I tried to adjust my position. She said, "Today is Monday, April 16th, 1984 and you are in the Monroe Regional Hospital," then turned and said something to my mother that I didn't understand.

My leg started announcing pain that demanded to be noticed. I tried to move and became very restless. A different woman came into sight and put something in my IV while mother held my hand and whispered in my ear, "Lie still. You need to stay still. You have been through a lot." I closed my eyes again and the voices got farther and farther away. I slowly drifted off, trying to remember happier times.

*   *   *

Frigid air bit at my face when my father first took me to Smith pond in the winter of 1965. Snow had fallen the night before, making the ground and trees around the pond sparkle in the morning sun. Soft mounds of new snow created a smooth, rolling landscape surrounding the ice below. The air was flavored with the earthy aroma of wood fires burning in old oil drums at the edge of the pond, drawing people in to get warm.

I was four years old when we first tramped through the crusty snow to that icy wonderland in Middletown, Ohio. My father had been there many times before, but that day was a special day for me. I was going to go ice skating. "Watch and learn," he told me as he tightened the skates on my feet and I started to stand. My grip tightened around his fingers and my feet wobbled with a new challenge. "It's ok. I've got you," he reassured.

Cautiously we stepped out onto the ice and as my feet started to move, with what seemed to be a will of their own, my grip clenched ever tighter. He peeled my fingers from his and soared away as I stood frozen in place, mesmerized by his every move and terrified that I would fall. I watched as he skated, gliding like a leaf in the wind, swooping and turning across the frosty surface as I stayed glued in place, afraid to move. I longed to be able to soar across the ice like he did and was determined to watch and learn.

For years to follow, I looked forward to the chance to skate on that pond. The annual invasion of winter ice and snow transformed the park into a new playground for skaters like me. The sound of the ice heaving and cracking would spread like thunder beneath our feet with a foreboding thrill of danger and adventure.

I would out skate the retiring sun and consciously resist hearing my parents call me to warm up by the fire. I pretended not to hear and skated farther away because I knew that my time on the ice was soon coming to an end. When my father was finally able to shepherd me to the log benches beside the edge of the ice, the struggle began to pull off my skates.

Cold feet and toes did not matter while I skated, but once the skates came off my toes burned and prickled from the rush of blood flowing back into them. They complained loudly that they had been squished into the skates and forced to heed my will. My cheeks were on fire, but I didn't care because the joy in my heart was worth the stinging aftereffects.

Years later, when the Winter Olympics were televised in 1972, I sat trans-fixed as I studied the figure skaters and listened intently to all the commentators' remarks. Later I tried to duplicate the moves I had seen, however, not always on

---

4

the ice. My mother's white speckled linoleum kitchen floor revealed the scars my skate blades inflicted with my attempts to replicate Olympic inspired moves. My performance was always better in the kitchen than on real ice. Perhaps my stable skating partner, the table, and the linoleum 'rink' gave me confidence. The table supported me well, much like I thought a real partner might, as I attempted to jump. In this make believe world, I improved with every leap, much to my mother's chagrin.

*　　*　　*

Pain and dizziness were apparent as I became more alert and aware of my surroundings in the neurological intensive care unit. My mother stayed at my side, with great determination to oversee my care and act as my private duty nurse. I had been in a coma for two and a half weeks as the result of a skull fracture and a subdural hematoma (swelling and bleeding under the skull, putting pressure on the brain.) From my perspective, it seemed I had only slept for a single night. They had given me a drug called Mannitol to reduce the swelling in my brain and save my life.

The nursing staff spoke primarily with my mother. "We rarely get patients who come out of a coma after head injuries like hers," I overheard a voice say, as I lie there with eyes closed trying to understand and remember what had happened. "She is a very lucky girl," someone said "I know." my mother answered. "We didn't think we would ever get to see light in those eyes again."

The days and the nights blurred together and I didn't know what time or day it was. I slept for long periods of time and would often wake disoriented, no matter how often my mother reminded me.

Surviving head trauma created real problems with my memory. Eventually I remembered being on a bike, but not being struck by a car. The retrograde amnesia was likely a blessing. Who would ever want to remember such a horrific experience? What I did remember was how much I loved to ride my bike.

*　　*　　*

My brother, Scott, and I were both born in July and our birthdays were often combined in one party for us both. My seventh birthday and his third were celebrated with the traditional cake and ice cream party. We had been running around the living room on a sugar high, playing Batman and Robin, when we were interrupted and ushered to the front screen door. I stretched up on tiptoes and peered out through the mesh window. What I saw made my heart pound in my chest. Attention was focused on my father pushing a bicycle up the sidewalk. It was not his size or my brother's, it was MY size.

It was love at first sight. The purple frame had upright handlebars with pink streamers, a pearly white banana seat and a sissy bar on the back. The bike beckoned to me. "This bike is mine?" I asked, with hope hanging in the air. "It's all yours." were the words that triggered tears to stream down my cheeks and onto my cake stained shirt. This was the first time I remembered crying because I was happy.

The bike had training wheels, but I was determined—since I was seven— I did not need them. They lasted about an hour before I begged to have them removed because seven year old big kids did not need training wheels, or so I thought. Fifteen minutes after they were removed I had my first close encounter with the pavement. Undeterred, I brushed off my knees and took the bike even further. The rest of the summer was spent riding up and down the alleyway alongside our house.

A few years later, my mother's dream to live on a farm in the country was granted. My alleyway was replaced with pastureland and cornfields—not the best place for a nine year old to ride a bike. Banana seats and sissy bars were exchanged for a saddle on a pony and a small tractor. Scott and I spent our summers playing outside on a rope swing hanging from a tall elm tree, tending chickens, picking cherries and creating imaginary fortresses in the nearby woods.

*   *   *

Intent on bringing me back from my initial vegetative state, my Mom worked tirelessly to try to help me regain as much function and memory possible. She decorated the area around my hospital bed with pictures of family and friends and tried to orient me to person, place and time every day. "Today is April 18th, 1984, and you are in the Monroe Regional Hospital in Ocala, Florida," she would tell me. "You had an accident that broke your leg and you have a skull fracture." Then she'd ask, "Do you remember where you are?" I would usually just nod and say, "In the hospital," and then giggle. She was very relieved to see that I was starting to be able to understand and follow directions.

Dedicated and driven, Mom did everything she could think of to help me feel comfortable in the strange surroundings. She brought personal items to the hospital like my favorite pillow and the teddy bear I had slept with for years.

Once the swelling in my brain subsided and I was neurologically stable, they scheduled surgery on my leg to install a fracture reduction plate and five screws to stabilize the shattered bones. After that I had a new cast that covered my lower leg only. This was an improvement over a full leg cast, but I wondered if skating would ever be possible again.

The day after Thanksgiving in 1975, long before anyone even heard of the big holiday shopping day called "Black Friday," my father introduced me to indoor ice skating. He discovered a skating rink on the north side of Dayton, an hour's drive from our small farm, but well worth every mile traveled in my opinion. The rink was just like ones I had seen on television with a surface smooth as glass. My fingers trembled with excitement as I hurriedly laced my skates in anticipation of gliding across the surface void of the bumps, ripples and cracks that I had grown so accustomed to on the pond.

Skaters of all abilities swarmed the entry gate, waiting anxiously for the ice smoothing machine called a Zamboni to leave. Once it left the ice, the entry gate swung open and skaters charged out to make their mark on the pristine ice. It seemed a shame when the hockey skaters marred the surface the instant their skates hit the hard white sheet of perfection.

After gliding around the perimeter and getting accustomed to the flow of people on the rink, I migrated to the center where the figure skaters collected. I began skating with them and emulating the moves my father did many times on the pond. I studied and worked to adapt my moves to mimic theirs. Again, my father's words echoed in my ears, "watch and learn."

Melodies drifted over our heads from the speakers above, prompting my movements, as if I were a puppet and the music pulled the strings. On the pond, the only music I skated to came from my heart and my head. I began matching my moves on the ice to the meter of the music. Between the smooth ice and the expressive instrumentals, my confidence began to grow. I became bolder and more adventurous, oblivious to any onlookers. The speed of my skates whipped my hair back and the feel of the ice took me to a world of my own. In a way it seemed I had just been given a new pair of wings and I soared.

A figure skating coach had been standing in the crowd and approached me from the edge of the rink. "I've not seen you here before. What club do you skate with?" he asked. "I don't belong to any clubs." I quietly replied, shrinking back, hesitant to talk to him, as he was a stranger. "We have a figure skating club here and I think you should come to our practice. There are instructors that would work with you," he said. Shocked and thrilled at the same time, I rushed to find my father and asked him to talk to the man. "She needs to become a member of the United States Figure Skating Association and then she would be able compete." he explained, "We have classes and coaches that can help." By the time we left, I had a hand full of papers to read and fill out clutched tightly to my chest.

All the way home, I was floating on air. Someone besides my parents thought I was good enough to skate with a club. It was the last thing I thought before drifting off to sleep and the first thing upon opening my eyes in the morning. My mind was filled with nothing but skating for weeks.

The cost of the lessons combined with the drive back and forth to the ice rink was financially difficult. My father worked as a firefighter and my mother *was attending nursing school, so money was tight, but somehow they made it happen. We soon discovered that learning to skate was easy for me and it did not take long to realize that I was much better at jumping than spinning. I had inherited my father's strong legs that gave me the strength to gather speed and jump. I learned to put more pressure into the ice and build the speed needed to accomplish the jumps.*

My first real competition on ice was brutal. I felt proud of my performance, however, after I finished skating, the primary judge shuffled up to me in her full length fur coat and matching hat, looking down at me over her lifted chin. Her first words were "Unless you have been in a major competition by the age of thirteen, you are wasting your time." She knew my age from the competition sheet in her hand. I was fourteen and her comment, combined with her tone, hurt. Did this woman think there was no reason to skate other than to compete in a major competition? In the blink of an eye, my joy in skating was crushed by a complete stranger. I later learned that her daughter was one of the skaters in my division.

After the shock dissipated, I realized that I skated because I loved it, not because anyone else liked or disliked the way I looked on the ice. It was the freedom and ability to express myself that mattered. That was the end of my lessons in figure skating but not the end of my love for skating. I felt as though I had "watched and learned" enough to know what I wanted.

* * *

The world seemed to be moving quickly and without me. Once the nurse's assistant finished changing the sheets on my hospital bed, vital signs were taken and food trays were placed in front of me long before I could understand what was expected of me. When someone spoke, I closed my eyes to focus on their words. I wasn't trying to shut out the words; I was trying to force their words into my brain.

The hospital staff told my parents that most patients in the neurological ICU who are fortunate enough to regain consciousness typically responded with odd, uncharacteristic behavior and would often curse without realizing it. Sometimes sweet little old church ladies would open their mouths and spew vulgar profanity without intent.

I didn't speak much or curse at all, I just giggled at everything.

"Here is your dinner," my mother would say as she opened the carton of milk on my tray. I giggled. For days, each time she said or asked anything, I gave the same response.

"Do you want me to cut up your Salisbury steak?" I giggled.

"You got a card from Cindy Lawrence. Do you want me to read it to you?" I giggled.

"Look at these beautiful flowers from Ted and Velma!" I giggled.

"They are going to try to move you in the bed now and it may hurt."
I giggled.

"You were riding your bike and got hit by a car." Again, my response was the same.

Giggling seemed to be the only response I was capable of giving.

Even though I had no recollection of a car hitting me, I did begin to remember the first time I started riding my bike seriously.

*   *   *

Riding my bicycle was my primary mode of transportation on the campus of Miami University, which had the bone chilling, bitter winds of the Midwest. I started riding five miles at a time from class to class and around the campus while enrolled in the same nursing school my mother had attended.

One blustery winter morning I discovered a handwritten invitation posted on a campus billboard above the rack where I locked my bike. It was announcing a bike club meeting at a local church. This would be my first exposure to an organized group of riders.

When I walked into the dark, richly decorated chapel, people were setting up rollers in the greeting area. Rollers are, for all intents and purposes, a treadmill for bicycles where a bike is balanced on top of cylinders connected by belts that respond to the spinning of the bike wheels. Imagine a running treadmill where the walking surface has been removed and the rider on the bike is the motor that turns the cylinders.

All eyes turned to see a rider named Aldo precariously perched atop his Italian bike, negotiating the rollers. He gradually increased the intensity of his pedaling until suddenly the wobbling transitioned into a smooth and steady hum. By balancing his bike on the rollers he had transformed himself into a cycling machine.

I stood transfixed as Aldo dominated the silver cylinders, pedaling like a man possessed. His legs bobbed up and down in a blur as the sound of the rollers flooded the room with a growing roar. Someone turned on a fan as sweat dripped from his furrowed brow hidden beneath a sweat band. His legs attacked the pedals like two alternating sewing machine needles, combined with the balance of a tightrope walker. All this captivated my attention and my father's words, once again echoed in my ears. Watch and learn.

With a mutual interest in cycling, we became fast friends. His real name was Jim Ross but he preferred to be called Aldo, as it was a good Italian name. Was he Italian? I doubt it. Although his angular features, thick dark hair and slight, yet muscular, build could have easily passed for Italian. He simply liked Italian bikes and their style of racing. He told me about an upcoming race that he planned to enter and suggested that I might consider racing in the women's event.

When I mentioned to my parents that I wanted to participate in a bike race, they were very supportive and encouraging. My father had raced motorcycles when I was very young and he appeared excited at the possibility that I might race. I had no idea what I was doing, but decided to go for it anyway.

Without any real cycling clothing or knowledge of where to find some, I studied what other people wore. We decided that I should have the proper uniform to be in a race. Riders wore jerseys made of Lycra with pockets in the back, black form fitting shorts, gloves with leather palms and stiff soled shoes. The helmet and gloves I had, but I didn't know anything about buying cycling clothing and the bike shops seemed to only have men's clothing so I decided to make my own.

Searching local fabric stores for anything that resembled what I had seen on other riders, I discovered swim suit material and was satisfied. The selection was limited, but I chose powder blue with little pink dots throughout the fabric for the body and made the sleeves and pockets solid blue. I found fashion shorts that looked like cycling shorts, but later realized, much to my discomfort, that there was no padding in the saddle area where it is crucial. After finding tennis shoes that had stiff soles and were narrow enough to fit in the toe clips on the pedals, I at least came close to looking the part.

On a cool morning in April, my parents accompanied me to my first race in Cincinnati. The course twisted and turned through an undulating wooded park called Burnett Woods. The trees, still barren of leaves, allowed spectators to follow the flash of racer's jerseys as they flickered through the trees like colored strobe lights. I surveyed my surroundings while standing in line to register under a covered picnic shelter, shivering from a combination of chill in the air and fear in my heart.

I knew nothing about bike racing, having never even seen a race before, let alone been in one. As I stood at the start with women on racing bikes who had jerseys that displayed the names of different clubs and sponsors, I realized I was in over my head.

I might as well have printed "Newbie" on mine, because I made all the classic first time racer mistakes. I shot off from the start with no warm-up or prep, pumping my legs as fast as possible and went straight to the front as hard and quickly as my lungs would allow. As we rounded the sweeping course, a male voice in the crowd shouted, "Sit on her Nancy!" Every lap I heard, "Stay on her wheel!" or some variation of the same message. I was in the lead and the only sound behind me at that point was the shifting and the breathing of a single rider. I knew it must be Nancy.

The finish was approaching and I spotted my parents on the side of the road, cheering, as we gained speed. Excitement built as I pedaled closer and closer to victory, but in the blink of an eye, Nancy passed me within inches of the finish line to win the race. My parents met me after the finish and told me how well I had done. Although relieved that the race was over, I was disappointed that

Nancy had taken advantage of me. I quickly realized that this had been another "Watch and learn" moment.

The satisfaction of victory was mine for barely an instant before it was snatched away. The fleeting taste of victory was sweet and motivated me to want to learn how to get it back. After that race I started training with other racers and learned a lot about drafting.

*　*　*

"Every day you were in a coma, it rained." My father told me. "But the day you woke up the rain stopped and the sun came out to shine." My parents spent weeks sleeping in a small motel close to the hospital and had come to know the nursing staff very well as they were at the hospital each day. They visited like clockwork; arriving to help with bathing and eating as well as trying to help me regain my memory and ability to speak once again.

One morning, my parents brought two more visitors with them. Upon entering my area Mom said, "Cindi, do you see who came with us this morning?" The first visitor stood tall above my bed with familiar brown eyes and red hair. He reached out and touched my left hand, looking uncomfortable seeing me in a hospital environment. His full name seemed to be erased from my memory, but I did remember the first letter of his name. "Ssss" I tried. "It's Scott," my mother prompted. "It's okay, Mom." my brother said "Don't push her."

Behind Scott another visitor waited to be introduced. His sandy brown hair, mustache and glasses looked familiar. He stepped forward, "Hey there." he said as he reached down and took my hand. His name had also been erased and I was unable to recall even the first letter. Then my lips parted, "I remember you." I said, "You have a brother named Mark." A grin peeked out from beneath his ever present mustache and my parents laughed for the first time in the weeks since the accident.

Before he left my bedside he leaned over and kissed me ever so gently on the cheek. I placed my hand over the spot his lips touched with wonder and couldn't respond. The next day when he came back to visit he kissed me again. "That was a kiss and my name is Ken," he whispered.

*　*　*

I first met Ken at a bike ride in Oxford, Ohio—not far from Miami University campus— in 1982. He was riding with his fiancée Sylvia, his brother Mark, and his best friend Mike Kearns. The three men looked like brothers as they shared riding styles, inside jokes and wore matching Dayton Cycling Club team jerseys with caps stretched over leather strap helmets. Riding with them was entertaining at the least. I learned that Ken had coached both Mark and Sylvia through several National Championships and that Mark could burp the alphabet and do the Limbo while riding his bike. Good things to know.

The pace was comfortable and I stayed with their group for most of the ride. Three quarters of the way through the tour, a cyclist in front of me unexpectedly slammed on his brakes and before it was possible to react, I found myself on the ground. The rider that caused the crash rode away completely unconcerned with what had transpired behind him due to his carelessness.

Mike, Ken, and Mark stopped to help me and made sure I was okay. They told me that I had not done anything wrong and said it was the fault of the other rider. "He's a jerk, do you want me to catch him and knock him down?" asked Mark. "No," I said, brushing off my bike. "I don't think he did it on purpose." Mike, a kind and true gentleman stayed and rode with me the rest of the ride while Ken and Mark raced up to rejoin the main pack.

At the finish, I waited for my father in the parking lot. "What happened to you?" he asked, questioning the abrasions on my leg. "Someone slammed on their brakes. I was too close and went down." I answered. "She wasn't too close; they shouldn't have put on their brakes like that." Mike piped in. I introduced Mike as the rider who stayed with me to assure I was alright after the crash. Mike then asked if we would like to meet the group at Taco Bell in Middletown and we agreed.

We drove to the nearest Taco Bell, purchased our food, and sat waiting. Alas, they never appeared. Discouraged, we went home not realizing that Middletown was a two Taco Bell town and they had gone to the other side where they waited for us. In retrospect, if we met as planned, my life might have been significantly different.

I continued riding and racing and soon won a race in Cincinnati at Union Station. It was a Criterium: a type of race held on a closed course, usually around a few city blocks, and no longer than half a mile. The race is composed of many laps and includes sprints for prizes within the race, called primes. Primes are announced during the race with the ringing of a bell and the announcer informing the riders what the prize is. "We have a twenty dollar prime on the next lap. The winner of the next lap gets twenty dollars!" The course in Cincinnati consisted of many tight sweeping corners and I timed my final sprint well enough to jump out of the last turn and win the race.

After the awards presentation, my father and I, still basking in the glory of winning, were approached by someone from the Dayton Cycling Club. He suggested that I should race for their women's team which included several international caliber women. He gave us the name of the team coach and told us that if we ever needed any bike parts we should contact Kenny. A few days later, my father told me that I should contact "that Ken guy" to order a pair of new wheels.

"Kenny" turned out to be Ken Blauvelt from the Oxford bike ride where I fell. He not only managed and coached the Dayton cycling team, but also drove the team to all the races. He was the "go-to" guy for anyone who needed bike parts. Having met him the year before and remembering that he was engaged to Sylvia, I found it rather awkward to call him. My father persisted so much that I finally gave in.

After we talked a few times on the phone about bike parts, the best deals on wheels and racing, Ken asked if I wanted to go for a ride with him. Another cyclist named Chuck had already asked me to join him, but I had not committed. Chuck lived on the north side of Dayton which was over an hour's drive away from my home. "No problem." Ken said. "I could come and ride with you on your roads." "Sure," I thought "Why not? It would save me gas and two hours of driving back and forth."

We rode on some of my favorite backcountry roads with rolling hills and farmland and saw very little traffic. We ended up talking the entire ride. He told me how he and Sylvia had broken up nearly a year ago. She was in medical school and things just didn't work out. He explained how he started riding in pursuit of a Boy Scout merit badge and he had been racing since he was fourteen years old. He had traveled with his brother Mark to nationals and cross country when he worked for Huffy. Before we knew it, we had completed the ride and the miles seemed to have flown by.

In July, Ken suggested that Aldo and I carpool with him to bike races. Ken liked to drive and for young, financially compromised bike racers with student loans to pay off, this made sense. After that, we started training together on a regular basis. He was eager to introduce me to a specially constructed race track for bicycles in Indianapolis. Major Taylor Velodrome, a 333 meter concrete oval with twenty seven degree banking that was designed for a type of bike racing where riders use fixed gear bikes, which have no breaks and cannot coast. People are often very intimidated by the thought of no brakes, but in reality riding the track with no brakes is much safer. No one could slam on the brakes like the rider did that caused the crash in Oxford.

My first experience on the track was in a race on a borrowed track bike. I was very nervous as we rode under the glare and glamor of the "Friday Night Lights" with spectators in the stands and even more lining the boards around the track, cheering.

The race, called an Australian pursuit, took place with multiple riders equally spaced around the track and they chased each other from a standing start. If a rider is passed, they are out of the competition. I was frightened and trembling as Ken accompanied me to my starting point. He pushed the bike as I walked alongside with my stiff cycling shoes clomping on the hard concrete. "Please Lord, don't let me fall. I don't care if I win or lose, JUST PLEASE DON'T LET ME FALL!" became my mantra.

As I mounted the bike and tightened the straps binding my feet to the pedals, I stood waiting to go. Suddenly the sound of the starting pistol shot through me like an electric shock and I responded by pedaling like my life depended on it. My lungs and mouth went dry from the effort and the lights from the track made everything sparkle and blur. Ken and Aldo cheered for me, but all sounds were muffled and unintelligible. When the signal came that the race was over, the need to go fast was immediately replaced by the need to remember how to stop. I had forgotten that track bikes do not allow riders to coast, so the pedals kicked me and quickly reminded me to keep pedaling. I did not fall and was amazed to discover that I had finished second place to a former national team member named Debbie Melton.

Throughout the rest of the summer Ken drove us to the track every Friday night and on Saturdays and Sundays we raced every Criterium and road race in the Midwest. I had started working at the hospital as a nurse in the pediatric unit and eventually made enough money to afford my own track bike so I no longer needed to borrow one. My life evolved and changed focus as I discovered my passion for speed on two wheels.

*   *   *

On his second visit to my hospital bed, Ken brought a Walkman and headphones with hopes that hearing familiar songs would help trigger memories. He, very thoughtfully, composed a mixed tape with all my favorite music then showed me how to wear the headphones and turned on the tape player.

The music was both comforting and distressing. Although it seemed familiar, I realized that I could no longer remember the words or the names of the songs. I hung on every note searching my mind, trying to associate a thought, a word or an image with each one. I knew I should remember the words, but they didn't come. I closed my eyes to let the music wash over me with the words filling in the blanks.

Prior to the accident, I loved to sing and knew all the words to many songs and musicals. I had often entertained myself on long, solo bike rides by singing the entire Jesus Christ Superstar album. I would sometimes serenade the cows as I rode beside pastures that lined the southwestern Ohio chip-n-seal roads.

*   *   *

During summer break from nursing school in 1981, I worked as a camp counselor at Camp Miami, a United Methodist church camp in the town where I grew up. We camped in platform tents with one that housed a female counselor with five female campers and another for the male counselor and his campers. Life was filled with campfires, songs sung in worship, praise and just plain fun.

The smell of pine trees and wood fires, hearing chirping crickets, navigating the woods by moonlight, and starting matchless campfires will always hold fond memories for me. The fires we used to cook and stay warm became a primary focus of our daily lives. One counselor, a seminary student from Africa named Solomon Avatri, could carry almost anything on his head. He had an

---

                                                     CINDI HART

amazing skill when it came to fire building and asked how long we would like our fires to burn and at what temperature.

Patrick Fee was my co-counselor for a few weeks that summer. He towered above the campers at six feet tall, with dark hair and mustache accompanied by piercing hazel eyes. He always wore a Greek fisherman's cap with blue jeans and was blessed with a booming "ready for radio" voice. Pat's love for life was easily recognizable in his willingness to play, laugh and celebrate every moment possible.

The campers loved him and often used him as a human jungle gym when they found an opportunity. He gladly shared his time and made them feel like they were the most important people in the world. Some campers were from the inner city and had never experienced backwoods camping before. The unknown environment could have been very frightening had Pat not been such a stable influence.

We taught the campers lessons about living with nature, unconditional love, and respect for God and each other. The counselors served as role models and attempted to teach them by example. Using songs to bring us together in unity and fellowship, our voices lifted up and entwined like the smoke from the campfire, reaching toward the star filled skies above.

We remained completely isolated from the outside world that entire summer and I learned so much about myself during that time. I realized that the campers depended on me for judgment and protection. My daily decisions mattered and I believed that everything I did could have meaning.

My confidence as a leader was born during that experience. After camp came to an end in August, we all returned to the harsh reality of the modern world and our college lives, but I felt that the lessons learned from my experience would stay with me for a lifetime.

Singing and music continued to be a strong thread in my life. Spending summers at camp gave me the confidence to sing out loud and blend my voice with others around the fire. One semester at Miami University, I accompanied a friend to an audition for a part in a campus musical called Dames at Sea. I had no plan to try out myself, but to tag along as moral support. However, once we got there my friend talked me into giving it a try. The director introduced herself as Cindy Lawrence, a recent graduate of Miami with a degree in Theater. I had never heard of Dames at Sea and knew nothing about the theater outside my role as Cinderella in a second grade play; my only singing experience had come from spending summers at camp and singing to cows while riding my bike. I simply went where directed, sang the music they gave me, and danced with the steps they taught. These seemed easy, thanks to my experience in figure skating and high school drill team where I found I needed to watch and learn quickly.

A few days after the auditions, we found a notice outside the theater department door that listed the names selected and roles assigned. My friend pulled me excitedly to the board so we could read through the roster together. He had gotten a part and, much to my amazement, so had I. I had been selected to play the part of Ruby. "Wow, I got a part in the show!" I said. "No," he replied, "You didn't just get a part in the show, you got the lead!"

Disbelief flooded my mind as I swam through the realization of the role I had been given. We started rehearsals with read-throughs and meetings with the music director and main director, Cindy. One of the actors was unable to carry out the commitment of their role and it was announced that there would be open auditions for his part. Thinking he would be perfect for the part, I convinced my brother to audition. Scott had an exceptional voice and musical talent and he was immediately selected as the right choice for the part.

Cindy and I spent long hours after classes, working on choreography and dance steps. She taught me how to tap dance and we frequently discussed life and love. We quickly became best friends; the kind that talk for hours on the phone without ever wanting to hang up. She became my sister for life.

The show ended up being a lot more fun than I imagined and the cast and crew had a great time being ridiculously campy in the presentation. Cindy and I brought out the best in each other, as only a true friendship could. She had music in her soul that was just looking for a way to get out. I shared my experience working at church camp with her and talked her into interviewing for a position at Camp Miami. She listened to my advice and was in turn given the position as camp director. It was there that she discovered her true path in life and decided to pursue her masters degree in divinity.

*   *   *

Interacting with family and staff in the hospital helped me regain my memory, although it was exhausting and frustrating at times. I initially experienced difficulty comprehending what people said, because they talked faster than my brain was able to understand. I also tended to favor my left ear over my right. The ringing in my ears was distracting and I assumed it was due to the head trauma. I constantly said things like "Huh" or "What" or simply guessed at what people were saying and ended up with some pretty entertaining twists on what was actually said.

It became worse when people spoke to me in a noisy situation. For example, it was difficult to comprehend what was being said when there was music in the background, IV alarms beeping or others talking at the same time. I studied faces as people spoke in an attempt to understand and remember what they were saying. After it became obvious that I wasn't getting all that was being said, many tests were ordered. After the results had been analyzed, it was determined that my ears worked fine despite the fact that there was swelling behind my right ear. That conclusion indicated that the trauma affected my brain's ability to differentiate a single voice from the cacophony of sound in the room, as the overlapping sounds became noise to me. I felt frustrated and embarrassed having to keep asking people to repeat themselves and tried with all my focus to understand what was said, although it was very difficult.

*   *   *

During the summer of 1983, after I graduated from nursing school, Ken and I began spending more free time together—on and off the bikes—and I got to know his family. His mother was about five feet tall and fairly round in stature. She wore metal rimmed glasses, and had curly gray hair with eyes that shined bright with warmth, compassion and obvious love for her family. Initially, it was hard to understand her because she was profoundly deaf and spoke with a deaf voice—classically high pitched and monotone.

Her parents had not wanted her to learn American Sign Language so they enrolled her in a new program in the early 1940's that taught lip reading. At a very early age, she went to a special school to learn how to understand speech by reading the faces and lips of people as they spoke. This was how she was able to communicate in the hearing world. Her name was Edna Ruth, but family referred to her as "Mumsy." After graduating as Valedictorian from a hearing high school, she attended college with no handicap support. There was no doubt that this woman was very intelligent and exceptionally gracious.

Later in life, Mumsy joined a church which included a large deaf congregation and became a Sunday school teacher. She decided that it was time to learn sign language so that she could communicate with others in the deaf community. This was about the same time that I decided to take a Sign Language class at Miami University and it created a strong bond between us. We were able to communicate silently and did not interrupt anyone else with our conversations. I think we both enjoyed the opportunities to practice our new language together.

Ken's father is not deaf and did not know sign language, but didn't need to. He had worked as an engineer with robotics, applying his logical and methodical thought processes in his approach to life. Ken has two sisters: Linda and Susie. Linda, a stylish business woman, with her hair fixed and nails perfectly manicured, found her perfect match when she married her high school sweetheart, Steve. They lived happily together two blocks away from her parents. Susie, the youngest sister, had an affinity for hippos that started as a child and continued as a passion into adulthood. Susie was a kind hearted lover of animals with a creative and artistic eye. Ken's Brother, Mark, was eight years younger than Ken, loved soccer, cycling and fishing. They have a close relationship as they share a love of bike racing, cross-country skiing and traveling.

*   *   *

A few months before my accident, Ken had invited me to his family's Christmas day celebration. They all warmly included and accepted me. Ken surprised me with a package that I knew at first sight was a pair of cross country

*skis. He had taught me how to ski using his equipment on community golf
courses that winter, so a package wrapped in toilet paper, measuring six feet tall
and three inches wide that curved to a point at the top was a sure giveaway.*

*New Year's Eve weekend we traveled to a small family-run tree farm in
Cadillac, Michigan called "Cool's XC Ski Lodge." The tree farm had perfectly
groomed ski trails extending over rolling fields into paths lined with pines. Skiing on a groomed trail, compared to learning on frost covered golf courses in
Dayton, was amazing.*

*The air was cold, crisp and still. The only audible sounds were the skis siz-
zling on the snow beneath our feet, the occasional thump from nearby pine
branches relinquishing their accumulated load onto the soft bed of snow below,
and the beating of my heart.*

*We skied every path available, relenting only when hunger drew us into the
lodge where Ma and Pa Cool had a warm pot of chili waiting on the kitchen
stove. A wood fire in a stone fireplace beckoned us into the main room. We
removed our boots to reveal a rush of burning in our toes as the blood returned
quickly and made its presence known, reminiscent of my days of skating outdoors
at the pond.*

*   *   *

I continued to improve, but the process was slow. They sent a speech
therapist to assess me, and she asked me to read a page of text. This was
incredibly frustrating, as it seemed impossible to get past the first sentence. By the time I got to the end of a sentence I had forgotten what had
happened in the beginning and was forced to start over again, which was
extremely, upsetting. I had always prided myself on my ability to remember things and I loved reading. I often spent countless hours perusing the
works of Louisa May Alcott in middle school and Charles Dickens in High
School. I had memorized and recited the witches' scene in <u>Macbeth</u> in the
fifth grade. Now I was stuck, unable to get through one stupid sentence.

Occupational therapists taught me how to use a fork to feed myself,
while asking questions regarding my orientation to person, place and
time. The routine went like this: "Good morning, what is your name?"
they would ask. "Cindi" I answered. "How old are you?" I often answer
with a giggle. "What year is it?" As uncertainty spread across my face like
a rash they would answer for me, "1984." and wrote on my chart each
time I failed to respond appropriately.

My mother talked to me every day trying to help trigger my memory,
sharing her memories of Scott and me growing up on the farm and saying
how proud she was of us both. Then she would mention bike camp. It
seemed like a lifetime ago with everything that happened, but in reality it
had been a little over a month since I had attended.

A few months before my accident, in February, my mother found a cycling magazine that I had left around the house and discovered an ad for a bicycle training camp in central Florida. She brought it to my attention and after looking at the schedule and the coaching staff bio, I recognized an opportunity to get training from some of the best coaches in the country. My parents were willing to take me to Apopka to attend the camp. What a fabulous opportunity to "Watch and Learn" from the best.

The Walden School of Cycling operated out of a Boy Scout camp called Camp Wewa. Rustic cabins surrounded a central dining hall used for meals and lectures. They were on sandy, leaf covered grounds near a lake that had reported alligator sightings. The cabin's limited accommodations included bunk beds and windows with screens that failed miserably at keeping the bugs out. Moss covered trees acted as a natural canopy, keeping the camp's environmental temperature much cooler than that of the surrounding farmlands.

With limited expectations, we watched with great interest as people started arriving. After I checked in, my parents said their goodbyes, as they were going to stay at the beach while I was at camp. Most of the attendees came from Michigan; the majority lived in the Detroit area. After dinner we all moved the tables and chairs around in an effort to change the dining hall into a lecture hall.

Once everyone had taken their seats, the man at the front of the room started to speak. "Welcome to the Walden School of Cycling. My name is Dale Hughes and I am camp director. Our Wolverine Sports Club has a rich history in bike racing and we are here to help you benefit from our experience."

"Mike Walden, our head coach was a racing legend in the 1940's and 50's along with Clair Young and Jim Smith, who are also part of the coaching staff. These three have been best friends since childhood, but when it came down to a sprint race, they were fierce competitors." Dale gestured to three older gentlemen sitting in the front row. The heaviest of the three, weighing over 275 pounds, stood up wearing a classic driving cap covering his bald head. Gesturing with a right hand that sported a pinky finger skewed far out from the finger's normal range of motion, he blurted "Ah, don't believe a word he says. I would knock any of them down if there was money on the line!" then he sat back down as the crowd laughed.

Dale continued, "Clair Young holds the record for winning more state championship cycling titles than anyone, ever. He continued to win races into his forties, racing against the young pups." With a glorious head of thick white hair, a tan weather-worn face and a sheepish grin, the shortest of the three stood and waved. "Jim and Terry Smith will be helping with skill drills on the golf course and the lunch stops. Jim will also be your bugle player." Dale announced as Jim stood, sporting wavy white hair and a well groomed handlebar mustache to match. "Just wait till you hear what we have in store for you in the morning!" he said with a grin and blue eyes that sparkled.

"These coaches have produced more National, World and Olympic champions than any other sports club in the US. Three of our female riders competed against one another for the world championships on the track, and at least two of them competed in the Winter Olympics in speed skating. In fact, Clair's daughter, Sheila, was the first American to win three medals in one year at the games."

After those impressive introductions, Dale explained the rules of the camp and started lecturing about the drills they planned to teach the next day. My head, already swimming, looked forward to the adventure ahead.

The next morning the clanging dinner bell, and a horrible attempt by Jim Smith at reveille on a bugle, rousted the troops. Campers dragged themselves out to the tennis court, as instructed, to begin group stretching. Mike belted out orders like a drill sergeant. One of his junior officers, Angelo, stood by his side to demonstrate the proper exercise technique. With my background in dance, drill team, and figure skating, this was very easy. After breakfast we divided into skill groups. Since the coaches didn't know me, and had never ridden with me, I was placed in the introductory group. This was fine with me as I was happy to be with any group as long as I was riding.

Christine Hughes, Mike's daughter, was the coach in my first group ride at camp. We pedaled out to an area designated for us to work on the basic skills of cornering and pace line riding. Thrilled to be learning things that I hadn't heard or seen anywhere else, the joy bubbled up inside and I started to sing while riding. After practicing the skills we had covered in lecture, we rode to lunch at a park in Umatilla where Christine approached me and said, "We need to move you up to a faster group. If you can sing while going up hills like that, this is not the right place for you." I was sad to leave the friends I had already made in that group, but moving to another would give me an opportunity to make even more.

Chris Mailing's group was indeed faster. He was a highly structured leader with a clear voice that commanded his troops. We rode in rotating pace lines through the undulating landscape that was covered by fields of orange trees; the pungent odor of their blossoms seemed almost artificial in the early spring breeze.

A couple of times I became so distracted by the joy of the moment that I forgot to slow down at the front of the pace line. This, evidently, was a cardinal sin. During one of these episodes, much to my surprise, Mike Walden drove up to me in a van yelling at the top of his lungs. "Back off and slow down!" he bellowed.

As if this was not enough of a shock, he was driving the van beside me on the sandy right shoulder of the road, alongside the orange groves. He made an impression on me, alright, and I was NOT going to make that mistake again.

In the evenings, the riders were critiqued and schooled in how to improve their form. For example, Mike had often yelled, "Keep your heels down!" when he noticed my pedaling style. I thought they were down until we viewed the video that Dale shot from a motorcycle during the training ride. Video never lies. My toes pointed down so much that I looked like I was riding in ballet slippers.

This helped a great deal to perfect my pedal stroke. In addition to the basics of bike fit and pedaling, they taught us how to corner, ride in groups, climb hills, and to master the timing of sprints and the mechanics of time trials. Once again my father's words came back to me: "Watch and learn." My eyes were now wide open and I was soaking it all in.

The fourth day was a short day, which gave us time to go sightseeing. Since my parents had dropped me off without transportation of my own, I got a ride with a group headed for Daytona Beach. The moment we arrived at the beach and the van doors swung open, I tasted the salt in the air. I took off in a full out sprint for the ocean as soon as my feet hit the sand. Much to my amazement, and to his, I found David Asslin, one of the strong riders from the fast group, running alongside me. Our eyes met, and with recognition of a kindred spirit, we became great friends from that moment on.

The next day David's group invited me to ride one hundred miles with them. By then I had advanced to the fastest group and loved every moment, every pedal stroke and every hill climb. Riding was obviously my passion. I celebrated my accomplishment and now had a new perspective on bike racing.

Camp ended the next morning, long before I was ready for it to be finished. When my parents came to pick me up, I found it difficult to leave all my new found friends and made sure to get everyone's phone number. Having bonded with this wonderful group of people, I felt as though I had become a member of a new family.

While I lingered on saying goodbye, Mike Walden approached my parents and said that he wanted to talk to them for a moment. "As you may know," he said, "I have coached several world champion riders. Many of my best have been women." My parents looked at each other, as they did not know this. "I have seen Cindi improve a lot this week with a little coaching," he continued, "I think she has great potential and natural talent and with the proper training and conditioning, she could be my next champion." My parents seemed stunned. He went on, "She needs to race as much as possible. What kind of training is she getting in Ohio?" "She rides all the time. She loves it," my mother answered. He nodded and said, "I'm planning on taking a few riders with me to race and train in Europe. Let's see if we can make this happen and get her on the team."

On the drive home I started writing down every detail that I learned from the coaching I had long sought. Once I got home and back to work at the *hospital, it did not take long to realize that I knew what I wanted: the 1984 Summer Olympic Games were going to be held in Los Angeles and they had become my new goal.*

*   *   *

Every day in the Neurological ICU, I worked to regain something: memory of what happened a few minutes earlier, ability to recall names or understand what I heard or balance on crutches with a heavy cast on my leg. After being in bed for a month, the therapists needed to teach me how to walk all over again. A few days before Easter, the physicians and therapists determined that I had progressed to a point where I was finally able to be released to my parents' care and return home to Ohio.

Sensitive to the fact that I needed to process everything that had happened and what was happening currently, we didn't rush home right away. After saying goodbye to the staff that witnessed my transformation from vegetable to a somewhat functional human again, my father wanted to drive the road where I had been struck by the car. I didn't know what I expected to see, but I did wonder what horrors would be revealed should my memory return. My parents wanted to see what I remembered, thinking that visual stimulation would help bring it all back. They retraced the events of that day, but I needed to retrace more than that.

*   *   *

After the conclusion of Walden's training camp we returned to Ohio where I went back to work as a nurse in pediatrics at Middletown Hospital. I tried riding in the snow with Ken and the Dayton Cycling Club. I attempted to share some of the valuable skills I learned at bike camp, but somehow the concept of riding in rotating pace lines seemed difficult for people to grasp.

One evening, while in a pediatric patient's room, I glanced up to the television overhead and saw the Olympics on the screen. I stood, transfixed, as Scott Hamilton figure skated beautifully and won an Olympic Gold Medal. A desire was ignited deep within me to make it to the Olympic Trials for the 1984 Summer Games in Los Angeles.

The timing could not have been better, as the hospital was experiencing an unusually low patient count and my manager had asked people to take voluntary time off. This provided a perfect opportunity for me to put all my focus and energy into training. Remembering Mike Walden's advice that there was no better training for racing than to race, my parents and I scoured the cycling calendars and magazines and found an early season Stage Race in Fort Myers, Florida. My father insisted on driving down with me for the competition.

The stage race consisted of a time trial, multiple long distant road races, and a criterium as the finale. A criterium is generally a race that is held around a city block, with many corners, and consists of many laps of the closed course.

My riding gloves looked rather tattered, so my father bought a new pair for the competition that had black crochet on the back and lightly padded leather palms.

The skills I had learned at camp gave me more confidence and the races provided the opportunity to test my abilities. I found that my Florida training had paid off as I place 3rd overall in the stage race and was learning more with every competition. The apparent pride on my father's face felt even better than having a gold medal.

After that race I didn't want to lose momentum. I realized the need to take advantage of as much training and racing as possible to strengthen myself and sharpen my skills before the Olympic Trials. After concentrated racing in southern Florida, we traveled north to Ocala. My training goal for the day was to get in one hundred miles of riding. We looked at the map and discovered that the route between Ocala to Daytona was about that distance. State Route 40 went through the Ocala National Forest and looked like a great straight-shot ride. My father and I decided that he would drive the van behind me with his flashers on until traffic backed up, then pull ahead to wait for me to join him further up the road.

The weather was predicted to be gray and overcast with a light drizzle of rain for the morning of Tuesday, March 27th. I started the ride wearing the wind jacket Ken made especially for me with little heart appliques on the collar. He had designed it to match the Dayton cycling team uniform and used a combination of bright orange, yellow and white fabric to make sure that drivers on the road would see me.

I settled into an even pace, confident that every mile I completed would take me closer to my goal of competing in LA. My father drove his van far enough behind to watch over my progress and still allow vehicles to see and pass me safely. When he thought traffic was backing up, he would pass me, as we had planned, and drive down the road a few miles to wait. His silver van passed and I could see him wave from the driver's seat as he reluctantly made his way up the road, disappearing from my sight as other cars followed by passing me. I kept my wheels balanced, like a tightrope walker, hovering over the narrow white line at the edge of the road to stay out of traffic. I recalled seeing signs for "Silver Springs" and thick foliage on both sides of the road.

*   *   *

As my father continued to drive, nothing looked familiar and I couldn't remember anything more. The landscape appeared new and unfamiliar. He drove five more miles before he came to a "T" intersection where a side road joined our road from the left. He slowed to a stop and asked, "Do you remember anything here?" I looked around, trying to see if there was something that was even faintly recognizable that would trigger a memory of any kind but nothing sparked even a glimmer of recollection. I felt like I was disappointing him.

He told me what had happened, according to the drivers' who witnessed the event that almost ended my life. His words painted images in my head as he spoke. I was riding east on State Route 40 when I approached the "T" intersection where we were now stopped trying to recall the events that took place. A beer truck had stopped at the stop sign, contemplating traffic. I was part of that traffic. The right-of-way was mine as I was going straight through the intersection, but the driver of the truck saw the cars driving slowly behind me and decided not to hesitate and be stuck waiting his turn to pass me. He quickly accelerated and pulled out into the intersection, attempting to turn left in front of me. He was obviously looking to the right, toward me, and not to the left, where there was a car traveling toward us at a high rate of speed. The oncoming car swerved into my lane to miss impact with the truck and instead struck me, head on.

*　　*　　*

My father had been waiting down the road with growing concern when I did not appear. He flagged down a car and asked, "Did you see anyone on a bike back there?" The driver of the car replied, "You mean the kid that got hit by a car?" All blood drained from his face as panic and desperation hit him hard. He jumped back in his van and rushed to where all the cars were stopped in the road. After skidding to a stop he ran to where a distressed group of people were standing in the street.

He shoved his way through to see a dark raincoat covering a crumpled body on the pavement. The only thing visible beneath the coat was a black knit gloved hand sticking out. In those first few panic stricken seconds, he did not know whether he would find me dead or alive. No one attended to me; they only stood and waited for the ambulance to arrive. He rushed forward and was shoved back and restrained by one of the onlookers. "This is a fatality, we can't touch anything!" "That's my daughter! You will let me through." He growled.

My bike was destroyed, but recognizable to him on the side of the road. Again, he was restrained from touching anything that would be considered evidence in an investigation. Trying to assemble the event in his mind, he asked, "What happened?"

A witness told my father that after the car swerved into my lane and hit me, I flew through the air and landed on the road about twenty feet from impact. My bike had been devoured as I bounced over the car and it landed in pieces on the road.

Having been a professional firefighter and a paramedic, my father had come upon emergency scenes like this before and knew them all too well. However, now it was different. This time HIS daughter was on the road bleeding, his daughter's life slipping away before from his eyes. He pulled back the raincoat shroud to reveal thick, sticky blood coating everything, including the exposed bones of my right leg, which stuck out of the skin in a compound fracture.

He attempted to touch me, but I began to thrash and fight wildly. At least this meant that I was alive. After flying over the car the back of my head struck the pavement, causing my skull to fracture. When the swelling in my brain surpassed the limits of cognition and consciousness, my fighting stopped. The emergency squad arrived, the Emergency Medical Technicians cut off every stitch of my clothing to examine for injuries, and then I was quickly loaded into the ambulance. Meanwhile, my father could only watch from a distance and pace.

Fearful that any moment could be my last, he wanted to stay with me every possible second, but the ambulance crew would not allow him to ride with them to the hospital. Since the accident was being treated as a probable fatality he was forced to follow the coroner's vehicle to the hospital instead. Much to the surprise of the ambulance crew and everyone on the scene, I survived.

*   *   *

Visiting the scene of the accident, as the encounter was recounted to me created a lot of confusion for me, as it was more than my brain could handle. I observed the area, imagining ghostlike images playing out the scene my father described. I didn't know what to think or feel. As he spoke, I incorporated the surroundings with what I had been told, and tried to recreate the accident in my mind as though I had only been a witness to the event.

My parents didn't want to shock my system too much, because dizziness and disorientation remained an issue: When I closed my eyes, I felt as though everything was spinning. They thought it only fitting that I should finally reach the destination of my ride, so they took me to Daytona Beach. We spent a few days adapting to being out of the hospital and trying to enjoy our time there.

When we returned home on Easter I wanted to get back on a bike even though I remained extremely dizzy, had a cast and was on crutches. I just wanted to ride. Most people assumed that I would never want to see a bike again, let alone ride one, but I did not remember anything about being hit. I only remembered the love, freedom and exhilaration I had when I was riding.

Determined to fight through my setback and get my body to the level that I had attained before the accident, I knew that there was a lot of work ahead. The fracture was slow to heal and I hated the crutches and the limitations they imposed. Attempting to eat at a salad bar, use a public restroom or visit almost any place with that heavy cast and crutches proved to be clumsy and made going out in public impossible at times.

My loving parents became overly protective. Balance and memory were still real problems: Trying to recall people's names and flipping the first letters of words around were issues for a time and my short term memory was almost nonexistent. I halfway joked that I felt "Dain bramaged."

To appease me and to speed up the healing progress, my father eventually borrowed a tandem bicycle. With great care, I was able to ride on the back with him pedaling and steering the front. To adjust for the cast on my left leg, we put one of my father's size eleven bike shoes over it so that my foot could turn with the pedals. I loved being back in the saddle. Beginning to reclaim the life I had nearly lost was very motivating.

After a referral to a Neuropsychologist for evaluation, I went through a battery of tests which seemed to last forever. They asked me to read sentences, answer questions, and look at pictures to recall later. Some tests were inconclusive: Since I was not a very politically active young adult, the fact that I was unable to remember the name of the Governor of Ohio wasn't necessarily due to my brain injury.

A few weeks later, we received a thick, business like letter with my name on it. I opened it to find the results of the neurological-psychiatric evaluation. I visually scanned it, gazing at the content and two words stopped me in my tracks: "mentally retarded." I blinked, looked at the words and then blinked again. I stood frozen in place, unable to believe the diagnosis staring me in the face. Flipping back to the address label I checked again to make sure the report was for me and not someone else. Devastation, outrage, and anger expanded from my core, engulfing me in dark despair.

Isolated and trapped at home, unable to ride, and labeled "mentally retarded," I went through periods of depression. Before the accident, I had focused on riding in the Olympic trials in Los Angeles. Now I helplessly watched my muscular legs shrivel, all the while thinking of all the training time I had lost. The Neuro-psych diagnosis of retardation glared at me, but also challenged me. My new goal became to prove them wrong.

In the hospital, the food tasted terrible. No one had told me that the type of head injury I had could affect a person's sense of taste. Bananas, tomatoes and many of the other foods I had loved now tasted metallic. I never realized before how many foods contained tomatoes. I lost interest in eating, and as a result, rapidly lost over ten percent of my body weight along with muscle. No wonder I was depressed: I had lost appetite, muscle and opportunity!

At home, I realized that although many things had been taken from me, the desire to ride was still great. I was determined to do everything possible to get caught up both physically and mentally to prove that the diagnosis was wrong. I am inherently stubborn and everyone would soon realize just how much I could accomplish when I was determined.

A family friend happened to be a physical therapist and he allowed me to work out on his weight equipment and even used a tens unit to send a mild electrical current through my muscles to cause intermittent contractions. This method of therapy helped prevent further atrophy of my leg muscles while trapped in the cast.

I started riding on a trainer (which turns a road bike into a stationary bike) in my parent's kitchen. I pedaled with my left leg and propped my right leg with the cast up on the handlebars, then after some time I began bearing partial weight on my injured leg. Once again the cast was squeezed into my father's cycling shoe and I was finally able to pedal with both legs.

The doctors said that my healing was progressing slowly because the fracture was close to my ankle, where the supply of blood was diminished. We set out to find a sports medicine doctor who would understand and treat me with MY goals in mind.

In 1984, sports medicine was a developing specialty. Many of my cycling friends told me to see a particular doctor of sports medicine in Dayton. My mother and I made an appointment to see this highly recommended professional and went with great hope that he would be able to help me return to the activities that had become my passion.

*　　*　　*

The sports medicine doctor looked at my leg x-rays and surgical record. "By the location and the extent of your fractures, it appears that you have lost some bone in the area. Also the fracture reduction plate will prevent you from participating in the sports you are now enjoying. You may need to reconsider your future," he declared.

Shocked, I asked, "What are you saying? That I can't ride, or skate or even cross country ski? What do you mean?" "Yes, you won't be able to do any of these things again because there is too much impact loading involved. You need to take it easy and find something else to enjoy," he affirmed. Outraged by his proclamation and his ignorance to the fact that there is no impact loading in cycling or cross country skiing, I exploded. "Do you even know what cross country skiing is?"

My mother, seeing my ire building, calmly challenged him. "Tell me doctor, what exactly is your background and certification?" she asked. "I am a board certified orthopedic surgeon." he shot back. "And how is it that you call yourself a sports medicine specialist?" she retorted. "I have attended seminars in sports medicine and I am the advisor to the University of Dayton Football team." he defended. "So you are not a board certified sports medicine physician?" she asked. He hesitated, saying, "I am an orthopedic surgeon and I specialize in sports injuries."

That was all we needed to hear. We knew that this guy did not have the knowledge necessary to address my issues and my competitive level in sports. We left his office with a hefty bill and the determination to find someone who understood my needs. With continued research, we eventually found an excellent, well-reviewed, certified Sports Medicine Orthopedic surgeon in Cincinnati.

The new doctor looked at things from an entirely different perspective. I told him what my goals were, and he assured me that he would do everything possible to get me back on my feet and competing in the sports I loved. Hearing exactly what I needed to hear, my spirits lifted and I finally had real hope.

The swelling in my brain subsided and my dizziness lessened with time, but I continued to feel frustrated with the discomfort and awkwardness of being on crutches. The only occasions I truly felt normal were when I rode on the back of the tandem. I spent as much time on that bike as possible, but was restricted by the availability of my father. He was not able to ride as often as I wanted; therefore he reluctantly began to let me go on short rides with Ken at the helm. We gradually began to ride farther and faster, and I absolutely loved it.

My bike could not be repaired, as it was destroyed in the accident. Every major component had been bent or broken. Eventually my parents found a replacement and bought it, providing a new set of wings to lift me out of confinement.

I remained manacled to the crutches for what seemed an eternity, but I stubbornly used them to get to the bike, where I could hand them off and pedal away, cast and all, as if I had never gotten more than a bruise. Finally able to get back on a single bike, I experienced an even greater sense of freedom. I acknowledged that I had a lot to accomplish in a short period of time, but as a naturally goal-oriented person, also knew that I needed to ignore my doctors' negativity and get my life back.

At first my mother paced the floor, nervous about my riding on the road again. She was afraid that if I crashed and hit my head, I might never get up. I needed a safer environment and realized that riding the track would provide a good place to start finding my way back.

There was a lot of time to think, as I was unable to return to work or do much of anything else. I tried time and again to remember what happened on that fateful day of March 27th. I imagined a lot of things, but they were based on what people had told me and not on what I recalled.

No matter how hard I tried, I had no memory at all of my encounter with the car or of being treated at the scene. There were a few things from my time in the coma that I do remember. I had a sensation of floating in a yellow cloud, cradled in love, having absolutely no pain and seeing the caring faces of people around me. Even though I didn't recognize the faces, I felt safe. I realized later, after hearing the details of the accident, that the end result could have been drastically different. Accidents as violent as mine often result in death, paralysis or head trauma so severe that people never wake up.

There's no way could I have been merely lucky. I truly believed that God had a reason and purpose for saving me, yet I had no idea what it could be.

Thoughts and questions about my future percolated in my mind, but the one constant was my bike. Internal drive to make up for lost time and training kept me pushing to ride more. Ready to test my limits once again, I searched for something that didn't have any major risk of crashing and realized that time on the velodrome seemed to be the best answer. This type of race only consisted of me, the bike, the track, and a stopwatch, with absolutely NO CARS.

Ken was happy to drive me to the velodrome in Indianapolis on multiple occasions, making special trips to help me train. After witnessing my drive, determination and improvement, he suggested that I race in the State Championship Track Race. "It's just a race to get you back on track," he said, his eyes grinning at the pun. "It's just a line in the sand," he finished. I thought he was joking at first, but his persistence told a different story.

When we returned to the track to race, I hopped on one foot to the start line where Ken stood holding my bike in wait. He helped me climb on the saddle and get strapped into the pedals and once again the thrill of riding surged through my body. Apparently, I had not forgotten how to start the way I learned from Mike Walden at camp just a few months earlier, though so many things had happened since then.

Much to my great surprise, I won the State Championships. At one point during the two hour drive back home, Ken looked over at me as I sat in the passenger seat, window rolled down and casted leg sticking out the window getting some air to my toes. "You realize that the time you set qualified you for Elite Nationals don't you?" he asked rhetorically. I looked at him, trying to figure out the significance of what he was asking.

Just to be able to race again was a major milestone for me. He continued, "If you would like to go, just let me know. They will be in Pennsylvania and I would be happy to take you."

Wiggling my toes in the breeze I contemplated his proposal, trying to understand the implications. "I think you should consider it. Since you qualified, you should go," he continued. "I wouldn't win or even be in the top 10." I replied almost apologetically. "Haven't you heard that winning isn't everything? You would be going to learn to race again with the best," he said, eyes fixed now on the road ahead. How could I argue with logic like that?

Agreeing meant that I would have barely six weeks to train. I spent every moment possible either training or debating the sanity of going to Nationals with a cast. My mother expressed her support and her concern as she still worried that the slightest bump on the head might cause a seizure or even end my life. The time finally came for my cast to come off and be replaced with a brace. Unfortunately, the crutches would have to continue to be my companions for a while. I brought a razor and shaving cream with me to the orthopedist's office. When they cut the seam down the fiberglass cast and pulled back the halves, it revealed an alarming combination of mottled skin and scars from where the plate had been installed and where the bones had come through. The skin and the muscles looked unreal, pale and covered in little hairs. I hopped immediately over to the sink and placed my foot in, ran warm water over it and started to wash the layers of skin and hair away. I wished that I could have washed away every indication that the accident had happened at all.

Fortunately, riding and the electronic stimulation had helped the fractures heal faster than we expected by increasing the circulation to my lower leg. I rode with a regular cycling shoe while remaining in a leg brace. Without a doubt in my mind, it was decided; I was going to race again.

Mike Walden suggested that I come to Detroit and train with him before Nationals. He arranged for me to stay with his daughter, Christine, her husband Dale and their growing family.

I packed both my track and road bikes on top of my yellow Pinto hatchback and headed north. To break up the monotony of driving I wore a big nose and Groucho glasses. It wasn't my normal traveling attire, but it was fun to watch the expressions of the other drivers as they drove by. A woman with long reddish hair, a big nose, glasses and a fuzzy mustache was really a sight to see. It really did make the time go faster.

I arrived in Detroit after dark and spent over an hour trying to find my way with the directions Mike had given me, long before cell phones and GPS devices were in use. When I finally stopped at a gas station in downtown Detroit, a man looking very much like Kareem Abdul Jabbar (glasses and all) told me, "Honey, you lost. You shouldn't be here at this time of night," and I believed him. He kindly directed me back to the interstate and I wasted no time getting there.

I drove till I found a payphone and called Chris and Dale, who guided me in for landing. Relief poured over me when I found their house, and even though I had arrived much later than planned, they still welcomed me warmly into their home. I felt honored to be staying with these friends who had been the superstar coaches at bike camp.

The next morning Dale took me to the store that Mike owned, the Continental Bike Shop on John R. Road. I stepped inside the well-worn door and was greeted by the aroma of bike tires and old wood. The floorboards creaked and the bell rang overhead, announcing my entrance, as bike history enveloped me like a fog. I wondered how many bike racers had stepped through that same threshold before. Mike greeted me wearing his driving cap and a big grin, then said in a barreling voice, "What took you so long?" and gave me a pat on the back. "Let me see your leg!" he commanded. I brought my right leg forward and he reached down and pinched my thigh. "You can ride in that cast?" he asked as he knocked on my brace covered with a striped leg warmer. "I have been." I answered. He shook his head and said, "Well, we've got a lot of work to do." "Let me show you around," he said with a smile, and he started to give me a guided tour of his compact collection of history and legend. It was like touring a cycling hall of fame.

In the back room where the mechanics were working, he showed me his speed bag. "How are you with working the bag?" he asked, pointing to the worn leather bag suspended from a board in the corner of the room. "You need to work the speed bag to get your upper body adjusted to the road shock on the bike through the handlebars," he explained. He proceeded to demonstrate slowly, and then increased his speed to the point where the bag turned into a brown blur, buzzing around his massive fists. "Now you do it," he demanded. I was starting to think that he might have also trained Rocky Balboa. I gave it a try and quickly found the tempo. The technique was all about timing and rhythm.

Later, Mike took me down the street to a local pub, which was a popular hangout for a group of older Belgian gentlemen who gathered to play bocce ball regularly. As soon as we entered, shouts of greeting rang out to Mike. "Who ya got wit ya dair Mike?" came the accented shout from one of the older gentlemen. "This is one of my riders. We are getting her ready to ride at track nationals," he explained as his friends pressed forward to meet me.

I had never heard of bocce ball until that day, but they would not rest until I agreed to throw a few balls. I was rewarded for my time with their laughter at my lame attempts. Clearly, I didn't know what I was doing and after having spent thirty minutes trying to perfect my speed bag technique, my arms felt like spaghetti.

It was an adventure just getting to the track with Mike driving his van. Once there he shared its history with me. "We built this track, all of it with volunteers. It was once the premier spot for racing and now it's falling apart, but we keep patching it up because it's a good track." He took a broom out of the van and started to sweep the broken beer bottle shards from the concrete surface. The concrete training grounds for cycling was obviously a huge labor of love, designed and hand made by the Wolverine Sports Club many years before. It was evident that volunteers had poured their blood, sweat, and tears into the foundation of what was once the incubator and nursery of many national and world cycling champions over the years.

Although now imperfect, with cement patches and tar filled cracks, graffiti tags and uncut grass, it continued to be Mike's domain and his love and pride for it was obvious. He told me to warm up on the track and then we worked on time trial starts. I could hardly believe that I was being blessed with quality one-on-one time with the "master."

Mike trained me in individual sessions during the day and in the evenings I practiced with the club racers on the track. On Wednesday evenings he told me that I should join a weekly touring ride with hundreds of cyclists snaking through the streets of the Detroit suburbs. He said that riding with a big group of riders with different skills would help me learn to navigate through race packs. Ride leaders blocked traffic as we rode in thick masses through the intersections.

I often met Mike at pancake houses before training sessions where we would sit and talk about training and racing. At one point in time he asked me about my accident. I told him, "I don't remember anything about getting hit; all that I know came from witnesses. I do remember that while I was in the coma, I felt absolutely no pain, and I know that one second one way or the other I could have been killed, paralyzed, or not even hit at all." I paused to take a sip of my hot chocolate. "There must be a reason for the way things turned out. God must have a purpose for me. I just don't know what I need to do. I wonder with each person that I meet if they might be my purpose." I waited to see what his response might be.

Mike just looked at me. "Well, as far as I can see," he said as he took another bite of pancake and swallowed, "The fact that you were even willing to look at a bike again tells me that you were meant to ride. So my purpose is to help get you to the championships and beyond. You get more strength back every day, and that's good, but there is one thing that the accident has taken away from you that will be really hard to recover. That's the killer instinct I saw at camp." He paused as he sipped his coffee. "If your purpose is other people, then you need to go back to nursing and forget about the bike. You have to be selfish to be a champion. You can't be polite and nice; you gotta be able to get mean. Can you get mean?"

I returned home the week before nationals to rest and contemplate whether I could get mean or not. As promised, Ken drove me to Trexlertown (referred to as "T-Town" by the cycling community) for the 1984 Elite Cycling Track National Championships in August. Major Taylor Velodrome in Indianapolis had been modeled after the T-town track, which helped me adjust quickly.

I recognized many of the riders from other races as well as those from the Florida's camp. David Asslin came from Connecticut to watch my race and greeted me with great enthusiasm. I hadn't seen him since bike camp and he wanted to see that I was doing well after my accident and to show his support.

The riders filtered into registration. As they arrived, I recognized many that we had watched with awe and envy during the Olympic Games or had read articles about in cycling magazines. The fastest racers in the country would be my competition. Momentary doubt crept through my mind again and landed in the pit of my stomach. I looked down at the brace on my leg, "What am I doing here?" I thought, "I am so out of my league."

Both Mike Walden and Clair Young were there, coaching and socializing with the riders and other coaches. As soon as Mike saw me, his face lit up as he yelled "Hey kid, come with me, I have some people I want you to meet." For an older, heavy man with knee problems, it was all I could do to keep up with him as he buzzed through the crowds. He knew everyone and was obviously highly respected and often feared in the cycling community.

Mike sat on the Board of Directors of the United States Cycling Federation and was never afraid to speak his mind. Clair was one of his closest friends and they had ridden together and coached each other's children from an early age. Clair was very quiet and kind, yet one of the toughest riders I ever met. Their combined history in the sport made Nationals at the track like a class reunion.

Negotiating my way around the infield on crutches, I tried my best to keep up with Mike as he introduced me to other coaches and riders, but all the names and faces became a blur as he moved like a bee from flower to flower. One look into his sparkling eyes, peering out from under his cream colored driving cap told me how much he relished every moment there. Once again my father's words came back to me, "Watch and Learn," and I realized that I was definitely in the right place with the right people.

The designated area of the infield where riders warmed up and prepared for competition was alive with activity. Magnetic trainers and rollers like Aldo had ridden were scattered around the paved portion of the infield. Some riders chatted in the shade while others seemed almost meditative as they warmed up in isolation. Massage therapists worked kneading riders' doughy muscles while coaches changed gears from those used to warm up to the racing gears needed to optimize performance during the race.

Many competitors trained to peak for that very day as the culmination of their hard work and sacrifice. For me it was a celebration of being alive and on my bike again. Although I realized there would be no win for me that day, I was determined to ride and I did.

Even though I attempted to disguise the leg brace by covering it with a leg warmer to make it look less dramatic and obvious, I still got a lot of strange glances from onlookers. I didn't like drawing attention to the fact that my leg was broken, but what else could I do?

Every race I rode that day proved to me that I was alive and where I belonged. I did not anticipate winning, and was happy that I finished at all. I was 22nd in the points race, which was not bad considering the fact that there were more than thirty in the starting field for the women's event. I left the track with a sense of accomplishment and a T-shirt.

A few weeks after nationals, my parents traveled with me to Windsor, Canada over Labor Day weekend for a series of criterium races in the "Little Italy" section of downtown. Track Nationals and training with the Wolverine Sports Club riders gave me the confidence to ride in a pack again.

The races were fast and full of skilled riders, including four recent Olympians. In the final sprint, the riders were packed curb to curb scrambling for the finish line, looking for a hole to sprint through or a wheel to hang on to. I finished a very respectable seventh place and earned a nice cash prize. Thrilled that my parents were there to see the race and share the moment with me, I rushed to find them.

While we stood breathless talking excitely about the race, three older gentlemen walked up to us, speaking in Italian. The oldest and shortest of the three spoke directly to me. One of the others interpreted in a thick accent and said, "He told me that he bet on you, because you are already handicapped." They laughed while pointing to the leg brace and patted me on the shoulder in congratulations then shook my father's hand and walked away. Overjoyed from just having placed seventh, riding in a field of over fifty women, I burst into laughter.

After Windsor, I raced every chance possible, searching for my killer instinct. Life started to return to normal bit by bit as I looked forward to being one hundred percent myself again, but knew there was a lot of work ahead. Without a doubt in my mind, I was ready and willing, but I was still working on being able.

When the Michigan weather turned cold and no longer suitable for outdoor bike riding I returned to Ohio and discovered an invitation from the Olympic training center in the mail. I was shocked. Now I would be able to improve my cycling performance and train with the best.

I called Mike and told him how excited I was. Happy to hear the news, he gave me some words of caution, "Listen to everything the coach's say, take what applies to you and leave the rest," he said. I wasn't certain what he meant, but I promised to follow his advice: another opportunity to *"Watch and learn"*.

After what seemed like a lifetime, my leg healed and I was allowed to bear full weight without a leg brace. I rode every hilly back road in southwestern Ohio to get stronger, and Ken coached the Dayton cycling club as the seasons changed. He introduced me to cyclocross, which was a type of off road bike race that I'd never tried before. In cyclocross, we would ride through muddy trails, jump off the bike, hoist it onto our shoulder, run and jump over three hurdles, and then jump back on the bike and ride as hard as the body would allow. Challenged on many levels, I quickly discovered that any type of running caused pain in my leg at the fracture site. I struggled as the pain increased, but remained convinced of the need for experience to help prepare me for the training center.

As I said goodbye to my family and boarded the plane for Colorado a combination of feelings made themselves comfortable in my stomach: hope that I could make my family proud, nervous that I would fail, fear of the unknown, and excited for a new adventure. Ken packed both my road and cyclocross bikes into cardboard bike boxes for transport on the plane. He made another jacket with hearts on the collar to remind me of him while I traveled alone. He thought of everything. All I would have to worry about would be riding.

After landing at the small Colorado Springs airport, I found signs directing me to the Olympic Training Center shuttle. I looked out the windows, trying to soak up every sight I could. As we passed through the security gates, I could see the Olympic Rings standing proudly inside the entrance to greet us. I felt like Dorothy entering the gates of the Emerald City.

My bikes were unloaded and delivered to the mechanics' shack and I was given a site map, a schedule, an athlete's ID, and directions to my dorm room at check-in. My roommate, Jill, a tall blonde from California, had already arrived. The dorms were former Air Force barracks with plain concrete block walls, two beds, one closet, and a sink. The community bathrooms were down the hall, and each floor had one common room with couches and a television.

We were required to attend the riders meeting that evening. It was the first time we would all officially meet to go over the training schedule, rules and expectations. We sat in institutional folding chairs arranged neatly in rows, and I looked around to see who I might recognize. There were several members of the 1984 Olympic track cycling team and the National team at this meeting. One of the Olympic riders, Scott Berryman, recognized my Dayton Cycling team uniform and approached me. He had started his cycling career in Dayton coached by Ken, who took him to the races and introduced him to the track much like he had done for me. Scott later gave me a National Champion Jersey. "I want you to give this to Ken. I want him to know how much I appreciate all he has done for me. I wouldn't be here if it wasn't for him."

After the coaching staff was introduced and we were welcomed, the topic quickly turned to the scandal looming over the Olympic cycling results in Los Angeles concerning blood doping. The head coach for the United States Olympic cycling team, Eddy Borysewicz, known in the cycling world as Eddy B, stood before us speaking in a thick Polish accent, professing that the riders made their decisions in Los Angeles on their own. He insisted that he had nothing to do with the blood transfusions at the Olympic Games and proclaimed that it was his decision to bite the bullet and take the blame and spare his riders the shame, as he stood before us with his arms outstretched to the side as if being nailed to a cross. Words spoken by Mike echoed in my ears "Do not get involved in the politics of the games and keep your nose clean."

Each day we got up early and gathered in the infield of the running track for warm-up and stretching exercises before breakfast. What an exhilarating feeling it was to go out in the cool, crisp Colorado morning air and know that the distant snow-capped mountain of Pikes Peak stood watch over us, ever present, ever silent, and always perfect.

The dining hall was everyone's favorite place to hang out. There was an excellent variety of healthy food and we were invited to eat whenever and whatever we wanted. A buffet suited for a multitude of different dietary requirements and ethnic cultures had items labeled to help athletes make decisions based on their needs. It was obvious that when a company announced that they would sponsor the Olympic team they truly meant it. Even the lawn mowers on the grounds were labeled with the name of their sponsor.

The weather conditions dictated what our daily training would be. Based on the wind and temperature, we would ride through the foothills into the countryside, cyclocross in a nearby field, or ride indoors on trainers. They tested us with all the latest sports science equipment: VO2 Max, lactate threshold, anaerobic threshold, strength, and flexibility assessments gauged our fitness and endurance.

It was a while before my body was able to adjust to the high altitude, especially since I was from the flatlands of Ohio and I could not make the transition to thin air as swiftly as I would have liked. On the first few rides through the foothills, I started lagging behind the group, gasping for air. I later learned that I had experienced exercise induced asthma, which was exacerbated by the cold, dry, thin air. Riders became acutely aware of constant scrutiny with which the coaches determined our potential as we tried to perform at our best in the frigid Colorado winter months. What the coaches told us were training rides often turned into competitive race pace sessions, trying to out-ride each other and gain the attention of the coaching staff.

Living at the training center provided a great opportunity for athletes to observe different sports in their venues and meet visitors from different countries. Our unlimited access to sports medicine and excellent nutrition freed us to focus one hundred percent on training in our sport.

Crash training at the gymnastics venue taught us how to run, dive, and roll with arms and head tucked to land on padded mats. The goal was to train riders' instinctive reactions to crash in a way to decrease the potential for injury. Unfortunately, the pain in my leg grew in intensity and plagued me while off my bike. I was able to ride, but running and jumping did not agree with my leg. Eventually every step I took caused pain where the fracture had occurred. Unavoidably, my stride turned into a limp and the coaches noticed and expressed concern. One of the coaches did some measurements and discovered that the leg I had broken now measured a full centimeter shorter than the other, so he built up the bottom of my cycling shoe to try to balance the difference.

The pain became even more distracting and I resorted to flying home to see my orthopedic surgeon. After x-rays and examination, he told me that the anterior tibialis, the muscle in my shin, was now scraping over the screws and plate in my leg resulting in pain and inflammation. We decided that the time had come to have the plate removed.

He cautioned me that the new bone would heal stronger than it had been originally, but the surrounding bone might flex and break around it. He chiseled what he called "fish scaling" into the older bone to cause stress and make it stronger. Again, I found myself back in the brace for a few more weeks and began to wonder if I would ever get back to normal.

It did not take long for me to get antsy to return to the bike. Much to my surprise, my parents picked me up from the hospital in Cincinnati in a motor-home. We now had a mobile training headquarters and I could not wait to get back on the bike and train again.

In February of 1985 we headed back to Florida to train with Mike and the team at Camp Wewa. What a thrill to see everyone and be able to ride in the warm sunshine. Bike camp had different riders coming every week for three months and I started helping with coaching and had the opportunity to race on weekends. Mike always told us, "The best training for racing is racing." and he was absolutely correct. By May I had become a lot stronger and we headed back home, but racing in Ohio would not be as competitive as it had been in Florida.

It had been over a year since I was struck by the car. My parents called me into their bedroom and I sat down next to my mother on the bed. "When you were hit by the car we thought we had lost you," she said. "They said at the time that it was doubtful that you would ever come back to us." She paused and sniffed quietly. "When you opened your eyes and I heard you speak," my mother's voice started to waver and she looked away from me as she paused to take a breath, "and to see you be able to feed yourself," again, pausing to collect her words, "we realized how much of a fighter you are and knew there was hope." Her voice cracked and she could speak no more.

My father stepped forward and said. "What your mother wants to tell you is that we were devastated when you were hit by the car, and having seen how far you have come in only a year, we want to help you pick up where you left off." My mother began to speak again, "We realize in order for you to reach your full potential, you need to not just race, but to race with the best in the world."

"There is a series called the Mayors' Cup, sponsored by Wheat Thins. The races are every weekend throughout the summer and each one is in a different state capitol. We think you should go." There was a pause and the thought of traveling to where the best races were excited me, but had seemed far beyond my ability to make it happen logistically. I looked at their expectant faces beaming at me.

"We want you to have this," she said as she glanced at my father then handed me a small red, rectangular box. I opened the box and inside there was a stack of twenty dollar bills. Speechless, I blinked and looked up from the box with questioning eyes. "One thousand dollars," she said. My eyes filled with tears of shock and surprise. "Since you don't have sponsorship from a big team, we want to sponsor you." she assured. Typically, sponsors paid for entry fees and travel expenses. My father was an injured firefighter/paramedic, now retired, and my mother worked as a nurse so they did not have much money to spare. I realized what their sacrifice and investment meant, and it instilled even more drive and passion in me to succeed. The flame that already burned within me grew with my determination to make them proud.

David Asslin and I had corresponded as pen-pals since our first meeting at Camp Wewa in Florida. From the moment we both charged out of the van at Daytona and ran to the beach we realized we were kindred spirits. At camp we had exchanged addresses and he later sent me many wonderful letters telling me about his life in Connecticut. I had written to him about my experiences at the training center in return. When I told him about my opportunity to race on the East Coast, he wasted no time in offering me a place to stay at his parent's home and the opportunity to train with him a few weeks before the races began in Hartford.

I accepted his offer and flew into the Hartford airport, where he picked me up. His family embraced me and I was invited to stay in his sister's room. Never having been to the East Coast before, I was not accustomed to the lifestyles east of the Hudson. One evening after dinner, I joked that people on the East Coast did everything fast. They talked fast, drove fast and even ate fast. In fact, by the time my salad course was finished, they were all done with their entrées and ready for dessert.

David happily acted as my tour guide around his stomping grounds in Middlebury while we rode through the lush, rolling, sometimes mountainous landscape. I began to think that the entire state was one giant park. We rode to Litchfield, where large white Colonial houses and picket fences stood as sentries on every corner. The town proudly displayed churches with white steeples and lush, well-manicured green lawns. After stopping at a small, locally-owned market to buy handmade tortellini and fresh strawberries, we decided on an impromptu picnic in the middle of a meadow surrounded by tall white flowers and our bikes. We then continued on through the Berkshires.

My life that week seemed so very different from the world I had experienced in the Midwest. David took me on an excursion to the city, New York City to be exact, where everything seemed to be a blur of high-paced humanity on every corner. We took a taxi which had me holding on to my seat, breathless and white knuckled and clutching the door. David put his arm around me to help keep me from sliding around as we snaked aggressively through traffic, fitting through holes that I did not see as valid options for the taxi. The lines on the road appeared to be mere suggestions for drivers, which they often chose to completely ignore.

When we walked through the streets of Chinatown, there was so much to see, hear, and smell that it was sensory overload. There were whole ducks, stripped of their feathers with heads and feet still attached, hanging upside down in storefront windows, and red and gold silk decorations everywhere. A cacophony of aromas from Asian spices, incense, raw meat and vegetables I didn't recognize, combined with the smell of traffic and sewage vents, assaulted me. The surrounding clatter of car horns, bike riders blowing whistles, Chinese music, and people arguing in foreign languages enveloped me.

We stepped into a small restaurant that served Dim Sum to seek shelter from the clamor of the streets. "Just wait till you see this." David beamed. "There are no menus, you just point to what you want and they count up the plates when you are done to calculate the bill." Small portions of Chinese foods on individual plates were displayed on carts as that were pushed through the restaurant and past our table. We selected and sampled things I had never seen before; my favorite by far was the crab claw. I wanted to see it all, taste it all, and hear it all but we had only one afternoon and by the evening I was exhausted.

Near the end of my stay with his family, David wanted me to meet his grandfather at their country club. The required attire for the club was semi-formal. As an official traveling bike bum, I had not packed any dress clothes. "No problem," David said, "You're about my sister's size, you can borrow one of her dresses." I'd never even been near a country club let alone strolled into one wearing a designer dress. David had been referring to me as his "Princess" throughout my stay and when I walked through the doors of that club on his arm, I felt like one.

David's dark hair, blue eyes with dark expressive eyebrows and very muscular build reminded me of Gene Kelly, one of my favorite actors.

When I met his statuesque grandfather, the family resemblance was clear. What a charming and gracious man he was.

Arriving at the country club and looking at the menu, I was out of my element. I had never eaten lobster so they insisted that I try it. David and his grandfather coached me through the proper way to confront the large crustacean. I must have been quite the sight, sitting in a country club in a semi-formal dress covered with a lobster bib while eating a giant bug. I quickly forgot all about the bib when the delicate sweet flavor of the lobster touched my tongue. It was delicious. I didn't want the dinner or the evening to end.

That evening was like a fairy tale and I could not thank David or his family enough. I must confess that I imagined what it would be like to live a lifestyle like that forever. But I had to follow my passion.

The Wheat Thins races were classics in the making. Each race course was located in a state capital, and the signs at the start/finish lines, the orange fencing holding spectators back, the announcer, and the support personnel all followed the same recipe with the same ingredients for success no matter where we went. Professional racers and teams had been solidly established and when the riders arrived at the start line, they knew exactly what to expect from the race course and from each other.

The races had huge fields of racers. There were over one hundred competitors on the starting line, which was exceptional considering that they were women's races. The race roster consisted of some of the best female racers in the world on teams that traveled and worked together. The advantages of being on a team quickly became apparent as I discovered just how the tactics of racing changed when you had teammates to help. Sitting in the race, watching and learning, it became obvious who the sprinters were: who would push the pace and who to take seriously when they attacked off the front.

My entire summer was spent racing and moving from state to state like a nomad on wheels. My parents were able to see me race in Atlanta and Knoxville. I returned home once the majority of the races had finished for the season. Later on, I went to Milwaukee with Ken for the Road Nationals where I faced many of the same women from the Wheat Thins circuit.

The feed zone for the Road Nationals had been designated at the top of the climb overlooking the lakefront. Ken served as my support person, and as the rules required that all food or water must be delivered to the rider in a feed bag called a musette, Ken personally created matching musettes for our team.

I felt comfortable in the race since I had competed with many of the same riders throughout the summer and was starting from a perfect strategic location in the field. When it came time to get a water bottle in the feed zone, Ken stood waiting with a musette for me. He extended the bag as I rode by and slipped my right arm through the strap quickly, moving the bag to my back to transfer the bottle to my back pocket.

Somehow I had gotten the wrong musette. The bag I received had apparently been made for one of the tall male riders on our team as it sported a very long strap. When I swooped the bag onto my back, the strap with the weight of the water bottle acted as a huge pendulum that swung out and into my front wheel, stopping the bike on the spot. I went down abruptly, crashing in the middle of the feed zone.

Ken and other support people ran to me in the midst of the chaos. Somehow, the other riders avoided my crash. Ken lifted me back onto the bike and pushed me off, but I never got my water bottle and spent the rest of the race chasing the pack. Lesson learned: Put your name BOLDLY on the feed bag and make sure the strap is the proper length before the race begins

Dale Hughes called me a few months later, to tell me that I had been selected to compete on the National Women's team that they were sponsoring; I did mental cartwheels. The team would compete in the largest stage race in the country in early April.

The final race of the season took place in Scottsdale, Arizona late that fall. My Aunt Janet lived in Phoenix so my mother and I flew out together. I was very excited to have them both there to see what I had been perfecting all summer. The women in my race rode smoothly and were relaxed as we glided through the corners, four to six riders wide, without hesitation or delay.

The riders were all seasoned by that time, comfortable in the race and aware of how to make their bikes perform in just the way they needed. Immersed in the middle of the field at one point, I looked up and saw my mother and aunt looking for me. Taking advantage of the moment, I sat up in the middle of the pack and waved as we passed by them, raising my head above the sea of colored jerseys and the rolling landscape of helmets, happy to be sharing the moment with them both.

My mother flew back home and I stayed in Phoenix with my aunt and her husband, Dick Powell, to train on the warm sunny roads of the southwest. Only eight years older than I, Janet is more like a big sister than an aunt. I have always looked up to her and envied her gorgeous, long red hair. Everyone in my family had red hair and even though I had been described by others as a redhead, I still felt dull by comparison. When I was little and Janet was a teen, my grandmother sometimes let me sneak into her bedroom and play with her Barbie dolls. When she discovered my invasion, she chased me out and I giggled at how I had annoyed her. Now, all these years later, Janet was inviting me to stay with her so I could pursue my dreams and I was thankful.

At first light in the desert, I would get up to eat a breakfast of oatmeal and fruit before charging out the door to go on long solo rides and explore my new surroundings. Every ride proved to be an adventure: I saw tumbleweeds, road runners, and even snakes. The Saguaro cactus stood witness to my rides and I named them as I passed because they each seemed to have their own distinct personalities.

The destinations of many of the rides were often decided when I spotted a mountain range in the distance, declared it my target and set out to reach it, eager to see how long it would take to arrive at the foothills. I loved riding in Phoenix and having the freedom to roam without worry made it even better.

The roads in Phoenix are set on a grid system which made it nearly impossible to get lost. I often encountered riders from local bike clubs and started getting invitations to ride with them. They told me about a ride on Thanksgiving morning at 5am that consisted of a large group who met in the middle of downtown to ride up South Mountain and watch the sunrise together. The excitement of the challenge lured me in and the opportunity to see the mountain sounded awesome.

Early on Thanksgiving morning, we gathered in the stillness of the pre-dawn morning on the empty streets of the city. Only street lights and lights on the bikes illuminated our way as the group snaked through the dark streets toward South Mountain. The road was a steady upward grade with constant switchbacks weaving in and out of the side of the rust colored mountain. Upon cresting the top, those of us in the lead sat and waited at a picnic shelter for the others to arrive. Watching the sun rise over the city and spread golden light over the brown horizon made me feel very thankful to be alive and able to see the morning glow from such a beautiful place. I was appreciative of my family and their support that helped me reach that point in my life's journey by bike.

A few of the experienced riders brought newspapers to tuck into the front of their jerseys in an attempt to stay warm on the descent. This was new to me, as I had not ridden down any huge mountains before. South Mountain would be my first. When I climbed I had paid very little attention to the left side of the road because I was in the right lane which hugged the side of the mountain and stayed focused on the rising road before me. On the way down, I became cautiously aware that there were NO guardrails on the outside lane to protect anyone from the threat of a sudden drop straight down the side.

The local riders began screaming down the mountain road with wild abandon, swerving back and forth at speeds greater than forty miles per hour. Reality hit me like I had run head first into a Saguaro. Never having ridden down anything so steep and so fast in my life, I imagined myself getting a flat tire at forty miles per hour, or even worse, sliding off the side of the road into the rocks and prickly brush that surely waited beyond the sheer drop below.

The smell of burning rubber rose from my brakes with my generous use as I cautiously controlled my increasing downhill speed. I'm not certain if the shivering I experienced came from the chill of the November pre-dawn, or from my fear of plummeting over the edge. I may have been one of the first to arrive at the top of the mountain, but my bike was the last to reach the bottom.

While in Phoenix, I rode every day with focus and determination. My aunt and uncle were very supportive and he gave me some motivational tapes to listen to while on the bike. They also shared with me the wonderful news that they were going to become parents. Honored to be the first in the family to hear this announcement, as they had just found out themselves, my joy for them was immeasurable.

The plan was to fly back to Ohio for Christmas, so we celebrated an early Christmas with my aunt and uncle's family in Phoenix before leaving for Ohio. My uncle's sister's family kindly included me in their holiday celebration and their fifteen year old son joined us for dinner wearing pajamas and coughing a great deal all evening. They thought that he was having issues with his asthma. I understood, as my brother Scott had severe asthma attacks and struggled with it often when he was young.

We flew back to Ohio together for Christmas at my grandmother's house. There, on Christmas Eve, Janet announced her wonderful news and we all expressed how happy we were for them. The house was alive with the smell of turkey, the sound of Dean Martin singing Christmas carols on the stereo and the colored lights from the tree warming the room. I had not seen my parents, brother, grandparents or Ken for months.

Exhausted and unable to gather enough energy to show enthusiasm about anything, I sat like a lump on the couch with my head on Ken's shoulder and wondered if I had over-trained in Phoenix. Later that evening I started to shiver uncontrollably and we discovered that my temperature was very high. I was more than exhausted, I was sick. Apparently, I had caught something from the coughing boy in Phoenix.

The next day I started coughing and coughing, unable to stop. Since it was Christmas Day, I had to wait until the following day to go to the doctor. My chest was x-rayed and I was diagnosed with a mycoplasmic lung infection, similar to pneumonia.

The doctor explained that I was quite sick and started me on massive doses of antibiotics. Even after taking all the medications prescribed, the coughing continued for two months. Again, I had taken one step forward and two steps back in my training. The plan was to go to Florida for camp in February to meet my new teammates that I would be racing with in Texas. I wasn't sure if I would be able to regain my strength in time to race.

Spending all of January coughing in bed had left me exhausted and weak. The only good news was that all the coughing gave me killer abs.

In mid-February we drove to Florida in the motorhome. Although the coughing had stopped, I was still weak from the lung infection. We arrived early to get some much needed road miles on my legs and I found myself both nervous and excited to meet new teammates. After listening to the motivational tapes my uncle had given me in Phoenix I was absolutely ready to get back to work and build my stamina.

Tracy was the first to arrive. She had short blond hair and a muscular build that reflected time spent in the gym. She spared no time firmly establishing who owned the team. Her father was the primary sponsor, and provided the van as well as our new team uniforms, which both displayed his company's name.

The next was Sally; a petite girl with short dark hair, whose build looked more like that of a runner than of a cyclist. I later learned that she was indeed a runner as well, and a collegiate gymnast.

Then Elise arrived with her thick black wavy hair, dark eyes and thick glasses. She was the veteran of the team due to her many years of racing experience. She was very quiet, and her strength was in endurance.

Clair Young pulled into camp in his motor-home with motorcycle in tow. He was going to serve as our team manager, but had no idea what he was getting himself into with this group of women. None of us did.

Armed with a new van, matching bikes, complete uniforms and warm-ups, we looked the way a pro team should. Our Florida training lasted over a month. We each arrived alone, but we left as a team headed for Texas to race in a large, international, month-long stage race called the Tour of Texas. I thought of it as the Tour de France, Texas style.

Even before we reached our destination, the competitive tension began to appear within the team. Tracy, a sprinter, and Sally, a road racer, were both very talented and strong. However, Tracy's father "owned" the team as he was our sponsor, and she never missed an opportunity to remind us of that fact. We left Florida and traveled in the team van, loaded with bikes on top and the team name and sponsors painted on the sides. At every fuel stop Tracy insisted that we get out cleaning the windshields, checking the oil, and filling the tank. She also demanded that we stop and buy large towels to cover the seats to assure we did not soil them in any way during our travels.

The race headquarters were located in Austin. Tracy's father arranged for the team to stay at her grandparent's estate in Horseshoe Bay about an hour away. When we arrived we were directed to our quarters. Tracy occupied a suite that contained a beautiful pink and cream colored canopied bed and private bath on the main level of the house. Meanwhile the rest of the team stayed in the basement and shared the shower and toilet there.

Happy to have a place to stay, we spent the first couple of days, shaking off the travel trauma by riding through rolling hillsides dotted with fields of bluebells and small, dog-sized deer with Clair riding with us on his motorcycle.

The competition began long before the races started. Tracy and Sally fought constantly in an attempt to establish dominance. Tracy may have held the upper hand in sprints and finances, but Sally proved to be a superior climber and endurance rider.

Clair stayed in his motorhome with Angelo and Rick, the two male members of our team who were racing the tour. Clair stood about five feet two inches short with thick white hair and powerful legs that could still put young riders to shame, although he was in his late sixties. He looked a little like Buddy Hackett, but had a quieter sense of humor. Clair took us out on training rides where we would pace off his motorcycle or practice sprinting up hills. He may have been quiet and reserved, but he knew the sport and what it took to win.

During our training sessions, Tracy and Sally tried to outrace one another. Unfortunately, on more than one occasion, crashes involving either of them seemed to always be the fault of the other. They complained either to Elise or me every chance we had alone and sometimes even called Mike or Dale long distance to express how unhappy they were with the other. They quickly learned that Clair didn't want to get involved in all the bickering and sniping. We all wondered just how much of an accident, it really was when Tracy stopped to gas up the van and drove away, leaving Sally in the gas station restroom. It might have been an accident, but either way it took more than ten minutes for Tracy to turn the van around and pick her up.

When we arrived in Austin for the riders meeting, stars filled my eyes. Rebecca Twig, Jeannie Longo, Inga Thompson, Connie Paraskevin Young (Clair's daughter-in-law), Betsy King, Betsy Davis and so many other outstanding international female cyclists were standing at registration. We decided to stop by Connie and Roger's hotel room after we all finished with registration. Just before we knocked on the door, Tracy stopped us with her arm stretched out. "You realize that we are about to enter the room of a world champion. Take note of their lifestyle," she said in a pointed yet hushed tone.

We knocked and Roger opened the door and welcomed us into the room. "Where's Dad?" Roger asked. Tracy piped in, "He's trying to find a parking place for his motorhome." He stepped aside as we entered. Connie sat on the bed, surrounded by papers; the dresser drawers were open, with clothing hanging over the edges, and there was a tray filled with food wrappers discarded to the side. The room was a wonderful mess and I loved it! We all looked at Tracy with a defiant look: "See, you don't have to have a spotless room or van to be a world champion!" In this rare instance, she was absolutely speechless.

The competition started with a time trial, called a prologue, designed to establish the initial ranking of the riders. After that, the majority of the stages became road races so we traveled from city to city racing in canyons and over rolling terrain with huge climbs.

In one memorable race in Texas, I was in an excellent position when the field came to a cattle guard crossing on the course. The cattle guards were made simply of loose metal pipes set in a cut out running perpendicular across the road to keep cattle from walking over it. When the bikes crossed them, the pipes moved beneath us. We encountered a few of these during the race causing the pack of riders to slow down before the guard and then everyone would sprint afterwards. I was riding in a very large field when someone ahead of me abruptly put on their brakes creating a domino effect. Before riders had time to realize what happened, there were about a dozen bikes tangled in the road around me.

Support personnel seemed to appear out of nowhere, picking up bikes, reuniting them with their riders and pushing them back into the race. One rider, a former teammate and Olympian from Dayton named Janelle Parks shouted "My knee, my knee!" drawing a lot of the support people in her direction. Meanwhile, a man from one of the support cars threw me on my bike without pause and pushed me off before attempting to notice or straighten my handlebars, which were twisted drastically to the right.

Stunned, but with adrenaline surging, I kept pedaling as fast as possible. Legs pumping, heart racing, lungs burning; I knew that if I stopped to make adjustments I would lose even more time. I kept pushing since stage racing is all about time.

I was approaching a steep downhill that ended with a sharp turn to the right at the bottom, where the smell of melting brake pads from the bikes ahead of me still lingered in the air, alerting me that I was not far behind the main pack. Braking was difficult with the handlebars askew, but turning right was nearly impossible.

The next thing I knew I was going straight where the road turned right; I went straight off the road. Spectators rushed to pick me up from the prickly scrub. I don't know what I had crashed into as I didn't have time to look, but I certainly felt the stabs of sharp needles through my Lycra shorts. Frustrated, I pounced around to the front of my bike, grasped the front wheel between my knees, then firmly and quickly jerked the handlebars into their proper alignment. Next, I grabbed the bike and charged back up to the road with it on my shoulder. Cyclocross training helps sometimes even in a road race.

I hopped on and continued my pursuit of the pack. This time I was mad. I caught the back of the field just a few miles from the finish line. I will never know just how well I might have finished if I had not crashed TWICE in that race. It could have been the anger or the adrenaline that pushed my legs harder than before. Perhaps this was the "mean" that Mike had referenced. In addition, I learned to never rush and let myself be pushed back into a race until I was sure my bike had been set straight again.

A week later, Tracy's father arrived in an oversized motorhome while we were in the garage fine tuning our bikes in preparation for the next day's race. As he stepped out of the motorhome we could see that he had another man with him. We didn't pay any attention to them until we clearly overheard him, saying to the other man, "You see those bikes? I own them. You see those girls? I own them too. They race for me." Until that moment, I hadn't realized that I was owned.

We raced more days than we rested, often three and four in a row, but we did get Easter off. Since we were not considered guests at Tracy's grandmother's house, Tracy told us, in no uncertain terms, that her family was going to have Easter brunch at the estate and we needed to make ourselves invisible. We decided to seek our Easter meal elsewhere. Our band of outcasts cheerfully climbed into the team van and drove into the small, isolated resort town of Horseshoe Bay.

On that sunny Easter Sunday morning, we ventured out in search of food. Every shop and restaurant in the area had closed for the holiday but at long last we discovered an open doughnut shop. We walked in and gazed at the glass display of sweet pastries with hungry eyes. The shop owner looked at us with surprise as he visually evaluated the three strange women standing before him.

"We can't tell you how happy we are that you are open!" we exclaimed. "We have been looking everywhere for something to eat and your shop is the only one open." "Today is your lucky day then!" he said, "Since I have not seen a single customer all morning, I was planning to close the shop early. Another five minutes and the door would have been locked." The relief or the hunger in our eyes must have been apparent. "You can have all the donuts you want. I would just have to throw them away. They are yours, no charge. Just let me know which ones you want." Thrilled, we thanked him repeatedly as our wide eyes watched the sugar crusted wheels being poured into white waxy bags.

We happily devoured the scrumptious fried dough and pastries, delighting in the knowledge that they were ours. Even though we had full knowledge that they consisted of nothing but fat and sugar, they felt so morally satisfying that we didn't care. We returned to Tracy's grandmother's house and went straight to the garage to work on our bikes because we didn't have anything else to do. A short time later, Tracy's step-mother appeared in the garage door entrance to the house, "We are all finished eating, you are welcome to come in now, there are plenty of leftovers," she announced. Even more delicious than the doughnuts was the ability to smugly refuse her offer, satisfied with our own unique Easter feast. It may not have been the healthiest of lunch choices, but it turned out to be great food for our spirits.

For over a month the battle to establish superiority raged. The stage race had a team time trial where we were to start with four riders and the team's overall time was determined by the time of the third rider. This type of synchronized team racing demanded teamwork and the members had to work closely together for the common good of the team. Each rider had to take turns pulling into the wind, thus giving the others a chance to rest in their draft. Elise, our fourth rider, unable to keep up the pace, dropped out halfway through the race, which left Tracy, Sally and me to continue and set the time for our entire team.

When a team loses a rider in a time trial it puts a lot more strain on everyone, as each person has to work more and rest less. Adrenaline surged with increased feelings of urgency, causing tempers to flare and our speed to decrease. Tracy and Sally continued arguing about who should be pulling and for how long, blaming each other for not working enough and not working well as teammates. It was my turn to yell at them. "You know this is a TEAM time trial. If we want to finish and have a team at the end, stop yelling and start pedaling!" They seemed startled. I think they had been so focused on each other that they forgot that I was even present. We reassembled and got back into a rhythm, but our time reflected everything that had gone wrong. At least we didn't crash like so many of the other teams had that day.

The final stage was a criterium held on the city streets of Austin. Races referred to as Crits were very different from the road races we competed in previously and were more technical, involving more sprints and turns. Due to the increased technical challenges, crashes happened more often in Crits and they favored the sprinters more than endurance climbers.

On the morning of the final race, rain began to fall. This was a great concern to many, as the top racers' times were so close that a crash caused by slick roads could affect the outcome of the entire stage race. The women all pulled together and protested. As a group we sat down on the start/finish line and refused to get onto our bikes until the officials determined that the stage race times would be final and the Criterium results would not affect the outcome of the overall results. After a fifteen minute delay, during which we sat in the rain, the announcement was made. The officials conceded and proclaimed that the stage race was officially over and all the times would stand. It was good to know that there was indeed power in unity.

After the Tour was over we packed up all our gear and headed east to race in every major cycling event we could find on the calendar. Joined by more of our regional team mates, we moved from race to race like nomads. In North Carolina, we competed on rolling countryside roads lined with fragrant pine trees in a race called "Tour de Moore." We did very well, easily dominating the sprints and controlling the peloton. Our one major flaw was that we didn't know where the finish line was located and were caught off guard in the final sprint by the local racers. Lesson learned: Always drive the course the night before, especially if it is a point to point race so that you will know where the finish line is located and how to time your sprint.

*　　*　　*

While training in Maryland, Angelo Chinni, one of the men on our team, and I fished off a pier for blue crabs using nothing but a leftover fried chicken leg hanging from a string. We walked out on the moss covered dock, smelling the salt air from the ocean peaked with the scent of fish, and submerged the chicken leg in the clear water below. We watched as the crabs circled around our bated string. Angelo said that when crabs grab hold of their prey, they don't let go and we could just pull them up and put them in the bucket.

Most of our team was skeptical and didn't think crabs could be caught with this method, but we proved them wrong. We returned from the dock with a five pound bucket full of blue crabs. Truthfully, we only caught two with the chicken leg; the rest was provided by a fisherman who, after emptying his traps, walked up to us and watched as we drowned our chicken leg with little result. We bought a bucket full of crabs from him and he seemed so amused by our lame attempts that we were charged next to nothing. Of course we waited to tell our teammates that detail until after they gazed, mouths open, at the crustaceans crawling in the bucket.

Maria, one of our new teammates, had a background as a track racer and had been the National Junior Women's track sprint champion on more than one occasion. She stood just a bit taller than me and had short jet black hair with purple highlighted stripes thrown in. Maria was a sprinter with a rebel attitude, along with a very powerful jump on the bike, and loved the sport purely for the fun and thrill of the race.

Racing with Maria was fun, as she was not only strong; she knew how to work as a team. One particular race in Florida had a large draw with a generous prize list. Maria and I blocked the field, helping Tracy ride off the front until she was out of sight; we worked to control the pack to keep others from jumping and catching her. This technique is referred to as blocking.

Eventually we found ourselves off the front with one other woman who did not work with us. She simply sat on our wheels taking advantage of our draft while refusing to take her turn to work and pull through to break the wind for us to rest. She was what would be called a "wheel sucker" because she contributed nothing. Since we were all working toward the same goal at that point, in an effort to guarantee a monetary prize, everyone in the breakaway is expected to do their share of the work to stay away from the main field that was chasing to catch us. This was a long road race and as we passed one section of spectators, I heard a man's voice rise above all others with a familiar "Sit on her Nancy!"

Oh my goodness, was that a voice from my past? Was this *THE* Nancy from my very first race? It was! I knew her strategy was to have us do all the work and then attempt to out-sprint us at the finish. Some things never change.

Maria and I decided that we were not going to make it easy for her this time. We agreed that one of us would ride steady with Nancy on our wheel and then open a big gap while the other accelerated up ahead. When Nancy realized a gap was opening, she would be forced to jump up and close the distance and we would just sit on her wheel as she towed us back up to the other rider. Then the other rider would repeat the process of opening a distance, forcing her to work to close the gap again. It was a little like leapfrog and allowed each of us to get a small break from pulling. We did this to force Nancy to work instead of getting a free ride in our draft. It only took a few gaps before she could no longer keep up and we took a solid jump away and left her far behind.

After the race was finished, Nancy and her boyfriend protested our tactics. Her eyes filled with huge crocodile tears as she pleaded with the official that we had worked as a team against her. I will never forget the look on the official's face as he explained to her, "You know that strategy and hard work are actually allowed in bike racing." He then quite visibly stifled a laugh and walked away shaking his head and mumbling under his breath. That is what teamwork is all about. Watch and learn, Nancy. *Watch and Learn.*

Another race that year was the National Capital Open, a prestigious event that took place on the ellipse behind the White House in Washington, DC. Called the NCO for short, the riders called it the National Crash Open. Although there are no real corners and the race was around the gradual radius of the ellipse, one might assume it would be a safe venue. But it was quite difficult because the sewer grates along the inside curbs had large gaps that could stop a front wheel in an instant and many crashes occurred when riders got pinched to the inside. They had to work harder to advance around the outside because they were forced to travel a greater distance. We just had to race smart and survive amidst the sprints and swerve to miss fallen riders.

It was an honor to race under the watchful eye of the Washington Monument in the shadow of the White House. Friends I knew from the National Men's teams and riders that I had not seen since the Mayor's cup on the east coast were there. I was thrilled to get to see their race, cheer for them and get caught up on how life and racing had been for them that year. From DC, we traveled to race in Pennsylvania, Ohio, and Indiana. In Indianapolis, we competed at the velodrome and I was reminded of my first ride there with Ken, scared and shaking at the thought of competing on the track. Now I was returning as a seasoned racer and the Russian national team was going to be there.

Mike Walden traveled down from Michigan to watch us race. Our women's team dominated the international racing in Indianapolis, both on the track and the road. Teamwork once again proved profitable. Maria and I rode at the front of the pack to control the pace so that Tracy could get away from the field. Then Maria and I would take all the field sprint primes and share the prize money with the team.

After winning the women's Circuit race at Brookside Park, we joined the men in their race. The plan was to get more race experience and training. Unfortunately, it was made very clear to me by one of the men that he didn't appreciate having us in his race. "You don't belong in this race," he growled as he rode in the tightly packed field. "Isn't it enough that you and your teammates just ganged up on my girlfriend in her race? If you think I'm going to be a gentleman and let you in this race, you had better think again." Then he tried to make me flinch as he faked a move in my direction. I was just in the men's race for training. There was no reason to get taken out in a crash just because I competed against his girlfriend and defeated her, so I moved out of his sight for the rest of the race.

Indianapolis was our final official destination as a team. The racing season was basically over so my parents came to watch us race one last time and drive me home to Ohio. As we sorted our gear and were saying final goodbyes in the parking lot of the velodrome, I heard Clair, a strong, quiet man of few words, burst out to Mike, "I will never travel with a group of women again!" just before he slammed the door to his motorhome and started his drive back to Michigan. I smiled, knowing that he had endured a lot having been surrounded by the "estrogen" team for an entire summer.

* * *

After track nationals it was clear that I needed a more powerful sprint on the track. In the match sprints I had raced against one of Mike's former world champions, Connie Paraskevin, and this event was her forte.

When Mike was with me during my warm-up he told me "You don't have a chance in hell of beating her in the sprint. Just make sure you give her a good ride and make it your best ride yet." I tried to take the sprint long, which meant that I had to lead out and jump early. She did what any good sprinter would do. She sat in my draft for a few moments, and then passed me at the finish. Later in the points race, Mike gave me more advice. "Stay high on the track, so high that you have paint on the knuckles of your right glove when you come down." Following his direction I ended up getting pushed up the track and did scrape the boards with the back on my right hand pinned between them and my handlebars. "I didn't mean literally!" he laughed as I showed it to him after the race.

Mike had often mentioned that speed skating and cycling were perfect complementary sports because they use the same muscles and often the same strategies in racing. Connie was one of his many world champions that had been a speed skater. When I returned to train with Mike in Michigan he told me, "If you want to improve your sprint on the bike, you need to start speed skating. Speed skating will build the muscles and the snap you need to sprint." As we walked through his bike shop he continued, "It will keep your racing instincts sharp through the winter months. Short track skating races are a lot like bike races on the track."

He pulled a pair of speed skates down from a shelf. "Have you skated before?" he asked. "I used to figure skate." I told him, concealing my joy at the thought of getting back on the ice. "Well, I won't hold that against you." he said, grinning as he handed me a pair of Planert speed skates.

They looked nothing like figure skates and didn't feel anything like them either, but I adapted to the long blades quickly. Returning to the rink where I had previously skated in Dayton, I realized how much I missed the freedom I felt, gliding at speed. There weren't any speed skaters in southwestern Ohio, so I traveled back to Michigan to skate with the Wolverine sports club on their ice to get instruction and coaching. Clair gave me a few pointers to help me learn what skills I should be honing to improve my performance.

Since I began skating far better than Mike had ever expected, he told me about the training program at the United States Olympic Education Center (USOEC) in Marquette, Michigan. This was a training center established to allow athletes to train full time while going to school, something that many elite level athletes had to sacrifice. They required that all athletes be enrolled in school full time to live and train in their facility. I had already gotten my degree in nursing so I decided to study exercise physiology to become a better, more competitive racer.

The USOEC had a special co-ed dorm on the campus of Northern Michigan University designated as the living quarters for athletes. The dorm accommodations were sets of two rooms connected by a shared bathroom. Students in many other sports trained there, including speed skating, boxing, XC skiing, biathlon, rowing, badminton, team handball, and Nordic combined.

My assigned suite-mate, Christine Klein, had fine blonde hair, radiant pale blue eyes, alabaster skin, pink apple cheeks and a warm bubbly personality. She was one of the sweetest people I had ever met. She had been homeschooled in Ketchikan, Alaska, where she had studied engineering in her undergraduate studies and was now working toward her masters in meteorology and museology.

Growing up in Alaska, Christine had become a long track speed skater, outdoors on a 400 meter oval track. She was not accustomed to warm climates and anything above sixty degrees convinced her that she was melting. Our dorm rooms overlooked Lake Superior and I never felt what I considered a warm breeze coming off that great lake, yet she often felt overheated in the early fall months.

The cyclocross bike was my only mode of transportation, so I rode to all my classes no matter the weather. Considering Marquette gets an average of two hundred and fifty inches of snow a year, there were some distinct challenges at times, including a blizzard my first winter there.

I loved the classes, living in a sports environment and studying as a returning student. It was a completely different experience than nursing school where we were in a competitive environment, at the mercy of the instructors, doing everything we could just to graduate. This time it felt as though I was paying the professors to teach me things that I wanted to learn and apply to my own life, and was determined to get everything possible from my education. Motivated by a piece of paper I received in the mail a few years earlier, there was something I had to prove. I had been declared "mentally retarded" and was going to prove them wrong.

At the end of my first semester I opened the envelope that held my grades with great excitement. I'm sure I startled quite a few people with my shriek of joy that poured out of my soul. Not only have I proven to myself that I was not mentally retarded, I proved it to the world and I had it in writing! My name was on the Dean's list!

We had speed skating practice every morning. The ice rink was part of the Physical Education and Instructional Facility (PEIF) building where all the exercise science classes were conducted and it was convenient since it was just a little over a mile away from our dorm. Skating started at 7am every morning, but I got there earlier because as a junior member on the team, it was my responsibility to help place the safety mats around the corners of the rink every day. Most crashes in speed skating happen in the corners and the crash mats help absorb the impact and protect the athletes from injury.

Short track speed skating was an exhibition event in the 1988 Winter Olympics in Calgary. I was determined to watch the techniques they used that were literally "cutting edge." I studied how they leaned in the turns, the path and rhythm of their strokes. I was going to *watch and learn* everything I could from them.

In the spring of 1988, I went back to Florida to coach and ride at bike camp. It quickly became obvious that speedskating had indeed helped my cycling since my sprint was stronger and my hill climbing had noticeably improved. It felt wonderful to be able to power away in sprints, even if they were just for fun.

To be closer to bike racing at the Velodrome in the summer, and not too far from my family in Ohio, I found an apartment in Indianapolis. After securing a job working as a nurse in a hospital near the track, I made new friends in the local cycling community and settled in happily, riding every opportunity I could find and living on peanut butter and pickle sandwiches.

It was a summer of independence, not living at home with my parents or in a dorm. I had my own Goodwill acquired, eclectic furniture décor in the living room and Cornell dishes decorated with ducks alongside the mismatched plastic cups in the cabinets as well as the cheapest flatware I could find in the silverware drawer. Living independently was a new adventure. The only downside to the adventure was that I didn't see my family very often.

*   *   *

When I lived in Ohio I had been able to ride my bike to visit family fairly regularly. My great grandmother on my father's side was full blooded Native American had been married a few times in her life. We referred to her as "Grandma-Mommy" as she had a lot of kids, grandkids, great grandkids (like me) and even great-great grandkids. She was 97 years old when I last visited her on my bike. She sat in a leather bound, high backed chair with her cherry tobacco filled pipe smoldering next to her. Her husband, Herbert Huff sat nearby.

Her vision was poor, but her hearing was sharp. I sat across from her in a folding chair in my cycling clothing and talked with her about school and life and riding for nearly half an hour before she leaned forward, took a long draw off her pipe and studied my face. She let the smoke sneak out between her teeth before she said, "Herbert, which one of my kids does this one belong to?" "That's Cindi, Herb and Sydney's daughter." "Oh, she said as she leaned back in her chair. " And they let you ride a bicycle?" I laughed as she took another puff on her pipe.

On my mother's side, I had my grandma "Gertie" and her husband Gene. Gene Earach might not have been my biological grandfather, but he was the only one I had ever known. He was short with dark eyes and olive skin with a very thick head of hair. He was very soft spoken if he spoke at all and loved to watch sports on television and jingle change in his pockets. My grandmother was the matriarch of the family and pretty much ruled everything that happened from the kitchen. It was there that we celebrated holiday meals and talked surrounded by smells of food cooking, mixed with the odor of stale cigarettes and coffee. It was at that table that my grandmother once burst out over dinner, "When are you and Ken going to get married so I can have some great-grandchildren?" I'll never forget riding to my grandmother's house as she was working in her flower garden. She stood up slowly, looking up at me in my Lycra clothing. "Oh my goodness!" she shouted, "Your anorexic!" "No Grandma, I'm not anorexic, I'm a cyclist."

* * *

My grandparents' happy life was interrupted one sunny day in early July when Gene was cutting wood in their backyard and chest pain stopped him. My grandmother called 9-1-1 and he was taken straight in for an emergency coronary bypass. After surgery he did not regain consciousness, he slipped into a coma. Their family doctor had warned them both that if they didn't stop smoking, they would both be dead in the next six months. Despite efforts to struggle free from the addictive grasp of nicotine, they could not get away from it. He never regained consciousness.

My mother and grandmother visited him daily, looking for signs of hope. Early in the morning on July 18th my phone rang and it was my father's voice, which caught my attention, because he refuses to use the phone. My first thoughts were of Gene. "It's Gene isn't it?" I said mournfully, bracing myself for his next words. "No, it's worse." was his reply. "It's your grandmother. Your mother found her this morning. She had a stroke." He paused. "She's gone." His words sucked all the air out of my lungs only to be replaced with gasps of grief.

The night before the doctor ran a test that indicated Gene was never going to wake up. My grandma Gertie, who was distraught learning that she would never have her love by her side again went home alone for the last time and suffered a massive stroke. Sadly, I lost both of my grandparents that summer seemingly on the same day. I had been very close to them both growing up and my heart ached with their loss. I felt that cigarettes had stolen both of them from me.

I felt guilty that I had not spent more time with them. That I had been pursuing my own dream of racing and I had missed so many opportunities to visit, but my mother assured me that they understood that I was building my own life.

* * *

Later that summer Ken decided that he was going to come to the USOEC to join me. He had been studying Human Factors Engineering at Wright State University, a profession that works with ergonomic design. He gave up that major when he enrolled at Northern Michigan University because they did not offer his program so he switched to computer science. He also contracted to be the speed skating coordinator and help manage the training program. I admired his commitment and the lengths he would take to be with me.

There was a delay in the preparation of the dorm for the athlete's arrival so we could not check in when we got there and had to stay at a hotel in Marquette. My hotel room was just a few doors down from the main lobby and someone must have been smoking nearby. The familiar odor crept into my room as I slept and blended with my dreaming subconscious, stirring memories of my grandparents. I dreamt that they were still alive and rejoiced as I rushed to hug and tell them how much I loved and missed them. Something pulled me from my dream and I woke up, aware that I had been asleep and realized that they really were dead and I would never get to see them again. Till that point I had not been able to grieve the loss that was hiding in my heart. They actually were gone and the realization felt like someone had opened the gates that held my emotions and I flooded the room with uncontrollable sobs of the agonizing truth. They were gone forever.

*   *   *

At the USOEC, the members of the 1988 US Olympic short track speed skating team representing the United States in Calgary joined us. Their form and training techniques were inspiring. I was definitely watching and learning all I could from them. Getting to know their personalities, training side by side daily and traveling to competitions with them on the weekends provided a rich experience.

In 1989, I traveled back to the US Olympic Training Center in Colorado Springs, where I helped develop the Regional Coaching Coordinators Program based on a lot of what Mike Walden had instilled in his coaching staff.

This was a new effort to provide coaches with standardized training at the regional level to help them oversee and direct coaches at the local level. We helped create the handbook to document the skills taught, setting the basis of training and expectations for cycling in the United States. My favorite part was meeting all the Regional Coordinators and teaching them the skills we had been teaching for years at bike camp, making it possible for them to pass that knowledge on to their coaches.

It was during this time that the United States Cycling Federation asked me to work as the coach and coordinator for the cycling program at the USOEC in Marquette. Combining all that I had learned from coaching for years at bike camp with my education in exercise science, I felt that I was ready to take on coaching at that level.

The next fall semester I moved into my office at the training center. We had a lot of snow fall that year, often making it difficult to ride outside. Therefore, my riders were introduced to speed skating, which served as a great form of cross training. Although there was some resistance at first, most of them picked it up very quickly.

Part 2 – Life beyond racing

Every spring, I left the training center and went to Florida to follow my growing passion for coaching. There was something gratifying about being able to teach someone a new skill and see them apply it. I was growing beyond looking at how I could improve myself and my skill, and learning I could pay it forward by helping others reach their goals.

Ken stayed behind in Marquette working with the skaters and continued his studies. In 1989, when I returned to the training center after camp, he picked me up at the airport and drove a direction that was unexpected, not toward the dorm, but toward the outskirts of Marquette. When I asked where we were going, he replied, "You'll see."

We entered the Northwood's Restaurant and saw tall beams of hand hewn timbers looming overhead and a large panoramic window framing the view of the deep woods beyond. The sun had set long before our arrival and the snow draped pine trees sparkled in the light from the lodge. He did not wait until we finished our meal before he brought out a small dark blue box.

"You probably have already guessed what is in the box," he said, as he gently took my hand in his. "I would be really happy if you said yes." Pausing for a moment to take it all in, not exactly prepared, I said "Hmmm." I couldn't help smiling, even though I was trying to seem serious. "What makes you think I know? Maybe I should see it first." I joked. His hands trembled slightly as he opened the small blue box, revealing a classic pear shaped diamond ring. "Okay, you're going to make me do this the old fashioned way aren't you?" He joked in reply. My heart raced and then I teased, "If it were really the old fashioned way you would have asked my father for permission first." "What makes you think I didn't?" he answered and we both burst out laughing, thankful for the comic relief.

Then he took the ring out of the box, held it out to me and calmly said, "Will you marry me?" He had asked me before. Sitting on the sand at Disney World after a dinner at the Polynesian dinner show. He had presented me with a coral ring while we watched the electric light show on the water. I had said, "Yes," but got cold feet and changed my mind quickly afterwards. This time, the ring was a diamond; he was determined. I seriously considered his proposal for a moment, a long moment. So many thoughts were going through my mind. Did I really want to get married?

Then I remembered how much I had missed him when I was in Florida. We had only been separated for six weeks and it seemed like forever. I thought of how dedicated, smart and loving he was and how he flew to see me when he heard that I was nearly killed by the car and patiently waited for my memory to return. He had waited for my returns so many times when I had been absent for months at a time to race around the country, train in Florida and at the Olympic training centers. This man had uprooted his life to join me in mine. I realized how rich life felt when we were able to share it and knew that there was so much more I wanted to share with him in our future.

One thing did hover in my mind and I asked, "If I were to say yes, would it be okay if I married you, but not your name?" All my life no one could pronounce my last name correctly. Cindi Lou Pfaff was the name my parents gave me when I was born. We pronounce it "Poff" and I had ALWAYS dreamed of the day when I would marry someone with a normal sounding name. Ken's last name was Blauvelt (pronounced "Blah-fvelt".) Taking his name would be like jumping from the frying pan into the fire as far as names were concerned. Heaven help us if we were to hyphenate the two names. I mean really, Pfaff-Blauvelt?

Much to my surprise, without hesitation, Ken replied, "What if I changed my name?" This concept was foreign and exciting to me at the same time. "Really, you would change your name for me?" I asked. He promptly responded, "I wouldn't have offered if I didn't mean it."

Elated at the potential, we considered different names for months, looking through phone books and trying names on for size. During road trips, we played with names that would pop into our heads, but eventually we started to get serious.

Bike oriented names were, of course, a major consideration. We narrowed the choices down to two choices. One was Madison, a bike race/relay that takes two people working in complete cooperation to achieve their goal. The other was "Hart" for all the hearts Ken had sewn on the cycling clothing he had given me as a reminder of his love.

I tried on both names, Cindi Madison and Cindi Hart. I liked them both. When I was saying them over and over again to myself I realized that Madison Hart sounded good together as well.

So six months before our wedding, with very little fanfare, Ken legally changed his name to Ken Blauvelt Hart. We would be Mr. and Mrs. Ken Hart and if we ever had a child, we would name him or her, Madison.

*　　*　　*

To maintain a fast and safe ice surface for speed skating, water is poured and spread over the track with large squeegees between races to heal the scars carved in the ice by the knife-like blades. Water makes the ice faster, reducing the coefficient of friction. Rubber blocks are used to mark the track corners and are supposed to glide freely over the ice in case a skater accidentally hits one.

Six weeks before our wedding I was skating and training for the World University Games Trials. This time either the ice was so cold that it froze a rubber block on contact or the block had been sitting in the water too long, which caused it to stick to the ice like glue. No matter how it happened, I hit the unyielding block and tripped at full speed.

Before I had time to react, I hit the safety mats, head first and felt my body crumple on impact. I was afraid to move, afraid I couldn't move. Surrounded by fellow skaters with concerned looks on their faces I was scared. "Don't move!" someone instructed. I had not stirred and did not know the extent of my injuries. After a short time, I had wiggled my fingers and toes and was helped off the ice. Amazed that I had not broken my neck I also realized that my injury was serious and that frightened me.

I was carefully transported to the sports medicine facility where x-rays revealed that I had sprained my neck. While sprains are considered mild as far as injuries are concerned, I realized once again that one small second in time could have changed my life forever. We take our bodies and our abilities for granted and I was thankful that I could move, although it was painful.

The doctor wrote a prescription for a muscle relaxant that knocked me out. Taking the medication made me feel as if all I did was sleep, eat, go back to sleep, get up and eat again; repeating the pattern for what seemed like a month. My head felt as though it was going to fall off the back of my neck if I moved and I knew I was done with skating for some time. Unlike being hit by the car, I remembered everything about this accident and knew it would be mentally difficult to skate very close to the blocks again.

There was no reason to stay at the USOTC and be tortured because I couldn't skate or train, so I flew home to stay with my parents in Ohio. During the weeks of healing, I had the opportunity to plan our wedding. By the time I was well enough to ride; it was time to go to Florida to coach and train once again with Mike and the rest of the staff at camp. It was very comforting to be back with my bike camp family where I knew I belonged.

I had established very close friendships with them and the riders over the years; they teased me about my upcoming wedding and told me that they were counting down the days they had left to talk me out of it. It was all in good fun and I enjoyed every minute we were together.

Planning a wedding is like putting a huge puzzle together, although there are no guarantees that all the pieces will fit. Not until you realize that you can change your puzzle pieces to whatever you like, will you get a clear picture.

We decided to get married on Memorial Day weekend 1990, because there was a very well attended bike race in Ken's hometown of Dayton at the time. Since we both had friends that were racers from all over the country, we thought it would be convenient for them. What cyclist wouldn't love a day of racing followed by free food and dancing in the evening?

Memorial Day weekend is a very popular time to get married and reserving a church on that Saturday was almost impossible. Our local church was not available on Saturday, which happened to be Ken's parents' wedding anniversary; however it was available on Sunday May 27th, which was my parent's anniversary.

Adapting to availability, we decided to get married on Sunday. Not quite the usual day of the week for a wedding, but I never claimed to be usual. When deciding on a minister and matron of honor, I called Cindy Lawrence, my best friend from college who was now a Minister. She met Rick Stackpole, the love of her life, at Seminary school after working at church camp. He had a passion for singing and church camps as well. They were married five years earlier on Memorial Day weekend and I was a bridesmaid in their wedding.

She was one of the first people I contacted when I was planning mine and I gave her the choice, "Do you want to be my matron of honor or the minister?" She answered, "I would be honored to stand beside you as your matron of honor, but I would be even happier to be the minister joining you and Ken in marriage." So we finalized our plan for the following year.

A lot of things can happen in a year. Cindy and Rick loved children and had been trying for a while to get pregnant, and as the stars would have it, Cindy was very pregnant by the time my wedding was to occur and could not travel from New York to Ohio. It didn't feel right not to have her there, but the new life she was nurturing was very precious. I understood and could not fault her in the decision she made. I knew so many ministers, having worked in church camps for several summers, but I wanted them to be there as friends, not working; so I asked the father of my high school friend, Charles Royalty, to be our minister.

Having grown up on a small farm, we were accustomed to doing most things ourselves: If we needed something, we made it. Why should my wedding be any different? My mother and I took care of making the pew bows together. She arranged silk flowers for the altar while I made corsages, bridesmaid's bouquets and designed my own dress. So much money had been spent in support of my training and racing that it seemed unreasonable to spend any more than necessary for a wedding.

Our friends from Marquette, Michigan had come to join us and agreed to sing during the service and DJ while Ken's sisters, Linda and Susie helped cater the reception. My father served as the photographer and my musically gifted brother, Scott, played his guitar during our procession.

I felt comfortable working on decorations and getting things finalized in preparation for the ceremony until the moment I was told that it was time to put on my wedding dress. "If you plan on getting married today, you need to let us take care of these details and go get dressed." Cindy Schwartz said as she pulled me into the dressing room at the church. She had been a very good friend in Marquette and had made my bridal veil and was working on my hair. I found it difficult to mentally change gears and put the dress on. I knew that once that happened, I would not be able to attend to any more details. This was it. *THE* moment!

"It's Show Time," my father said with a rare grin on his face as he poked his head in the door of the dressing room. I looked at my bridesmaids in their mauve dresses as they gathered their flowers and exited. The time had come and I was ushered to the door of the chapel. Queued up at the entrance to my new life, my father greeted me with camera in hand and as previously planned, I would walk to the altar on my own. Music began to fill the chapel and I watched as the last of my wedding party made their way down the aisle before me. The view beyond the doors yielded glimpses of the backs of a great number of people who filled pews that seemed empty only minutes before.

The music changed and I began the procession I had imagined my entire life. Everyone rose and turned toward me. Met with a wave of shining eyes and smiling faces, I saw so many people who, at some point had touched and shared my life, and were now here to share this special moment with us. This was an experience unlike any race I had ever known.

I began to walk through the portal to my new life and heard my father's voice whisper "Break a leg kid!" I took two steps forward and suddenly felt restrained, not by doubt or fear, but by the fact that he was standing on my dress. After a moment, noticed only by the two of us, I quickly returned to my original goal. I looked ahead to the altar where my future stood, waiting for me to join him. No longer able to see other faces beaming at me, I continued to feel their love. I came to the pew where my Aunt Janet and mother stood. My mother was holding my threadbare teddy bear that I had given her the night before. For so many years that little bear had comforted me and was my sleeping companion. It was a symbol of my childhood and that seemed to be the appropriate time to return it. My focus turned back to Ken, waiting patiently for me to join him.

During rehearsal, I had asked Ken if he wanted to memorize our vows instead of having Reverend Royalty spoon feed them to us. He never responded, so I thought that meant he didn't want to memorize them. So I didn't worry about it. When we stood up at the altar, facing each other, looking into each other's eyes and holding hands, Reverend Royalty started us in our vows and Ken took over. He had memorized them.

My eyes widened in surprise, and fear. I hadn't expected that from him. It was a good thing that we wrote our vows together and that he went first so I had a reminder of what I was to say when it became my turn.

After all the photos were taken in the chapel, we joined our friends and family at the reception at the church. Time seemed to be flying by so quickly and I wanted to stop and talk to everyone. So many dear friends had traveled a great distance to share in and be part of our life changing event. Mom kept reminding me that I should sit down and eat, but there were so many people I wanted to see and thank that hunger was the last thing on my mind.

After we cut the cake, the garter and bouquets were tossed and the dancing began. Although our first dance as husband and wife was special, the most memorable dance for me was the one where my profoundly deaf mother-in-law danced the chicken dance.

I had taken care of planning all the details of the wedding and made a deal with Ken that he would plan the entire honeymoon. Wanting it to be a surprise, I trusted him to decide where we would travel. My only request was that we would not go anywhere cold or where we would have to understand Spanish, as we had both studied French in school.

Ken and my mother conspired and managed to keep it all a secret. My bags were packed for me in advance so I wouldn't have any clues about what to expect. At the airport my parents greeted us with our luggage and helium filled balloons left over from the wedding with "Just Married" floating above our heads, announcing to everyone that we were newly-weds. Mom gave us a care package full of leftovers from the reception to take on the plane. After we said our final goodbyes and boarded, the flight was delayed for two hours on the tarmac. We didn't mind a bit because this was the beginning of our honeymoon and the thoughtful care package of wedding leftovers was greatly appreciated.

Somehow, Ken managed to pull it off and we boarded the plane without my having any idea what our destination was. When they announced that it was necessary to fill out immigration paperwork, I was surprised and delighted to learn that we were in Bermuda.

On the small island nation, we discovered pink coral sand beaches, peeping toads, and snorkeling in turquoise ocean water. We enjoyed elegant formal meals with Ken dressed in a tuxedo jacket with shorts and knee socks, and me in one of the semi-formal dresses my mother had packed. Visitors to Bermuda were not permitted to rent or drive cars for two good reasons. The island was only about 25 miles long with roads that were unable to handle the added traffic and the fact that people there drive on the opposite side of the road, British style, and the number of tourist accidents would be difficult to handle. So we took scooter rides around the islands. Every sight, sound and smell etched itself in my memory as time stood still in the celebration of our love and future ahead.

I had one moment of panic during our honeymoon, however, that made my heart stop. We were snorkeling around some of the gorgeous coral reef coves, observing the dashes of yellow and orange fish beneath us and reveling in all the beauty. In one snorkeling location we discovered impressive rock cliffs, jutting up from the ocean floor, surrounding alcoves in a guardian-like fashion. This did not create a concern when we entered the water, but unknown to us, the swells of the ocean waves above us were over five feet high. The tide started coming in unnoticed as we were enchanted by our underwater exploration, drawn in by the flash of never ending fish and the site of coral in the clear turquoise tinted water. The visibility underwater was outstanding, with pink sand below creating a great backdrop that made the other colors all the more magnificent.

At one point I looked up above the water and could no longer see Ken anywhere. Scanning in all directions, I found no sign of him. The increasing undulation of the waves created what looked like walls of water around me as I searched frantically. I popped up, tore the snorkel out of my mouth and began yelling his name as I thought if he swam too close to the rocks; the waves could easily have thrown him into the bluffs. Hearing no response, terror shot through me like a bolt of lightning. Panicked images flashed before my eyes, as I feared he might have been smashed into the rocks, drowning at that very moment. I didn't want to be a honeymoon widow! In desperate panic, I screamed his name as I bobbed up and down in the growing swells, with salt water splashing in my mouth.

Then I spotted him. His blue swim trunks were on the surface and his snorkel was upright. He was safe and completely oblivious to the terror I had just experienced. I kicked my fins as hard and fast as I could and headed toward him.

As soon as I was close enough, I reached out and touched him and he lifted his face out of the water, feeling the urgency in my touch. He removed his snorkel. "What?" he said, noticing the look on my face change from panic to relief. "I thought I had lost you!" I shouted above the waves. He seemed surprised, "I'm right here," he assured. I told him how I had panicked when I was unable to find him and thought that he might have drowned. "I would never leave you like that. You are stuck with me forever," he replied.

*   *   *

A New Life – A New Home

After graduation from NMU that spring, we returned home to Ohio to find that Ken's target job market was completely flooded with experienced computer people. Thankfully, we were able to stay with my parents while I worked as a nurse and Ken looked for work in his field.

When he was unable to find any employment opportunities in Ohio, we broadened our search. Somewhat familiar with Indianapolis, having raced there every Friday night through so many summers, we decided to check it out. Ken got an interview on the north side of town and I accompanied him.

After the interview, I suggested that we stop by Visiting Nurse Service on our way out of town so I could submit an application. When we got home two hours later, there was a call waiting on our answering machine. The human resource's person from VNS wanted to know when I would be available to start. Wasting no time, I called back to let them know I could start as soon as my husband found a job in Indianapolis. It still felt very strange referring to him as my husband. She asked, "What kind of work is he looking for?" "He works with computers." I told her. "Well, as luck would have it, we need someone in our computer support department." she responded.

Before we knew it, we were in orientation together, ready to make Indianapolis our new home. We secured a three month lease on an apartment near the velodrome and set out searching for a house. On Sunday mornings we eagerly opened the newspaper, mapped out all the open houses of interest in our price range, then plotted a route that would allow us to ride our bikes and check them out. It was important to us that our new home was close to good riding roads. We finally found a suitable home and made an offer.

It was a brand new spec home that had a hideous mauve carpet which probably scared a lot of people away. As a result, it had been sitting on the market for a while and they were willing to swap the carpet out and come down to a price that we believed was reasonable and in our range. The day our three month apartment lease ran out happened to be the day we closed on the house. We laughed when we considered that for a time that day, with all of our belongings packed tightly in a rented trailer, we were temporarily homeless.

Life was good; we drove to work together, ate lunch together, went home together, then rode and trained together in the evenings. Some people asked how we could stand being together so much of the time. I told them, "It's really easy when you marry your best friend."

Since we had become homeowners, we decided to warm up the decor of our home with a few plants. When the plants didn't die, we dared to take a risk and adopted a pet. He was a black and white humane society rescue cat that we named Pettit, in honor of the long track ice rink in Milwaukee by the same name. When we introduced him to our friends, they didn't quite understand the reference to speed skating. Some thought we were telling them to reach down and stroke his fur when we said, "This is our cat. Pet it"

We joined a small church that met every Sunday in the cafeteria of a nearby insurance company building and soon made friends that became our new Indiana family. My job advanced quickly and I found myself being promoted to nursing manager. A short time later they offered a new position to me and I became director of nursing for the home care division.

As life became more stable, we wondered about our next new challenge in life. After many years on birth control, how long would it take for my body to get back into fertility mode once the decision was made to bring a new life into the world? Needless to say, it took a lot longer than I expected or hoped to become pregnant. Things resorted to temperature taking, plotting and timing. I have never been a very patient person and waiting month after month to find that the timing had not worked was often emotionally crushing. You don't always realize how much you desperately want something until you decide you want it and it doesn't happen.

Nine months after we made up our minds to change our reservations from a party of two to a party of three, Ken and I were having lunch at the Omni Hotel, downtown. We had been there for a little while when I asked him, "Ken, if you are not too busy, I would appreciate it if you would coach me through an event next November." He looked at me a bit puzzled. Then, I watched as the gears in his head start turning. He began searching his internal files for events in November. As quick as a blink his eyes flashed with acknowledgment, and then his mustache moved as subtly as a Mona Lisa smile and I knew that he understood and was happy.

We decided not to tell anyone through most of the first trimester because we wanted to make sure for ourselves that it was real. I think we needed time to savor the knowledge that we were going to be parents before we would be ready to announce it to the world.

Arriving at bike camp, I wrestled with the timing of when I should tell my parents. They had been part of the camp staff for many years by that time, my mother as camp nurse and my father as a videographer / photographer. I didn't want to tell them before camp, as I didn't want my mother to worry about me any more than she normally did. As a nurse and an exercise scientist, I made sure to take it easy when riding, drank plenty of fluids and ate small, frequent meals.

I decided that the anniversary of my life altering crash in Florida, March 27th, would be a good day to tell them that we would be bringing a new life into the world. My mother was thrilled, but it took a little more time for my father to become comfortable with the idea.

On the last day of camp, during the traditional end-of- camp dinner with the staff, I experienced my first real episode of severe morning sickness. I decided to tell Chris, Dale and Mike our news as we were saying our last goodbyes. They were all excited for us, especially since we had considered them a big part of our family for so many years.

As our pregnancy progressed, I realized that we had to make some decisions. Many of the hospital deliveries I had witnessed were not my style. I wanted to be able to get up and walk around and have control over the situation. I decided that the clinical environment of a hospital was not my best choice. I chose a beautiful freestanding birthing center that had at one time been a house that was now operated by nurse midwives and overseen by an obstetrician.

Mom had been insistent on my going to a hospital for the delivery. After she toured the hospital and then the birthing center with me, she agreed that the center seemed to be a much better choice. However, she did insist that the nurse explain the details of patient treatment, as well as how the staff would be prepared with policies and procedures for any emergencies that might occur regarding the mother or the child.

When I went for my first prenatal checkup, I was excited to get to hear the baby's heartbeat for the first time. Even with nausea and my growing abdomen, it didn't seem "real" until that moment. The soft rhythmic swooshing sound is something that reaches into your soul and the wonder of life is almost overwhelming. Tears streamed down my face uncontrollably. WE REALLY WERE GOING TO HAVE A BABY!

I felt excited by the thought that soon we would have a child who would be able to *"Watch and Learn"* from us.

*   *   *

When my mother and Aunt Janet asked what we planned to name the baby, I told them that Ken and I had decided, before we were married, that our child would be named Madison. They both questioned, "What will you name the baby if it's a girl?"

In the early '90's, girls were not named Madison. My mother's name is Sydney; a name reserved for boys until it became popular for girls in the late '90's. My well-meaning mother and aunt argued that if we branded a girl with a name like that, she would encounter hassles like my mother had endured in school. But Ken and I were insistent and agreed that it was a name of strength.

In early May, we scheduled our first ultrasound and Ken, the gentleman that he is, dropped my mother and me off at the obstetrician's office door while he parked the car. They took us in right away, but Ken was delayed in the parking garage. The ultrasound technician went to work without waiting and in a short time we heard the "swoosh, swoosh, swoosh" of the heartbeat echoing from the machine. This distracted from the cold gel on the skin of my firm, round belly. She began sliding the plastic probe around while studying the morphing, black and white shapes on the monitor, and then she paused, looked at us, smiled and asked, "Do you want to know the sex of your baby?" The excited look in my mother's eyes told me that she was just as anxious as I was to get an official declaration. "Yes." I told the technician. Then she declared, "It's a girl."

All the wishes I made at the sight of the first star each night and all the pennies tossed into wishing wells had been granted. Tears of joy filled our eyes just as Ken walked in. "What's going on?" he asked, "What did I miss?" Because he had been kind enough to drop us off, then park the car, he had not gotten to hear the news with us. I felt guilty. The technician pulled up the image on the screen and he was able to see it changing before his eyes as she moved the sensor.

"Can you guess the sex of your baby by looking at the image?" she asked Ken. He looked at the screen and the technician indicated the area where he should be looking. "You should be able to tell around here," she told him, pointing to the screen. He replied, "You mean around that hamburger bun area?" We all burst into laughter. "What?" he said, as he stood looking very confused.

When I was five months pregnant, I raced at the velodrome in the State Championship time trial events, racing only against the clock to assure that I would not be knocked down in a race involving other riders. As you can imagine, I was a bit embarrassed to wear an aerodynamic Lycra skin suit when it appeared as though I had swallowed a cantaloupe. My father watched with a smile and teased as I rolled up to the start. "And now for our Tandem event!" he announced. "You know, if you win a medal here, you are going to have to share it with Madison," he said in my ear as I focused up the track. Amazingly, despite my condition, I won a gold medal in the short time trial and a silver medal in the long one. In my mind, I thought of these being Madison's first medals.

*   *   *

Later that summer, I experienced something called round ligament syndrome. The round ligaments are supportive ligaments attached to the uterus that are supposed to stretch during pregnancy. It appears that for women, who are very physically fit, these ligaments are a bit tighter and do not respond well to stretching thus cause pain. Unfortunately, I happened to be one of them.

The discomfort was almost debilitating. I called my nurse practitioner and she told me to rest with my feet up and it would pass. It did not. I am not a patient person, but I tried my best to do as she suggested. I tried resting on the couch, sleeping on my side, and even massaging the area where it hurt. Nothing worked. Deciding to try what my instinct told me would make me feel better; I went for a bike ride.

After ten minutes of riding, the pain subsided. It made perfect sense. I should have known from my experience as an exercise physiology; that repetitive movement warms stretches and often relaxes muscles and ligaments.

With that revelation, I vowed to myself, that I would continue riding as long as possible. Throughout the pregnancy I "watched and learned."

- I learned firsthand that trying to coach people who have large protruding stomachs, to get their knees in when they pedal, doesn't work because it is mechanically impossible.
- I learned that by leaning forward on the bike I was often able to relieve the pressure on the supportive structure in the pelvis.
- I learned that, when you are pregnant, your stomach becomes public property and total strangers touched my stomach without warning or permission.

- I learned that many people seem to think they can tell without the benefit of an ultrasound whether you are carrying a boy or a girl, and at least half of them were wrong. Many people look only at your abdomen and never seem to find your eyes with their gaze.
- Women I had never met in the past looked at me and smiled with an assurance and warmth I had not seen before.

With one month to go, an ultrasound revealed that Madison had not turned head down as expected and desired for a safe delivery. Breech position was considered a high risk presentation. Remarkably, I was in this same position when my mother gave birth without any difficulty or complication. My feet were up around my ears as I backed into this world. I found it quite interesting that they were telling me that Madison was trying to arrive the same way.

Breech deliveries were not allowed at the Midwife birthing center and women who presented for delivery in this condition required a C-section in the hospital. This definitely had NOT been in my plan. I went home and did everything I could think of to get my precariously posed offspring to turn around. I propped pillows on the couch to create an incline with my feet up and my head down, but nothing seemed to coax her into turning around. Our little girl was already proving she could be just as stubborn as her mother.

The obstetrician overseeing my progress mentioned an alternative solution. "There is a non-invasive option called an external version." She said. "It is not an easy procedure and there would be some discomfort, but if we can get her to turn around the C-Section will not be necessary." Ready and eager to give almost anything a try, I agreed.

We were directed to a large room where curtain dividers surrounded a sturdy mobile bed. After an injection of a drug to help my muscles relax, the obstetrician placed her hands on the outside of my skin that had expanded to accommodate an eight and a half month pregnancy. It quickly became very clear that she possessed the longest, thinnest, boniest fingers on the face of the planet as she attempted to push and pull the baby inside me from outside my abdominal wall in an effort to get Madison to turn around. I had seen videos of psychic surgeries that looked like someone could reach inside a person and pull out organs without breaking the skin. I almost expected to see her pull something out of me when she removed her hands because it felt as though she had reached deep inside my body.

Accustomed to pain from exercise, I did not anticipate the intensity of the pain that hit me. THIS was completely different. I found myself trying to breathe slowly and attempting to relax while it felt like the doctor was reaching through my belly button trying to touch my spine. After many attempts without success, she gave up. "I've tried all I can to make her move," she said, visibly fatigued by the physical effort it took for the procedure. "If you are willing, we can try again and I will schedule another doctor to help me. I think having four hands working together from different directions will work a lot better." I agreed but remained determined to have my child by natural birth, so we scheduled a second appointment, where an additional pair of hands would work with her to get the job done.

A week later I went back to what I referred as the OB torture chamber. Traces of yellow/green bruising from the last session remained on my belly. When my obstetrician introduced me to the doctor teaming up with her, I immediately looked at his fingers.

The two worked in tandem and this time employed ultrasound to discover a fibroid tumor, greater than 7cm in size that Madison used as a pillow. As I once again trained my focus on the ceiling in an attempt to relax, the physicians worked diligently together, pushing and pulling to no avail. Finally, and not without a lot of sweat from everyone involved, they reached our goal and we all breathed a sigh of relief. Madison would be ready to take on the world head first.

A week before Madison's due date, our dear friend Aldo came to visit from Ohio, as he was to participate in a cyclocross race in Indianapolis. I had always loved photography so Ken and I went to the race to take pictures of him in action. I waddled around with my camera, looking for the best angles to capture the light then started snapping photos. Aldo rode well, even on the rough terrain of off road racing, but still reminded me of the first time I saw him on the rollers at Miami University; steady, strong, skilled and well balanced.

That afternoon, while having the photos developed, I had a feeling that was foreign. It was my first contraction. I didn't tell anyone because I knew that Madison wasn't due for another week. "Maybe this is a false alarm, Braxton Hicks contractions, perhaps." I told myself. That night they became more regular and consistent and I was unable to sleep. Ken slept soundly next to me and I didn't want to alarm him.

At midnight, I realized the contractions had gotten pretty steady. With pains roughly five minutes apart, I got up and went downstairs to start cooking in preparation for the days ahead when I might not be able to cook. In the middle of my making turkey Tetrazzini, my father came downstairs and asked what I was doing up at that hour. "Looks like we are going to have a Halloween birthday," I told him sheepishly. "I'll get your mother," he said without hesitation and quickly did an about face disappearing back up the stairs.

She came downstairs in her robe. Having been fast asleep, she now appeared wide awake. "How far apart are the contractions? Have you called the nurse practitioner yet?" she asked while blinking under the bright lights in the kitchen. I lied and told her they were about 7-10 minutes apart. "Where is Ken?" she asked. "He's asleep upstairs. We don't need to bother him." I replied, "We need to wake him up. He should be here helping you." she demanded, "We don't need to wake him yet. He is going to need his sleep." I pleaded, but my words were ignored as another contraction became obvious.

There was no stopping her and before I knew it, they were all downstairs looking at me through sleepy eyes and watching as if I would pop at any moment. Mom told Ken to start timing every contraction while she documented them in classic nursing fashion, frequency, duration and intensity. I continued to cook and decided to make fruit salad as well, one of my favorite holiday dishes in honor of my grandmother.

Realizing that the contractions were getting more frequent, Mom started pushing me to call the nurse midwife. I kept stalling, not wanting to bother her in the middle of the night. When I thought it a fairly reasonable hour to call, I gave in and called at 6 am. The nurse on the phone calmly asked me how close the contractions were occurring and I told her that they were five minutes apart. "Do you think you can take a hot bath now?" she asked. "Sure." I replied to the suggestion that I had not expected. "Who ever heard of taking a bath while having contractions," I wondered.

"Do you think you can eat anything?" She asked over the phone. "Sure," I replied again. "Eat something and then if you are up to it, get in the tub for about 15 minutes. As soon as you get out, call me back and tell me how you are feeling," she instructed. I ate a piece of pie from the fridge and then got into the tub. The warm water worked its magic. I was amazed at how rapidly the contractions slowed to ten minutes apart, but as soon as I got out of the tub they returned to five minute intervals.

By 7: 30am we had packed all we planned to bring to the party. Casual onlookers might have gathered that we were headed out on an expedition. Ken put the XC Ski machine in the van at my request, and then I put the fruit salad and the baby seat in the back. We brought backpacks with clothes, cameras and food, looking like we had arrived ready to move in.

The nurses welcomed us with warm smiles, but were surprised when they saw Ken moving the rather large Ski exercise machine into the bedroom. Fortunately, the size of the large master-suite with its king sized bed, provided plenty of room for it,

Another family occupied the second bedroom and the mother- to-very- soon- be was having a hard time with her labor. We heard her moaning loudly and crying out from the other side of the house. I had sympathy for her because her pain seemed to last our entire stay.

At my request, Ken set up the ski machine next to the bed. I stepped on it and started skiing through my contractions while he sat on the bed watching and waiting and my mother sat nervously in the rocking chair. Carla, the midwife, said she had never seen anyone ski through labor, but thought it was a very good idea to help labor progress, so she approved. My conservative mother fussed around the room nervously, not as certain as Carla that skiing though labor was such a good idea.

The harder the contraction, the harder I would ski. It made absolute sense to me since I knew how to work through pain while exercising. Lying on a bed, focusing on a spot on the wall and breathing was just focusing on the pain itself. That may have been the more conventional method of dealing with labor, but it did not make sense to me and was not my preferred path. I was never one to be conventional.

When my contractions started becoming more intense, my skiing pace slowed. It was then decided that I needed to move to the hot tub. The warm water once again soothed and slowed the contractions just as it had earlier. In the midst of one of my contractions in the tub, I suddenly felt great relief from the pressure that had been building. Ken was trying to add more hot water to the tub at the time, as it had cooled to a tepid temperature. When the nurse came in to check on us I reported, "My water broke." This prompted the nurse to ask "The hot or the cold?" And I replied, "No, MY water broke!" We all laughed.

After a quick examination, it was clear that we would meet our daughter, Madison, very soon. We had a birthing plan all written out to include soothing music playing during delivery and had decided that we wanted our voices to be the first that she would hear. The labor progressed very well, except when Carla told me that it was time to push. She said that I was doing it wrong and needed to hold my breath and push. Many years of training as an athlete made it seem counterintuitive that I should hold my breath to push. It became second nature to me to breathe when I used my muscles. I kept breathing like I was lifting weights. Through the haze and confusion Carla's voice reached through to me. "Just listen and follow my directions," she said firmly in my right ear. My view of what was happening started getting narrower and blurry. "Take a deep breath and hold it," were the instructions in my ear. I did. "Now hold it and push." Again I obeyed.

Madison was born at 11:27 am under water and was quickly dried off and delivered into my arms. She had a shock of red hair and a mix of very purple and white skin. She didn't cry right away, so they started rubbing her little feet briskly as they toweled her off. They had Ken holding an oxygen tube up by her face when she took her first breath and cried. Looking down at her I melted as she reached up and pointed her index finger near my face. Recognizing that her fingers were just like mine, I thought to myself, "You are my purpose, aren't you? You are the reason I didn't die when I was struck by that car."

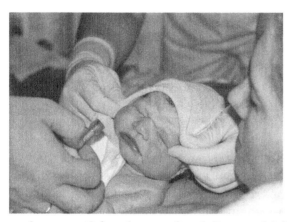

We were dried off, cleaned up and moved to the bedroom of the birthing center. They offered Tylenol to ease any post-delivery pain, but I refused, not wanting to take anything. I just wanted to go home with my perfect little girl and newly expanded family.

They wouldn't let us leave until four hours after delivery, which was the standard protocol. We arrived home at four o'clock that afternoon to discover that my father had put balloons on the light post in front of our house to welcome us home. It did not take long before some of our neighbors came over to meet Madison. One of them mentioned something about Halloween and with a sudden jolt of panic we realized our mistake. "Oh my goodness this is Halloween!" in our excitement, we had forgotten to stock up on additional candy. What would we do when our meager bowl of treats ran dry?

Ken went to the window and watched as the official start of the neighborhood Halloween parade snaked its way around the corner and across the street. There must have been over 250 of them and we were not prepared at all. To our great relief it began to rain heavily and we finished with only two costumed visitors coming to the door.

*   *   *

I was blessed to be able to stay home with Madison for a few months. There were times that I would just sit and look at how beautiful and perfect she was. I was totally taken in by her and feared that I would do something wrong to mess things up.

I started a new job at Wishard Hospital when Madison was four months old. It killed me to be away and leave her at home, knowing that this would be a time where she was growing and learning new things by the minute. Amazed that I still felt she was part of me made leaving her seemed foreign and awkward. There was a little twinge of guilt with separation anxiety mixed in. My mother remained available to care for her during the day and I knew she would be in loving hands. Even though my head knew this was the best arrangement, my heart still felt pangs of envy that I would not be there to see Madison reach many milestones while I was at work.

The new job was a career change for me. Previously, I had served as director of nursing which proved more stressful than I had anticipated. In my new role as clinical informatics specialist, I was tasked with helping hospital medical staff learn how to use an electronic medical record system that was developed and refined by Regenstrief Institute; a pioneer in medical informatics.

With a new job and a new baby, I had no vacation time and it would be the first time in ten years that I would be unable to participate at bike camp in Florida. My parents attended as part of the staff, but I was forced to sit out that year.

Upon returning from camp, my parents filled us in on all that we missed and delighted in telling us about a woman they met from Indiana, who said that she had competed in the Indiana State Cycling Championships and was beaten by a pregnant woman. My father boasted that she actually lost the race to his daughter and his granddaughter.

In the spring, we started riding again and pulled Madison along with us in a special trailer behind the bike. We made sure to select the sturdiest one we could find. In addition to the normal safety straps, we put her in her pumpkin seat and secured it inside the trailer with a five point seatbelt system.

It wasn't long before we realized that pulling the additional weight of the trailer and fighting the wind drag caused by the trailer, just didn't work well on a single bike. We each felt guilty when one of us pulled the trailer, going slower and holding the other back. There was a better way to work around the disparity. We decided to buy a tandem and it worked much better than we ever expected. Everyone was all together and happy.

That fall we started speed skating again in Indianapolis with a group of cyclists who were using speed skating as their wintertime training. The group had very little leadership and was not well organized. Essentially, it was open speed skating. There was one gentleman, who offered coaching, but his coaching style was very outdated and the techniques he taught conflicted with everything Ken and I had learned at the Olympic Training Center. Instead of complaining about it, we decided to share what we knew in an attempt to help the others improve.

One evening, we brought Madison out onto the ice. She was not yet able to stand on her own or walk, so we placed her in a walker. She was suspended in a harness that enabled her to use her feet to scoot around. We heard squeals of delight as her feet skittered to find traction when brought her out on the ice for the first time. We skated behind her, gently pushing to increase speed and her eyes sparkled as she skimmed over the ice, red hair peeking out around her cap in the breeze. Madison clearly loved the feeling because the moment we stopped, she began bouncing up and down, fussing until we started to push her again.

*   *   *

The next year we planned our return to bike camp. This would be Madison's first year to join us and I was looking forward to introducing her to our camp family. A few weeks before time to leave for camp we were shocked and broken hearted to learn that Mike Walden had suffered a massive stroke and had not survived. I was devastated! For so long he had been such an important and valued member of our family. Sadly, he never got to meet our Madison and I never got to say goodbye.

It seemed almost impossible that camp could go on without him, but over the years his efforts had trained everyone well. Dale continued to be the organizational mastermind, so the show went on in Mike's honor.

Not long after bike camp, Ken's job became a victim of downsizing. Once again, he found it difficult to find a new job in computers. Ironically, the job he did find was back in Ohio. He took the position and spent his weekdays working at a hospital there while Madison and I stayed in Indianapolis to try to sell our house. Every day, as I left for work, I backed my way out of the front door with Madison in one arm and the vacuum in the other. I wanted to leave fresh vacuum marks on the carpet so that when I returned after work I might see footprints to determine if the realtor had shown the house to prospective buyers. When there were footprints, I walked around and stood where they did in an effort to see what these prospective buyers might have seen. Much to my relief the house sold in about three months. Any more and I may have gotten too obsessive.

I turned in my resignation at the hospital in Indianapolis and we moved everything to Ohio. My parents suggested that we stay with them until we found a home there. Both sides of our family were thrilled that Madison would be moving closer and this gave me time to search for a job, ride my bike and resume training to get back into racing shape once more.

That year Dale won the bid to build the Olympic Velodrome in Atlanta and my father was to be part of that effort. Mike would have been so very proud of everyone.

The track Dale built was revolutionary and my father worked closely with him in its construction. I was thrilled to think that I would be able to ride on it in Atlanta.

Going to the Olympics in Atlanta was a giant family reunion. Claire and Dorothy Young were there to support Connie, who was competing in the Match Sprints. I discovered so many people that I knew and had trained and raced with over the years.

Dale and my father were very proud of the track made of unconventional materials. Supported by a steel frame, the riding surface was textured marine grade plywood using non rainforest wood. The surface was similar to dimples on a golf ball and created a hum when riders got up to speed. The sound unsettled many and led to assumptions and criticism of the track with some people stating that it would be slow due to that type of surface, too slow for an Olympic Games competition.

It measured 250 meters long and the corners had 45 degrees of banking. Standing at the bottom of the track and looking up to see the wall like corners was intimidating to say the least. My first experience riding on the banking sent my heart racing. The severity of the banking would cause the wheels of the bike to slip if at any time your speed dropped below fifteen miles per hour. Having this happen once, even for a fraction of a second,

was enough incentive to cause a rider to pick up the pace and get up to speed quickly.

While we rode on the track, Madison danced around proudly in the infield wearing her miniaturized replica of the US team skinsuit. We watched her bright red pigtails bounce as she danced and played, splashing in puddles and spinning in circles. The entire US Olympic pursuit team knew her by name and gave her lots of attention when they took rest breaks during training. On the last night of practice, before the games were to begin, I slipped a Sharpie marker from my pocket and stopped at the finish line. When no one was around to see I wrote Mike Walden's name there. He was responsible for

getting many of us to this point, to this moment, and he deserved a place on the finish line.

The stage was set. Let the games begin! Once the riders started racing in the time trials, Olympic and World records began falling like dominos. With each new record, Dale and my father celebrated the undeniable fact that the track was a complete success. In their own way, they had won an Olympic Gold medal in track building and design.

The track nestled in the shadow of Stone Mountain on the eastern outskirts of Atlanta, was a temporary structure, not set up with any permanent buildings. The only restrooms open to the public and athletes were port-a-johns. At one point I was standing by the results/display board high above the ground, overlooking the track to get a good view to take a panoramic photograph and realized that the VIP trailers with real restrooms and running water were just behind me. As I had unlimited access to the venue, I decided to make use of them.

Upon approach I noticed an Olympic escort and her charge, a very stern, dark haired woman who appeared to be in her fifties heading for the same destination. She did not look familiar so I thought she must have been the wife of some foreign dignitary.

The uniformed escort opened the door to the well-appointed restroom and announced that she would be waiting outside. We entered and I went into my stall as the older women went into hers. I took care of my business and went out to wash my hands. She did the same. I rolled down the cloth like paper towels and the woman promptly took my towel, dried her hands and causally, yet deliberately, handed it back to me and walked out the door without pause. Shocked and wordless, I shook my head as I thought, "This woman is exceptionally bold and spoiled."

When I rejoined Ken and my father in the infield, I shared my strange encounter with them. As we sat in the middle of the track watching some remarkable racing, Dale called on his handheld radio. "You will never believe who is here!" he said with excitement in his voice. "Two rows down, (we followed his directions with binoculars) four seats in, is Princess Anne of England!" I recognized her immediately. "She took my towel!" I blurted out when I saw her. My father joked that I had experienced a royal seating or possibly a royal flush and this could be my real life Princess and the Pee story.

We witnessed exuberant triumphs and devastating disappointments in the Olympic Games. There was a senseless bombing incident at Olympic Park that tragically took the lives of two people. A huge, dark cloud seemed to hang over everyone at the Games from that point on, as we struggled to understand why someone would do such an evil thing.

After the track races ended, we moved to the road race venue. We had a great time standing on the start/finish line talking to people who lined up to watch the race from the other side of the barriers. We answered questions and helped teach spectators about the sport. Ken and I cheered for Frankie Andreu, who was racing in the men's road race representing the United States. He had grown up under the coaching guidance of Mike Walden and at one time had been a primary competitor of Ken's brother Mark when they had been racing as juniors. Frankie's sisters rode as part of the women's team that joined us after the stage race in Texas, and his dad, Frank, came to bike camp on multiple occasions. They were all good people worth cheering for.

After the Olympics ended, Ken and I returned to reality. I took a job as an administrator for a hospital based home care agency. Once again, I was working in an environment where I had to be responsible for all the operations of the agency, from recruiting to marketing, training to payroll. This 24/7 obligation interfered with the amount of time I wanted to dedicate to my family and to training. My mother babysat Madison during the day when I could not be there. She was able to watch her grow and listen to her language skills develop as they played together, witnessing Madison discover the world around her. I regretted missing some of the little things in her early development.

"Watch and learn." was still a part of my life. Through parenting, I learned a lot from Madison. One day I realized that many of the issues I was dealing with at home, applied to people at work. I learned that everything I needed to manage employees, I had actually learned from parenting and watching my two year old grow and interact with others. For example:

- Deal with people in black and white, concrete terms.
- Answers should always be either yes or no, and never maybe.
- Never play favorites. Everyone must be your favorite.
- Never promise anything you cannot deliver.
- Always follow through with punishment and reward alike.
- Small rewards often bring greater results, much better than threats.

- Close supervision keeps everyone focused on the goals and ensures safety.
- Everyone wants to be heard, so listen even if you have heard it before.
- Strive to be a good role model so others have a path to follow.

Parenting is a challenge, but the rewards are much greater and well worth the effort in the long run.

In the spring of 1997, after we returned from bike camp, Ken developed an annoying pain in his left calf that would not go away. My nursing experience set off a red flag in my brain. He was positive for Homan's Sign, an indicator of deep vein thrombosis. I administered a simple test in which I told him to flex his foot, pulling his toes towards his knee. This resulted in a shooting pain up his calf. Panicked and insistent, I took him to the doctor where an ultrasound revealed several blood clots in his lower leg. He was admitted to the hospital and treated with IV blood thinners. I worried that I might lose him and imagined all the worst scenarios involving blood clots and the damage they could do when they break loose and travel around a body.

The threat to Ken's life was all I needed to wake me up and realize that I was not living the life I wanted; we were just marking time. My job was consuming my time and energy and we had searched high and low for a suitable home in Ohio without success. I was unhappy and uncomfortable there, even though we were close to our parents and siblings. I wanted to go home again to Indiana.

After Ken was discharged from the hospital and his blood viscosity was back to normal, we began discussing our lives and future, remembering how comfortable we had been in Indianapolis. We took a weekend trip back to Indy and visited our home church to catch up with our friends there. Afterwards, we took a drive through our old neighborhood just to see if anything had changed and if there were any houses in the area for sale.

While driving through the neighborhood looking at houses, I saw something that didn't register. Blinking my eyes, I recognized Jill Warvel, a key computer programmer and developer of the electronic medical record software that I had previously supported when I worked at Wishard Hospital. I blinked again; she was standing in a driveway with her sailboard. She didn't live in that neighborhood to my recollection.

Excited to see her, I shouted to Ken "Stop the car!" and without a moment's hesitation, I jumped out to greet her. "Jill!" I shouted as I ran toward her. She quickly turned to look at me. "Cindi? What are you doing here?" she returned. "We were driving through the area to see if there were any houses for sale because we are thinking about relocating. We want to come back home again in Indiana." I said, imitating the song that Jim Neighbors sang every year during the Indy 500.

"What is the chance that we would run into each other here?" she asked. "This isn't even my house. I just got back from vacation where I was sailboarding with these guys," she told me as she began to introduce her friends. "So do you have a job yet?" she asked. "Because Marc Overhage is looking for someone with your kind of experience to help with some projects at Regenstrief and I know you would be perfect!" she said enthusiastically "Really? That would be awesome!" I responded. "I will tell him that I ran into you. He remembers you well from our meetings at Wishard. I'm sure he would like to talk to you. Call Theda and set up a call with Marc." she urged. I was so excited that I gave her a big hug and said "Thanks! I will, that sounds perfect!"

Back in Ohio, first thing that Monday morning, I called Regenstrief Institute and spoke with both Theda and Mark. Jill was right; they did want me to join them. I had really appreciated working with the programmers in the past and knew this job would be a good fit. Ken then began his search for work as well. With a very good feeling, the best in a long time, we contacted the realtor who helped us buy and sell our original house. She was very interested in working with us once more and provided piles and piles of information on houses that might fit our needs.

We had been searching for a suitable home for over two years and knew exactly what we wanted. I found three houses in a neighborhood near our old one that seemed interesting. We loved living close to Eagle Creek Park on the North West side of Indianapolis in our first home, with quick access to country bike riding roads and even closer access to the interstate. Although the houses I found were out of our price range, I decided to look at them anyway. Ken was busy with work, so my parents and Madison came with me to look at three candidates.

The first was beautiful, and had a bump out room that was a library with a décor dedicated to the Civil War. This was particularly interesting to my parents, who were both Civil War re-enactors and history buffs. After touring the beautifully decorated Tudor style one story home, I felt that we needed to continue our search. I had always wanted a two story home with a basement.

The second house had a very tiny basement that was more closet-sized than basement-sized. It was as if they had decided at the last minute that they needed a tornado shelter and added it. Obviously this was not the one.

The third house we toured looked familiar. Not long after entering the large house, I realized that Ken and I had ridden our bikes by that very house while it was under construction. It had no walls at that time and the floors were still rough plywood. The frame was not a standard 2 x 4 wood structure, but consisted of galvanized steel beams. We had stopped and walked through, trying to imagine how it would look and how we might use the various rooms. I remembered saying out loud to Ken "This house would be perfect for us, if we could find a way to afford it."

It seemed surreal to think that I was standing in the same house again, walls up and painted, and floors carpeted. It was indeed perfect, but priced well over what we thought we could afford. This was the first house we had seen in over two years that filled all our requirements. When we finished looking and walked to the car, my father gave his opinion. He said, in as few words as possible, "What are you waiting for? Just write the check."

Ken had not seen the house since it had been completed so we returned to Indianapolis with him to look again. He agreed it was perfect, but unfortunately, out of our price range. We told our realtor the situation and the negotiations began. As luck would have it, the house had been on the market for over two years and we were the only people to make an offer. Our prayers were answered and we moved into our new home soon after the papers were drawn and signed.

It didn't take long to start settling back into life in Indianapolis, easing into our new jobs, including potty training and pre-school for Madison. After we felt situated, we reached a point where we were able to return to skating. Heather Thompson, a delightful young speed skater from California, had started coaching in Indianapolis while she attended Marian University and was on their collegiate cycling team.

Heather was very kind, skilled and patient with the skaters. When she graduated and returned to California, she left a large void in the skating community. There were many people that asked us to coach in her place. Ken and I decided to try to take things one step further and organized a not-for-profit speed skating club that the group decided should be called the Indy Speed Sports Club. Our goal was to combine the sports of cycling, speed skating and cross country skiing in a model similar to that we had admired in the Wolverine Sports Club that Mike Walden helped develop and coach.

Interacting almost daily with our athletes, we grew to love the members of our club. So many have come and gone over the years, but most all of them have felt like family to us. It was my hope that Madison would feel like she had an extended family locally that way.

One of the pledges I made to myself when Madison was born was that I would try to expose her to as many varied opportunities as possible. If she didn't want to participate in the sports that Ken and I coached, I wanted to support her in whatever she might want for herself.

One day Madison came home from kindergarten imitating martial arts kicks and punches that she had seen older students perform at school.

I eagerly jumped at the opportunity and asked if she would like to take a class in Martial arts. She enthusiastically replied "YES! YES! YES!" while jumping up and down as if she had springs on her feet. I had been waiting for her to show interest in something, anything that I could help her develop. Just the year before, we prepaid $70 for a dance class that she never attended. When we took her to the first class, she balked and refused to take one step onto the dance floor.

Not to be deterred, the next day after her enthusiastic interest in martial arts, we investigated the new Taekwondo School near our home. We entered the studio where kids her age dressed in white uniforms and colored belts filled the room. She watched, wide eyed, as they kicked and punched in what appeared to be a well-controlled environment. We looked at all the pictures on the walls.

After I got sufficient information from the instructor, Madison declared that she didn't want to have anything to do with Taekwondo. "Okay," I replied. "You are old enough now. It's time for you to make a decision. Will it be dance or Martial Arts? You choose." I declared. She delayed in responding. "But, but," she stammered without committing. As I drove home from the Taekwondo School, I saw my opportunity. It was leverage I did not want to use up until that moment: McDonald's.

"Madison, I'll make a deal with you. If you do well, I will take you to get a Fun Meal after your classes." I offered. Madison had only once been allowed a Fun Meal and that was when her grandfather, Herb, took her with him to McDonald's. She made her decision and exclaimed "I WANT TO DANCE!" I sighed in relief that she had made a commitment.

Madison got up very early the next morning bouncing into our room, proudly wearing her pink sparkle tutu and ballet slippers. I explained to her that she could not wear them to school. I called to get information about the dance studio after our visit to the Taekwondo School and the McDonald's declaration. The dance school year was to begin the following day, so we decided to go a day early to meet the teacher, check out the building and register. When I came to pick her up from school, her teacher greeted me and stated that Madison had talked about going to dance class all day. I was very happy to know she was so excited.

When we arrived at the building she looked around with a panicked look on her face. "Where are we?" she asked as she started to pull back on my hand, stopping our forward entrance into the room. "Dance Class," I replied and her eyes surveyed the room. Madison blurted out "I don't want to dance here."

As we entered, she held back every step, hiding behind my legs like trees in a game of hide-and-go-seek. I tried to introduce her to the teacher who explained that currently only two little girls were in her assigned class. Madison refused to look at her or let go of my legs as she buried her face in the back of my thigh. Apologizing to the instructor, I took Madison over to the ballet bar and mirrors where I goofed around and danced a bit myself. NOTHING! She refused to budge. A little, mouse like squeak rose from her lips as she quietly announced, "I changed my mind. I don't want to dance." "Okay, Madison, you have made up your mind. Taekwondo it is." I announced. "Yes, please, I want to do Taekwondo!" she replied, brightening considerably.

The following day Ken and I returned with her to the American Taekwondo Institute, arriving a little early to give her an opportunity to observe the class that would be hers. Sitting on my lap, eyes wide, she watched as the other children kicked and giggled. She looked at everything in the room as Ken and I talked about how much fun it would be. When Sir Eric, a very tall, kind instructor came over and sat with us, she curled up like a baseball bug in my lap and whimpered. She refused to look at the man and he didn't know what to do. He then called over the owner of the school. Master Burns was really good with her, but still she would not budge. He told her that he had two young daughters of his own in the class. Frozen in place, she did not respond.

I stood, but Madison did not change positions. Even then, she clung to me like a baby koala, so I carried her over to the wall where the mats were stacked, peeled her from my body and put her down on the mats. Still, she refused to move from her position. Master Burns sat next to her and tried to engage her in some form of communication and he was very good. Much to our surprise, when he challenged her to tell him what she knew about the different levels and colors of belts displayed on the walls above the mirrors, she answered his questions correctly, despite the fact that she remained in her fetal position facing the opposite wall.

At that point the Master called over his eleven year old daughter, Danielle, who was a black belt. He asked her to show Madison all the Taekwondo toys: punching and kicking dummies and pads. Madison sprang to her feet and accompanied Danielle on a tour of the room. Danielle demonstrated the correct ways to kick, block and punch and Madison replicated her movements. Ken and I stayed out of sight to eliminate any opportunity for our daughter to back out again. She didn't even notice. There was no "Where are my parents?" look of fear or panic. She fit right in.

That night we missed our practice at the Velodrome because it took almost two hours to get her out of the building. We were mentally exhausted, but she was signed up, had a uniform and eagerly awaited her first real class.

After we got home, she put on her uniform and kicked the heck out of every pillow she could get her dad to hold. She even wanted to sleep in her uniform. When we took her to her first real class, she rushed right in and lined up with all the other kids and did everything she was told. What a difference another child can make.

She remembered the Fun-Meal promise and was not going to let me forget it either. "Did I do good enough for my reward?" she asked. That evening she got her Fun-Meal.

After three years of dedicated practice and competition, she advanced through all the belt levels, competed in local, regional and national competitions and earned her "Full Splits club" patch. I attended virtually every practice and competition and loved watching her in her forms, with her long red braids whipping around as she swiveled on her feet and kicked. Forms were her best event and she was near perfection. Sparing was not her favorite, but she preferred sparing over board breaking. She was small and light and didn't have quite what it took to break big boards. Without a doubt, I was a very proud Mama. She went on to get her black belt before her ninth birthday.

Long before her birth, Ken and I knew that with our optical histories, the day would come when Madison would need glasses. We just hadn't expected her to need them as early as kindergarten. We realized that the time had arrived when she began to have difficulty reading because she had been a voracious reader.

To help prepare for the inevitable, we tried to talk up glasses, explaining how pretty they would look and how they would help her to see everything more clearly. Deep down I knew that all the encouragement in the world could not protect her from the cruelty of other children who would see her as "different."

At the optician's office, she did well for a five year old. She sat in the huge monster chair with equipment that could best be described as something out of a science fiction movie and bravely followed directions. She giggled while peering through the blur of changing lenses.

As she squinted to read the lines on the chart, I wanted to help her, but she was on her own on this one. After the exam, the expected proclamation came: she needed glasses. She tried on every pair of sample frames they had and looked through empty frames, fingering them all. Finally, with some parental guidance, the selection was made.

We were told that it would take a week for the glasses to be ready. A five year old doesn't understand the concept of waiting for the opportunity to see clearly once again. Every day she urged us to call and see if they had come in early, to find out if the delivery had been made. Once we learned they were ready, we could not drive fast enough to satisfy her. She ran to the counter to get them and when they were placed on her face there was no "Wow!" or "Cool" just silence as she looked around the store.

Her brain was trying to adjust to the change in her reality. She told us that they made all the little things seem bigger and closer and all the big things smaller. The floor looked closer and walking seemed funny and awkward. She had to dodge things that seemed too close, but we assured her that her eyes would adjust to their new helpers and things would get better soon.

That night at bedtime she took the glasses off carefully and put them to bed in their special case, adorned with cats from outer space. The actions of a child so young, gentle, caring and respectfully handling something that was changing her life touched me.

The next morning she greeted us with bright, shining eyes and new glasses perched on her smiling face. The sight of her wearing the glasses was a great relief, knowing that we would not have to remind or nag her to put them on. Experience told me that she would be facing the scrutiny of other children and I wanted her to feel good about herself. Therefore, I dressed her in a bright, cheerful dress and fixed her hair in one of her favorite styles. She needed to be armed for the battle ahead.

I wanted to take attention away from the fact that she would look different that day, but I knew that would be impossible. Suddenly she asked, "Do I have to wear these to school?" I replied, "Yes, sweetie, you do." "But the kids will laugh at me," she whined. "They won't be laughing; they will be noticing that you have something new, something that they don't have and that will make you special today. The other children will get used to them and you will too, then they won't even notice and even you will forget you're wearing them." I told her.

The dreaded moment of truth came as soon as we walked down the halls of her school to her classroom. Madison tried to hide behind my legs, but she was spotted despite her efforts to conceal herself from sight. A child in a purple overalls shouted "Madison! You have glasses!" as others ran to see her up close. "Yes, I know," she answered as she rolled her eyes and turned away from them. Another student asked, "Why are you wearing glasses?"

We could not walk through the hallway without little heads turning to look at her. When we got to the threshold of her classroom we peered in. The students stood in line like little soldiers ready to march off to the next room. Madison stepped into the room and they broke rank and engulfed her.

The same questions popped up from the cluster of pigtailed girls encircling her. The same, except for Megan Norris. Megan, who had been wearing glasses since she was an infant and had long hair like Madison's, abruptly plowed through all the questioning children with arms opened wide, embraced Madison like a long lost sister. "Aren't they wonderful?" she exclaimed with a joy that was undeniable. Hidden out of sight behind a door, I breathed a deep sigh of relief.

Trying to remain in the shadows, I watched the group dynamics from a distance. Megan had her comforting arm around Madison's shoulder as they shuffled down the hallway together. I heard a boy say, "I think she looks goofy." Megan stopped him in his tracks, got in his face and proclaimed "SHE DOES NOT!" Then another girl chimed in "I think they're neat!"

I was relieved knowing that she was not alone and would be protected. I returned to work with confidence that she would be alright without me. The hurdle had been cleared and Megan had helped us both. What a blessing Megan Norris was. She knew how difficult it was to be ostracized for being different and now she was no longer alone. At that moment she and Madison became sisters.

I will never forget that first image of the girls walking down the hall, Madison with her head down, and Megan with her protective arm around her shoulder. This courageous girl cushioned a traumatic day in my child's life as well as mine. There was nothing I could do to make this any better. I remember thinking that no matter what I had been through in my life, nothing was worse than watching your child in pain. Megan was an answer to a mother's prayer. Thank you, Megan.

*   *   *

In 2002, one of the speed skaters I coached, Brian Olah, asked me to come and help him coach Special Olympians for the Indiana State Games. I was initially uncertain whether this would be appropriate as my previous role in Special Olympics had been at the state games in the Upper Peninsula of Michigan, as a volunteer.

Brian introduced me to Scott Furnish and David Breen at the Special Olympics Indiana state office. They were both friendly and welcoming with just the right sense of humor and appreciation of sports. I attended some of the training sessions on the ice to help coach. This experience was very different than anything I had expected as they had combined training for figure skating with speed skating. I had to revert to my days as a figure skater and teach at a level that I had not been involved with for quite a while. Teaching special needs students how to skate proved necessary before they could learn how to speed skate, and eventually, how to race.

The athletes were very willing and receptive to learning how to race on the ice. When it came time for the Special Olympics state games competition, I was asked to be the chief official and I accepted. It was very rewarding to see the athletes I had helped train, in competition with other skaters from around the state.

After that, there was no turning back; I was hooked. In the years to follow, my involvement with the Indiana Special Olympics grew, as part of the sports resource team and as a coach. Working with the athletes, it became apparent that they should have more than just six weeks of training every year.

Therefore, I extended invitations to any Special Olympians who were interested, to join the Indy Speed Sports Club. This was a way for them to become part of an organization where they would be embraced as a regular member of the team. It appeared to be a perfect opportunity for everyone involved to *watch and learn*.

My regular skaters would have the opportunity to interact with these skaters and come to recognize them as valued members of our society. The Special Olympians in turn would feel acceptance and camaraderie with our team skaters; a win-win situation.

Mandy Hoopingardner was one who chose to accept my invitation. As a twenty-one year old woman with Down's syndrome who had been figure skating for many years, she adapted to speed skating quite well and became a wonderful addition to our team.

The classic traits of a person with Down's syndrome prevailed: fairly short in stature with very small hands and feet, overshadowed by a very large spirit. Her hips were exceptionally flexible and she had almond shaped eyes, which are perhaps the most noticeable trait for persons with Down's syndrome. She had dark hair, brown eyes and a small mouth crowded with teeth that made some of her speech difficult to understand. However, the more we got to know her, the better we were able to understand her.

When Madison was seven years old, she skated and played with Mandy at the rink. They cheered for each other and teased one another, on and off the ice. We crowded into one big van on trips to competitions and they would happily share music and play games along the way. They were best buds.

To help Mandy with her skating, we created a cheer that helped her remember what she needed to do to skate her best. We chanted "Feet together, feet together, go Mandy go! Feet together, feet together, go Mandy go!" and it helped develop her rhythm and reminded her to keep her feet together. This simple technique gave her the encouragement she needed and motivation to keep racing and stay focused.

Mandy had a distinct flair for the dramatic and we could always tell when she was elated and definitely when she was disappointed. It was not difficult to interpret what was going on behind those dark eyes as her beaming smile spoke volumes.

It was bittersweet to watch Madison and Mandy grow up together. Madison grew and changed so much in a few short years while Mandy remained essentially the same, devoted to her coloring books, children's games, and romance novels. Although she did not change, Madison had been changed by her relationship with Mandy. They interacted well together and Madison was not ashamed to play with her.

One day Madison came home from school and shared a story with me that was indicative of just how Mandy had affected her life. Madison was in middle school and the students sat at lunch tables grouped by class. It just so happened that Madison's honors class was assigned to sit next to the special needs class and thanks to her relationship with Mandy, she had no problem interacting with friends, irrespective of which class they attended or what they may have looked like. "I always try to sit on the end, as close to the special needs class as I can, so that I can talk to Kelly and Mauren." She told me. "The other kids in my honors class don't understand. They ask me, 'Why do you even talk to them anyway?' And I answered back, 'Because they are my friends!'" My heart swelled and I recognized what REALLY makes a mother proud has very little to do with grade cards.

In the fall of 2003, Scott Furnish encouraged me to apply for the Team USA head coach position for the Special Olympics World Winter games in Nagano, Japan. I was somewhat hesitant and doubted that I would be accepted since I had only been working with Special Olympians for two years. He reassured me that I had a lot to offer as head coach, especially with my experience in nursing, exercise physiology, and coaching at the elite level, so I applied.

In early 2004, I received a phone call at work informing me that I had been chosen to be their head coach and I was elated. A few months later I learned that Mandy, Katie and Wes, the other Special Olympians that I had been coaching in Indianapolis, were selected as athletes to be on Team USA in Nagano as well. I was overjoyed.

* * *

PART 3 – The Real Race Against Time

One April afternoon in 2004, after a long day of dealing with computer network issues and teaching medical staff how to use the electronic medical record, I looked forward to coming home. I sank down into my comfortable leather couch and relaxed for a rare moment.

Madison had already arrived home from school and had positioned herself on the jade green Oriental rug on the living room floor in front of me. She was flat on her stomach, boxing with the cat. Over time I had come to realize that the cat liked battling with her, trading punches and standing her ground with Madison. The orange cat, better known as "Purzit" issued threatening low-toned verbal reprimands. "Madison," I interjected between swipes and exchanges of jabs, "Stop aggravating her." I said superficially, knowing that this was a regular occurrence between the two of them.

"I know Mom, but she started it!" she defended. A cat, she was, but to an only child, she was Madison's lone playmate at home. Ears down, perched on her haunches with front paws extended, she swiped at Madison with all her strength and landed some pretty good punches. "See!" Madison said after Purzit scored a solid hit, "I'm not doing anything to her. She started it; she is the one who wants to fight."

It was at that point that I noticed an itch. It could have been caused by my hair or my clothing, but it didn't matter. What did matter was that it prompted me to reflexively attend to the itch over my left breast. I found more than just relief from the itch. I felt something unfamiliar, something I had never before noticed when I had done self-breast exams. It was a firm area beneath the skin.

Startled, I felt again. It was not my imagination. There was something there and I could feel a mass. As an athlete and a nurse, I was very aware of my body and its quirks. I was dazed and in denial. This was something that I never expected to find, at least not in MY body.

In bra fitting terms I considered myself an A minus, so it was very easy to do a simple and quick self-breast exam; there was not a lot of territory to cover. As a cyclist and speed skater I had always been thin and considered myself aerodynamic. Fortunately for me, Ken and I met through cycling and had trained and coached together for many years. Even before we married, he told me that he had always been a leg man.

With my internal panic button activated, I left the feline boxing match in the living room and went straight to my bedroom. It was there that I discovered the mass had brought a date to the party. The first mass, I noticed, was roundish and felt like a cross between an old fashioned miniature bottle cap and a squashed bug. However, upon further investigation, I discovered a second mass that felt smaller and perfectly round like a pearl.

I switched gears for a moment, scanning my memory banks as a nurse. Non-fixed and mobile: more than one with a rapid onset. It must be a fibroid and a cyst. "Don't panic. Let's wait this out and see if this is hormonally influenced." I told myself. That evening, as we were in the bathroom brushing teeth, I thought I would mention it to Ken. "Not to alarm you, but I just thought I would let you know. I found a couple of weird things, like lumps in my left breast. I think it could be a fibroid." He did not appear alarmed or even concerned. I knew the calm even-keeled demeanor of my husband and I would have been surprised to see him react any other way.

*   *   *

Before we moved back to Ohio, when I was working at Wishard Hospital, they had insisted that all their management staff take the Myers-Briggs personality assessment test. The test's results described me so accurately that I brought the test home for Ken to take. We ran the analysis on his results and discovered, much to my surprise, that in every single category, we were exact opposites. People always say opposites attract and in our case it certainly proved true. My results stated that I was an ENFP, which, when translated, described me as a Coach and Motivator. It indicated that I was a communicator and a people person. Ken's test results proclaimed him as an ISTJ and described him as a Judge as he is logical, analytical and very dedicated and fair.

When posing for pictures, people often tried to prod Ken to smile. "I am smiling," he always said, through lips drawn behind an ever present mustache. You have to look closely and be alert to the subtle nuances that are Ken's smile, hidden in his hazel speckled eyes and dark eyebrows. Madison always joked, "Beware the evil eyebrows!" as that was how she could tell when he was angry. His eyebrows then were peaked in sharp points at the top, somewhat like the top of a triangle. She has seen and known that look a little too often.

In 2002, on a day or two before Christmas, we were awakened by an early morning phone call. Ken took the call as if it had been a call from the phone company. "Uh huh" (Silence) "Yeah" (Even longer silence) "Which hospital?" (More silence as I stared at him with growing concern) "Uh huh. Thanks. You too." he said. Then he turned to me to answer my questioning expression. He told me the details that he had just learned. His sister Linda and her husband Steve lived a few blocks from Ken's mother who we affectionately referred to as "Mumsy." They got a call from her through the deaf relay in the middle of the night. Ken's father had been in the hospital for open heart surgery and was to be released to come home the next day. Mumsy was alone at home and called to tell Linda that she couldn't breathe.

They rushed to her home and found her unconscious on the floor. With great panic, they checked for a pulse and discovered there was none. Linda and Steve took turns doing CPR until the ambulance arrived and took her to the hospital. Ken paused as if that was the end of the story.

Grasping at whatever threads of hope I could find after assembling the picture in my head, I said, "She's going to be okay, right?" searching his face to try to read what he was thinking. That was when he calmly said, "Mumsy's dead."

The bones in my legs could hold me no longer upright as I burst into uncontrollable sobs. He held me up so that I would not melt into a quivering puddle of tears on the floor. He tried his best to console me. It was then that I realized that even though he has strong feelings, he expresses very little. That is okay with me, because I seem to have enough emotion for both of us.

Until that call there had been several times when I caught myself thinking how blessed my life was; watching Madison grow up, seeing her interact with her grandparents and aunts and uncles, sharing my life with Ken. "These are the good old days, aren't they?" I often wondered, but never said aloud because I was afraid I might jinx it. Somewhere in the back of my mind hovered a fear that something would come along to change that. When Mumsy died, I thought that was the thing I had feared and I felt such a great loss in her absence.

*　　*　　*

A month had come and gone since I first discovered the lumps. They were ever present in my mind and had not gotten any smaller or softer. We were preparing to host a women's cycling training camp at our house and my mother was visiting from Ohio before anyone arrived. As an employee health nurse for Middletown Hospital, she routinely gave pre-employment and annual employee physicals, which included breast exams, and was meticulous in the detail of her examinations. She took pride in her job, attempting to ensure the health of everyone she examined. I tried to decide how I could best ask her about her personal breast history without triggering any alarms. I found a moment when we were alone in the hallway upstairs. "Hey Mom, I have a personal question for you. Have you ever had any fibroids or cysts in your breasts?" I asked, straight to the point. Her answer came quick and sharp. "Yes. Why do you ask?"

"I found a lump in one of my breasts and I think it could be fibrocystic, so I was wondering if you have had any fibroids or cysts. I'm just checking to see if I have any family history." She jumped into clinical mode. "I have had a few fibroids, but you need to get this checked out." With concern in her eyes she said. "Can I do a breast exam now?" Really, how many people do you know that get breast exams from their own mother? How could I say no? She was thorough and professional. She washed her hands and even draped me. After she finished, she said, "You are probably right, they could be fibroids or a cyst but you need to get a mammogram anyway."

"Awesome." I thought. "No reason to worry."

The attendees of the training camp started arriving and I switched over into coach mode. Mom was going to watch Madison for us as she had done so many times before. Most of the members of the team lived in Ohio, but a few were from Indiana. I very much enjoyed bonding with them and sharing our back country roads.

*   *   *

I had met JoMay at bike camp in Florida. She was a reserved but brilliantly insightful woman and was responsible for our team coming together for pre-season training. The camp went well and the women worked favorably together. I had not met several members of the team before, so this was an excellent opportunity.

Brooke Crum was a real stand out. She was only thirteen years old, but had amazing foot speed combined with great power. It seemed very obvious that she had all the makings of a great sprinter. Everything she did just screamed to me that she was born to race on the track, yet she had never even seen one.

I had been coaching Abby Nicks in speed skating for several years and introduced her to cycling and racing at the track. The two girls had talents in opposite directions. Abby was a distance rider and could take very long pulls and excelled in time trials, riding smoothly and efficiently. As a speed skater, she had great attention to detail and form, and loved to skate and compete. Her love of sports was infectious and coaching her was a pleasure. We had traveled together so much that she was a big sister to Madison and at skating competitions, a lot of other skaters assumed she was my oldest daughter.

Brooke was powerful in sprints, but didn't like to go very far. She had no fear challenging anyone to a short distance drag race or muscling her way through a field of riders. My thought was that Abby and Brooke would make wonderful, complementary teammates. We finished the camp with much hope for a great season of racing ahead.

*   *   *

Once the camp was over, my mother pounced on me. She started every conversation with "Have you made an appointment for a mammogram yet?" then evolved into, "I can make an appointment for you, where is the number for your doctor?" Of course I was annoyed by this. After such a great camp, I did not want to think about mammograms or masses. I had a promising racing season ahead with a new team. My mother had initially told me that it was probably nothing to be concerned about. Why was she being so pushy now?

Mom returned to Ohio and I returned to work the next day. She began calling my cell phone with increasing frequency. I was working at one of the outpatient clinics when she called. "I am going to call you every five minutes if that is what it takes to get you to schedule a mammogram." There was no doubt in my mind that I was stubborn by genetic design.

I finally gave in and asked one of my favorite physicians, one that I was working with that day, Dr. Cindy Reed. "I'm very sorry to ask this, but my mother is harassing me to get a mammogram." I told her. "Could you please write me a referral so she will get off my back?" She looked up and said, "Sure, I can do that, but I would need to do an exam first." "Great!" I thought sarcastically, "First my mother feels me up and now someone I work with is about to do the same. Thanks Mom!"

With my insurance card scanned and registered in the system, I was now a patient. Like so many before me, I was given a scratchy gown and ushered into a room to await an exam. I felt very awkward, but could tell I wasn't the only one feeling that way. When Dr. Reed entered the room, she started to giggle a little too, but got over it quickly and was very professional and did a great job. At the conclusion, she agreed with my mother that I should have a mammogram as soon as possible.

Two days later I was at St. Margaret's Breast Center for my first mammogram ever. Waiting, I felt totally humiliated and angry with my mother for putting me through unnecessary stress and testing. When ushered into the room that housed the device I had heard so many women refer to as the "crushing plates of torture," I wondered how in the world they would be able to do a mammogram on someone with breasts as small as mine.

More curious than scared or worried, when the technician began to take the first image I tried to look down at the vise-like machine that was about to flatten the scant amount of breast tissue that I had. This was evidently the wrong thing to do, as the technician yelled at me. The whole process had to be repeated because I had either moved or my head had gotten in the way. For the second attempt, I stayed as still as a statue.

In the waiting area I sat in the tent-like gown awaiting my results. Other women in the room looked equally elegant in their faded turquoise patterned institutional apparel. I was witness to looks of relief as most were assured that everything was fine and they were free to go home and return next year for another routine boob squishing encounter.

"Mrs. Hart?" The technician called my name "There is definitely something there that we need to look at with an ultrasound. We need you to go in this room on the left and someone will be in with you shortly." This came as no surprise, because I could feel something. Two something's actually. "Great," I thought to myself. I am so going to relish telling my mother about all the torture she was putting me through, just to get confirmation of what I already knew.

A tall, thin blond, blue eyed boy who looked all of nineteen years old walked into the darkened ultrasound room. "I'm Dr. Stanley, a fourth year radiology resident and I understand that you had a mammogram that discovered an abnormality." Being very accustomed to teaching doctors, I turned on my clinic reporting brain and told him, "I have two palpable masses. One is 2 mm and the other 2.5 mm. They are mobile and non-fixed." He looked at me with a startled look on his face and interrupted, "Did you say palpable?" "Yes," I replied. He asked, "Are you a clinician? My patients don't usually say, palpable." I explained that I was a nurse who trained physicians in the use of the electronic medical record system that he was currently using.

This may not have been the right thing to say because "Doogie Houser" now seemed even more nervous and awkward. "I need to locate the mass before I can do the ultrasound," he said as he touched me as if my breast was the meringue on a pie and he didn't want to leave any fingerprints. I took his hand firmly and said, "It's right here," placing his fingertips right on the area where the guilty buggers were causing me to go through all of this drama in the first place.

He completed the ultrasound then stated that he needed to show the results to the staff physician who was overseeing his training. I expected this, as it was standard procedure for the resident to take their findings to the staffing physician. It wasn't long before they returned. The doctor stated that my masses were indeed 2 and 2.5 mm in size, and then added something that I had not expected. "Could be fibroids, could be cancer. We are not certain, so you need to have a biopsy." "Cancer?" I was mildly shocked. But then I thought they were just trying to cover all the bases. "Fine!" I thought, "More torture."

They scheduled me for a fine needle biopsy the next day in a room that happened to be one I walked past every day at work, but rarely noticed. That room became important to me, as it was part of a process that would predict my fate.

Take my word for it; there is nothing "Fine" about a fine needle biopsy. In this procedure they take a syringe and repeatedly poke the heck out of you. I began to think that the doctor and the student performing the procedure were woodpeckers in some former life. Still very sure that the masses were just a fibroid (the squashed bug shape) and a cyst (the perfect pearl) and both were benign, I was even more convinced when the doctor who was poking me stated that the pearl had disappeared. "See?" I thought. "Just a fluid filled cyst that burst when you pierced it."

They told me that the biopsies would be sent to the lab and we should have the test results in 3-5 business days. I was not worried, because I knew the results would be negative, so I went about my life as usual. Well, as usual as I could with a sore and swollen boob.

Two days later I was coaching at the velodrome with Ken and Madison and many of my favorite riders. When we returned home, I noticed the answering machine light blinking. It was a message from Deb Rusk, my friend and Primary Care Physician. She asked that I call her back when I got the message. I knew that this was just a formality and she was simply calling me with the results of the biopsy.

I had coached Deb's sons in speed skating and they were close to Madison in age, so the first part of the conversation was directed to catching up regarding our kids. Then she said, "I don't normally call patients at home with their test results, but since I know you, I know you can handle it." She paused, and then said, "You have ductal carcinoma and I have scheduled you to see the best breast oncologist and breast surgeon in the state. They will take very good care of you." She paused, and then asked, "Do you have any questions?" There was an even longer pause as she waited for my response. Playing her words over again in my head and wondering if I had heard them correctly, there was no room or time in my mind to have any questions so I said "No" and thanked her for calling. Stunned, I sat in silence for a few moments. There was a lot I had to process.

Ken was sitting next to me at the table. I took a moment to consider my words. They seemed so foreign. Words I never thought would be coming from my mouth. "It's ductal carcinoma." He looked at me questioningly, eyebrows knitted. "That means I have breast cancer." I said. The rest of the evening was a blur as we both sat at our computers searching every reference we could find for ductal carcinoma.

The following day was Friday. When I first woke up and stretched my legs in bed, everything was fine. It all seemed like a bad dream, but the concept continued to haunt me. I got up and went to work as I normally did, but what I was feeling was far from normal. My mind was so disconnected from my body that it seemed to be on autopilot while my brain was stuck in some sort of processing loop. As I walked in to work, I felt dazed and one thought kept running through my brain. "I have cancer. I have cancer. I have cancer." It seemed as though I was trying to talk myself into believing it. As I walked through the familiar corridors of the hospital and saw people that I knew, who said, "Hi, how are you?" as they often did, I replied, "Fine," as I always did. Inside my head I was screaming, "I HAVE CANCER!"

Sitting in my cubicle, my mind raced with all possibilities related to cancer, I felt lost and overwhelmed. I then recalled seeing an article in the Regenstrief newsletter, which included a picture of the Regenstrief Race for the Cure team. A co-worker named Mary Jayne had a pink survivor shirt in the photo. I remembered complimenting her hair almost a year ago. And she laughed, saying, "It is a wig." To which I replied, "I couldn't tell. It looks great." I didn't think much of it then, but now it meant everything, so I made a beeline straight to Mary Jayne's cubicle.

She was sitting, calmly working at her computer when I knocked. "Hey Mary Jayne, do you have a moment?" I asked, already trying to figure out how to open the conversation. "Sure." she replied and I entered her area and sat down. Searching for words to start was difficult. "I believe we have something in common." I said. "I just found out last night that I have breast cancer."

She responded by giving me a hug. "I'm so sorry." she replied genuinely. Then, with her hands on my shoulders, she stood looking me in the eyes and asked, "Who are your doctors?" "They scheduled me with Dr. Miller and Dr. Goulet." "Good. They are the best. They are my doctors and will get you through this." She didn't sugar coat anything. She didn't look at me with pity; instead her tone was straightforward, honest and caring. Mary Jayne told me what to expect and what to do, which was exactly what I needed. This woman, my friend and coworker was my oasis in a desert of fear and confusion.

The next morning was Saturday and Ken and I were hosting a get-together to celebrate the end of the speed skating season with our team. Ken and I hadn't talked much about my diagnosis since the phone call. I think he was waiting for me to bring it up, while I was still trying to figure out how I felt and what I was supposed to do.

So much was going through my head as we puttered around getting the food and the house ready for the party; putting tablecloths on the tables, chopping vegetables and working on decorations. Suddenly, like a pressure cooker with the gauge just starting to shake, the realization built up in my chest and my throat. I felt like a caged animal and started to pace. The process loop had stopped and reality settled in. All the alarms were blaring in my head and the fight or flight instincts were engaged. Ken was standing in the kitchen when I blurted out, "I have to go for a bike ride!"

With a shocked look on his face, he replied, "You can't! We don't have enough time for a ride." I looked at him, trying to suppress the wild rage I was feeling and burst out, "You don't understand. I HAVE to go for a bike ride, NOW!" I turned and ran upstairs, changed into riding clothes and before he knew what was happening, I was on my bike flying down the driveway.

As soon as I turned onto the road the tears began to flow. The gauge on the pressure cooker released and the gasps and screams were almost convulsive as I rode in fury down the hills. Tears streamed sideways into my hair and blurred my vision as I choked, coughed and roared out a combination of anger, fear and sorrow. If screaming alone could eject the cancer from my body, I would have been cleansed from head to toe. I was oblivious to anyone or anything around me, but that was okay because I knew those back country roads and my bike knew where to go.

I pressed on, fighting the fact that I had cancer. So angry and outraged, I questioned God. "How could this be happening to me? I thought I had done everything right, everything I should to take care of my body. You were supposed to do your part and protect me from things like this. I thought we had a deal!"

Questions surfaced regarding what I could have done wrong. Was it something in the food I ate or the water I drank? No one else in my family had ever had cancer. I didn't drink, smoke or even consume caffeine. I ate a low fat diet and exercised more than most normal human beings. "HOW COULD THIS BE HAPPENING TO ME?" I screamed out in a second wave of frustration, dressed in confusion, topped with anger.

Stomping on the pedals at full speed as if trying to out race the cancer and not let it catch me, I felt no pain in my legs, just the pain of realization that this was not going away and this was not a dream that I would wake up from. My throat throbbed from the mounting pressure of the screams and my lungs burned from the gasps. This was a rage unlike any I had ever felt before and it drove me to ride faster and faster. Riding uphill at twenty-three miles per hour, I passed a man on a time trial bike as if he were standing still. I passed him like a crazy woman determined not to let cancer win the race.

I rode it out, cried it out, and screamed it out and when nothing was left after the last tear had been shed and the pressure was somewhat relieved, the bike turned back toward home. "Lots of people get cancer and live." I thought as I pedaled. Now, I just wanted someone to cut the cancer out of me so I could be done with it. I had a life and family, especially my daughter, worth fighting to live for. When I returned home Ken was pacing the floors. His expression told me that he was not sure what had just happened. I hugged him and said, "Let's do this thing," and I wasn't referring to the party. "And by the way," I added, "I think the guy I saw on the hill is probably going to sell his tricked out time trial bike after I passed him today."

*   *   *

One of the first to arrive to the party was David Kaplan. Ken and I had coached him in speed skating, then introduced him to bike riding as a way to train during the summer months. This dear friend had great wisdom and was very caring, so I was compelled to tell him what was happening to me. For some reason I thought I owed it to him. He was very supportive and understanding and it was a great comfort to know he was on my side.

Telling my mother was not going to be so easy and I dreaded it. I had been so annoyed by her insistance to get a mammogram, and to realize that she was right all along made it even more difficult. I felt that I had failed her and was once again flawed and broken. She knew I had the mammogram, now she wanted the results, but I refused to tell her over the phone. She thought I was still just angry for all the harassment she used to get me to schedule it. Oh, I was angry alright, but not with her.

My initial appointments to meet my cancer team were over a week away. I had been invited to a Sports Medicine Symposium in Salt Lake City to discuss altitude training and its benefits that weekend. Since I was already registered, Ken decided it would be good for us to drive there and think everything out on the way. We asked Mom to come over to watch Madison while we were away.

I was given my biopsy results and copies of my mammogram to hand carry to my new doctors. Trying to figure out how to tell my mother was painful all over again. While alone driving in my car, I practiced telling her, but every time I did, I broke down in tears. I decided to let her read the results herself instead of just blurting out, "You were right; I needed to have a mammogram. I have cancer!"

When my parents arrived, I welcomed them and let them settle in. It wasn't long before she asked me, "Did you get the results of your mammogram yet?" "I did." I replied. "They are over here at the table and I've decided to let you read them for yourself." I handed her the results over the kitchen table and she looked them over carefully and I watched her expression as she read them.

The pale, freckled face that had been there for me throughout my life seemed unusually still. I held my breath waiting for her response. Then she looked up at me, her hazel eyes welling to capacity with tears, and she said, "This is not what I wanted to see, but I am not at all surprised." The pitch of her voice rose as she choked back tears with those last few words. She stood and wrapped her arms around me and we sobbed until we separated to find tissues and collect ourselves.

"I feared from the moment I felt the lumps that it was cancer, but I didn't want to scare you," she said between stifled sobs, dabbing at tears with her crumpled tissue. "Scare me?" I responded, in a half laugh, half scoff. "I believed you when you said it was probably nothing. I am a grown up and asked you for your professional opinion. You DID NOT need to protect me."

"I will always want to protect you," she said as her face unsuccessfully tried to suppress her emotion. We hugged again and my words poured out like tears, "I'm sorry, so very sorry. I didn't mean for this to happen." feeling guilty that I had cancer and had let her down, as if somehow it was my fault, not knowing why.

On Memorial Day weekend Ken and I were going to Salt Lake City to the high altitude symposium presented by the Olympic Committee. We planned to stay at the hotel where the symposium was to be held and it happened to be our 14th wedding anniversary, so getting away turned out to be a bonus. Ken drove almost straight through while I had time to compose my whirling thoughts while staring out the window at the changing landscape. I appreciated having this time without distraction to contemplate my mortality and think through all the possible scenarios and solutions that now faced me; faced us. I knew I needed this time to prioritize my life and get things in perspective.

When we arrived at the symposium we enjoyed visiting with friends we had not seen in a while. Ryan Shimabukuru had lived a few dorm rooms down from me when we lived at the U.S. Olympic Education Center; he was now the national long track speed skating coach. He had always been friendly and a delight to associate with, both on and off the ice. Many referred to him as "Ryan the Hawaiian" because he came from Hawaii. He possessed a rare talent as a speed skater coming from a tropical island state. This was exactly what I needed: a full immersion distraction.

Ken wanted to be sure we visited the sites in Salt Lake City. We gazed at the Mormon Temple and it gave me a great sense of peace knowing that I had family already praying for me. We visited many of the 2002 Olympic Games venues during our trip, then Ken took the long way home and we stopped at Yellowstone National Park, where I got to view Old Faithful and the Grand Tetons. I had an emotional realization that I was looking at these natural wonders, not knowing if I would ever live to see such splendor again.

While we were gone, my parents decided that Mom would spend the summer with us while I went through treatment. In fact, she went with me to my first oncology appointment and every one thereafter. "When are you going to tell Madison?" my mother asked. The thought had been weighing heavily on my mind during the trip. "I want to wait and find out what the doctors say before telling her anything." I told her. "I don't want to upset her. We need to know what is going to happen before we go there."

*   *   *

For some unknown reason, my appointment with the surgeon was scheduled before my oncologist. Dr. Robert Goulet entered the room with sparkling blue eyes and a round head devoid of hair. He wore a tasteful bow tie, which added to his charm and his handshake felt genuine, warm and welcoming. The first words out of his mouth were, "I hear you are a cyclist. My son and I recently finished touring Italy on our bikes."

Instantly connecting, I handed him my biopsy results and radiology images and asked him about his bike.

He did a breast exam with skill and confidence, giving me assurance that he knew his way around a breast with respect. Afterwards he looked at the results which revealed the details and stage of my cancer. "We are going to have to do a skin sparing mastectomy." He told me directly. I did not expect this. I had expected them to remove the lumps, but not to take the entire breast. He explained, in detail, that with a staging of 2B, the entire breast and all associated tissues would have to be removed, including the areola and nipple. This was going to be far more complicated than I had ever expected.

Not long after Dr. Goulet left the exam room, Dr. Kathy D. Miller entered and introduced herself as she sat down on the stool next to the exam table. Her calm, clear voice remained steady and soothing. She took my hand and looked directly into my eyes as she spoke. My mother sat in the corner taking copious notes of everything said while I sat there attempting to let it soak in. This was so surreal and reminiscent of my experience in the hospital with the brain injury. Everything seemed to be moving faster than my brain could comprehend.

When she said I had to go through chemotherapy, I bristled. I have just been told that I must undergo a mastectomy; shouldn't that be enough? I thought and then questioned, "Are there any other options?" She paused and leaned closer to me and asked, "How old is your daughter?" "Nine years old," I replied. Looking even deeper into my eyes, Dr. Miller firmly pressed, "If you want to see your daughter graduate from high school and you want to walk down the aisle at her wedding, you *will* do this chemotherapy."

She had pulled out the big guns and hit me right where I lived. I got the point, loud and clear. So much of my thoughts had been about how this would affect Madison. She proceeded to talk about the protocol for chemo, but I could not process her words. This is why no one should ever go to an appointment like this alone.

Dr. Miller continued talking as I started to be sucked down a tunnel to another place where everything around me became a blur and the sounds were muffled. I asked myself, "Who am I, really?" Pictures of my life flashed on the movie screen of my mind. "What am I willing to give up, and what am I willing to fight for?" were thoughts echoing in my head. Sudden recognition cleared the fog and I acknowledged that at my core, "I am a wife, a mother and an athlete and I will not allow cancer to take any of that away from me." Although I had to lose my breasts and my hair, I would NOT give up my identity.

As I returned to the conversation, Dr. Miller told us that she would start my chemotherapy the next week. This news was confusing. I had assumed that they would do surgery first, get the cancer out of my body as soon as possible and then start chemo. She explained that there would be a distinct advantage to administering the chemo first. "This way we can monitor the tumors to determine if this medication works. If they don't shrink, we can try a different drug. If we remove the tumors first, we would have to throw the whole kitchen sink at them and hope something would work." This made perfect sense to me. Now it would be their turn to *"Watch and learn"*.

They gave us instructions and a schedule for chemotherapy. My mother took all the information and organized it. Chemotherapy seemed like another slap in the face. When you think of chemo, you picture poor, sick bald people. How could I be so vain as to imagine that losing my hair might be justification enough to refuse this treatment? All my life I had long reddish brown hair and it was one of the first things people noticed. Madison and I had that in common and now it was going to be taken from me as well.

Of course, my mind raced. How would this affect Ken and Madison? Would I ever be attractive to Ken again? How might this change my athletic performance? Would this limit my ability to coach Special Olympics and take away the opportunity to take Team USA to Japan? I loved my life and I was NOT going to let THIS get in the way of what I loved.

After the decisions regarding my treatment plan and the implications had some time to sink in, it seemed appropriate to tell Special Olympics Team USA my change in health status. I knew that this would be a very difficult call to make because I believed that I would be letting them down. When I spoke with Melanie Ferlito, the Team USA director and discussed my issues and my plans, she did not hesitate for a moment to assure me of her confidence that I would be able to pull this off. That was what I needed to hear. They had faith in me and my ability to beat this disease and continue to live on my terms, which in this case included coaching; a big part of the life that I loved.

Within a week, my first chemotherapy treatment was scheduled and Madison had to be told. I wanted to choose my words carefully. How do you tell a nine year old girl that her mother has cancer? We had no idea how she would react. I thought it through, over and over, trying to put myself in the place of a child her age. How would it make the most sense and not be so frightening?

When I was ready, Ken and my mother were there to support both of us. I sat down in a chair so I could look into her eyes. Ken was to my left and mother stood behind Madison. She had no idea what we were getting ready to tell her and looked concerned, likely thinking that she might have done something wrong.

She shuffled a bit, her long red braids swaying, and looked from face to face nervously checking expressions to see if she was in trouble. I began, "You know our bodies are made up of many cells, millions and millions of cells, and every cell has a job to do to keep things working." She nodded with a look that said, "Why are you telling me this?"

"Every once in a while there are a few cells in the body that decide they are not going to do their job anymore and every job in the body is important. They decide they are going to do their own thing and that gets in the way of others that are trying to do their job. Then they decide to have a party and make more of themselves and that starts making trouble for the whole body. These cells grow very fast and need to be stopped before they take over everything and the body doesn't work anymore."

"Doctors have discovered medicines that can stop these trouble makers from growing, and hopefully stop them from ever coming back. The only problem is that these bad cells are not the only cells in the body that grow fast. The cells that make hair and fingernails and cells in the stomach also grow fast. The medicine stops the bad cells from growing, but sometimes stops the good ones too. A lot of times it can make a person's hair fall out for a little while and they might throw up some days." I looked at her, watching the wheels turning behind her hazel green eyes.

"Some of these bad cells are in my body and I need to take medicine to stop them from making trouble." I paused to see if things were registering. "These cells are called cancer and the medicine is called chemotherapy." I paused again waiting for a response. "Do you understand? Do you have any questions?" I asked, holding my breath waiting for a response or reaction.

Again, there was a pause and silence. I had been bracing myself for all kinds of questions like, "Are you going to die?" or "Why don't you look sick?" But she said nothing. After a few moments Madison shifted her weight and looked at the floor, then back up at me. "Yes," she said timidly "Can I go jump on the trampoline now?" The oxygen rushed back into the room and we could breathe again. "Yes," I chuckled, "You can go jump on the trampoline." There was a great sense of relief as we watched her scurry out to the backyard to play on the trampoline.

Apparently, like her mother, she needed time to think things out and process what was happening. She did it while jumping and I did it while riding. After she finished on the trampoline she came to me with questions, asking, "Is cancer contagious? Can you catch it from somebody?" "No," I told her, "it's not contagious. You can't catch it from other people." She appeared confused. "Well, there is this girl named Carolyn who sits on my school bus." she said, "She is the only one at school who is allowed to wear a hat. No one will sit next to her or play with her because she has no hair. Everyone is afraid that she has something they can catch."

"Sit with her on the bus tomorrow." I told her. "Tell her that your mother has cancer and see what she says." After I came home from work the next day, Madison ran up to me, very excited to tell me what had happened. "Mom, you were right!" She said almost breathless with excitement. "She has cancer too! She has a brain tumor!" Madison ended up sitting next to Carolyn for the rest of the year and they became good friends.

Now that Madison knew my situation, I decided we should have a family portrait. I'd had long hair ever since I was in kindergarten and liked it that way. I wanted a photo of our family together before the ravages of chemotherapy changed things.

David Kaplan told me that his wife, J.J. would do a photo session for us. She was a talented professional photographer with a studio called "Color My World" and was kind hearted with an artistic eye. She gave us direction regarding what to wear and told us to meet her at Holiday Park in Broad Ripple. We posed in different places around the park, while she rapidly snapped photos as we joked around and tried to play. It was fun and the perfect escape from the realization that I only had twelve hours before I was to have my hair cut and start the first of many chemo treatments.

After we finished the photo shoot in the park, mom insisted we go look at wigs. I was not emotionally ready for this. Sitting in front of a mirror and putting on a cap to hold my hair while trying on shiny plastic hair that would never look like my real hair, turned out to be more than I could handle. Choking back tears, I realized I didn't want any of these wigs; I didn't want any of this. I just wanted to go to sleep and wake up to find it had all been a nightmare.

That evening, when I went in to kiss Madison good night she had her nose in a book. This was not unusual, as she loved to read. What was unusual, was the fact that she would not let me pull the book away from her face to give her a kiss. She clung to her book as if it would make her invisible and hide her from all that was going on in our lives. A small little voice came from behind the book. "I don't want you to do it," she protested. "Do what?" I asked. With no response I returned, "You don't want me to do what, Madison?" Her voice cracked, almost pleading, "I don't want you to cut your hair."

At that moment, I realized that cancer was already having a greater effect on her than I had expected. She did not want me to see her face on this eve of change in our lives. Our hair had been a connection between the two of us for many years; part of our identity as mother and daughter. It appeared that she feared this connection would be broken. Calmly, I assured her, "I don't want to cut my hair either, but I really need to. I am going to donate it to Locks of Love so someone else can use the hair that is only going to fall out anyway." "I don't like it!" she squeaked from behind the protective barrier of her book. I pulled down her blockade and she closed her eyes refusing to look at me. "I don't like it either" I said, "but this is the best thing to do. I'm still your mom and that will never change. I will need you to help me with my hair when it starts falling out. Can you do that for me?" She silently nodded agreement and I kissed her good night. She rolled her face to the wall and I left the room with silent tears of my own.

The next morning when I sent Madison off to school, she was more hesitant than usual to leave. I gave her an extra hug and asked her, "Should I take armadillo with me this morning to keep me company?" Armadillo was her favorite stuffed animal, given to her by my father when he finished building a Velodrome in Texas. "No!" she shouted. "He's mine! Besides, you don't need him. You'll have Nana with you and won't need Armadillo!"

After Madison had gone, Mom and I went to a local quick cut hair shop where I told the stylist my plan to make a donation to Locks of Love. She brushed my hair back into a ponytail. The requirement to donate was ten inches, which was not a problem; I had plenty. She turned the chair to show me in the mirror. I didn't want to see so I closed my eyes and listened to the scissors chewing through the bundled hair. It felt so very surreal. I watched as she released my hair and swung it forward around my face. My head felt light and my hair moved easily. Who knew that ten inches of hair could make that much of a difference?

My mother was trying her best to boost my confidence by telling me how good she thought it looked. "Maybe you should have gotten your hair cut years ago, it looks that good." I knew she was trying to lift my spirits, but it didn't work. I knew the rest of my hair was not going to last long and so did she. Dr. Miller told us that hair usually starts falling out fourteen days after the start of chemotherapy.

We went straight from the hair salon to the IU Simon Cancer Center infusion clinic. Harp music floated through the lobby and paintings created by patients lined the corridor walls. Checking in at the front desk and searching for a place where we could sit together, proved to be more difficult than we ever imagined. The number of people waiting to go in and get poisoned was staggering. It was standing room only. I ended up sitting near a column and trying not to be obvious, as I looked around the open area at all the faces in different stages of treatment.

Sorting patients from family or supportive friends was fairly easy. Most patients had a dull pallor and some form of head covering. There were a few others that were not as obvious. Institutional wristbands were the only way one could tell they were patients. Maybe it was their first time, just like me.

I found myself looking at each patient, trying to guess their story. In my mind, I divided them into categories; a young man in his twenties, looks physically fit; testicular cancer; older woman, wearing a pink scarf: most likely breast cancer; young girl around 18 or 19 accompanied by her mom: Leukemia; an older gentleman with a newspaper and likely his adult daughter by his side: prostate cancer.

When they called my name we collected our survival supplies: laptop, phone, Mom's purse and cup of ice. You would have thought we were going on an expedition. They ushered us through the threshold into another large room were we found groups of people clustered about in high backed institutional lounge chairs with IV bags on poles hovering over them. Out of the corner of my eye, I noticed an open door through which I could see a pale, fragile looking woman lying on her side swaddled in white blankets. A knit cap covered her head as she shivered in little spasms, most likely the result of the potent treatment she had received. The thought crossed my mind and I wondered if that would be me someday soon.

Quickly I looked away in respect of her privacy, but mostly to escape the reality of that moment. I felt like a stray dog that had just been captured and was being walked through the animal control shelter past all the other lost dogs. They escorted me to my chair in the center of the room and welcomed me like wait staff would in a restaurant. My assigned nurse for the day introduced herself.

The menu for the day would be an appetizer of normal saline followed by a course of steroids. The entrée would be Taxotere with a side of anti-nausea meds. They also served dessert. Popsicles were given in an effort to help reduce mouth sores. Just lovely!

The nurse produced a needle and other supplies to start the IV. She placed a rubber tourniquet around my arm to restrict the blood flow, causing the veins to enlarge, making them easier to find. I had always had a vein very willing to cooperate in my left arm, and once again it stepped forward and volunteered for duty.

After the saline and steroids had run their course, my nurse appeared with my entrée. She attached the bag of poison to my main line and started the drip, then the hum and click of the IV pump began. Pulling up a chair, she sat next to me and asked questions about Ken and Madison then told me about her two children. When asked what I liked to do in my spare time, I told her about my cycling and mom chimed in with a few proud anecdotes.

As the poison made its way through my body, I grew progressively cold and started to shiver. Prepared for this, they produced blankets that had been heating in an oven nearby. Soon I was wrapped snugly in toasty white blankets, most likely the same type they had used on the young woman in the private room I had spied when I first walked in.

The nurse sat with us for about five minutes, making idle conversation. When all appeared to be progressing well she checked my vital signs, glanced at the infusion site and excused herself so she could check on other patients.

Mom then turned to her book and I opened my laptop and began watching a romantic comedy with Ben Stiller and Jennifer Aniston, trying to lose myself in the lives of other people and not focus on what was going on that moment in the life that did not feel like it belonged to me. After the pump chimed that my bag was completely drained the nurse came over and shut everything off, removed the IV, applied direct pressure to the site and gave us discharge instructions while she applied the bandage.

On the drive home mom kept looking at me. I could feel her eyes studying me as I drove. It was as if she expected my face to turn green or suddenly see me start spewing green pea soup all over the car, even though I hadn't eaten anything like pea soup, and I don't even like pea soup. Thank goodness nothing like that happened. Nothing felt any different physically, but it seemed weird waiting for the unknown to happen.

When we got home, Mom insisted that I lie on the couch and watch television while she watched me like a hawk. Although she pretended not to, I could still feel her hovering nearby, ready to spring into action with a basin should one be needed. The anti-nausea medicine apparently did its job. Nothing happened, my blood continued to pulse through my veins and my heart continued to beat. My head was a little fuzzy at times, but I was okay.

Sitting still and waiting for things to happen have never been my style. Thinking about what was going on inside my body caused me to want to get busy. I needed to get my life back. I needed to get on my bike.

Xeloda was my oral chemotherapy. I looked it up on the internet, and learned that it was used in the treatment of metastatic breast and colon cancers. That meant it killed cancer cells that had spread throughout the body. They were giving me the really strong stuff!

It did not take long before the Xeloda made its presence known in my body and showed everyone who was boss. The first place I noticed its effect was in my mouth. Sores started to develop in the ever thinning lining of my cheeks and were so painful that I could not open my mouth enough to put anything bigger than a spoon inside. If it stretched any wider it felt as though the thin, fragile tissue would tear. Needless to say, eating became unbearably difficult.

It didn't matter what I ate because there was no taste in anything. It seemed that sense also fled the scene when it heard that chemo was involved. With taste removed from my diet, I found myself pacing the floors, looking through cupboards trying to find something, anything that had some semblance of flavor.

I learned to eat for texture and to reduce trauma on the tissue in my mouth. My diet consisted mostly of soups, Ensure, and milkshakes. Concerned, my mother insisted we call the nurse practitioner and tell her that the side effects had become intolerable and I was losing weight. Once again, my mother was right.

After the call, the nurse phoned in a prescription for something called Mary's Magic Mouthwash. This was a solution mixed by a pharmacist that would help numb the mouth, as well as help it heal. She also reduced my dosage of Xeloda. Then I was told the reaction was not unexpected or unusual. I certainly would like to have known this information in advance so I could have been more prepared.

My mother accompanied me to the second infusion as well. We walked past the chairs in the open area and they were all occupied. This resulted in my being placed in a private room. Somehow the fact that the treatment rooms were all filled, yet the waiting room remained crowded with people disturbed me. I realized that cancer is an out of control disease and we have an urgent need to discover its cause, whatever that might be.

They started the IV saline and a pre chemo steroid ritual once again. The nurse sat down next to me and hooked up the real poison as she started talking to me about bike riding and life in general. As the poison entered I could feel the cold grip of the fluid make its way up my arm.

A few minutes into the infusion, I suddenly noticed an odd feeling in my chest, one I had never felt before. "I feel strange." was all that I had to say before the nurse hit an alarm and had my chair completely reclined. My lungs felt fuzzy and tingly. I looked up, startled, as three other nurses ran into the room. Mom was on her feet. "I'm sorry," I said to the wide eyed faces now peering over me with very concerned looks. "Did I do something wrong?" I asked. "I've stopped the Taxotere and started a new bag of steroids," my chair side nurse reported. "You caught that fast." the other nurse congratulated. They were all happy that I had not gone into respiratory arrest.

It appears that a lot of people have allergic reactions on their second dose of chemo. The first time they are infused with the chemicals they are sensitized to them, but don't have a reaction and are usually fine. It is more likely that the second dose causes problems as in my case. "You had a reaction to the medications and that is why we were taking it slow and watching you so closely. That is the reason I had the second bag of steroids ready," she said, after the code team had left the room. "Does that mean that I will have to go on a different drug from now on?" I questioned.

"No. Now that we know that you are sensitive to it, we can run things more slowly and make sure we have all the protective drugs ready. You will stay on Taxotere but it will be given at a much slower rate causing you to be in the chair even longer," she explained.

One of the side effects of Taxotere is narrowing of the tear ducts causing them to be stiff and inflexible. This can result in tears overrunning the eyelids and this will make a person appear to be crying. I soon had to explain the tears to many people who thought I was getting very emotional at times while talking to them. This was one more frustrating reminder that I was no longer in control of my own body.

One very hot evening at the Velodrome I was riding with David Kaplan, Joe Niccum and Mikk Carr. We were doing sprint intervals when my eyes started tearing beneath my sunglasses. As the tears fell and collected around my lips I licked them and was surprised to find that they tasted like plain water. "Where was the salt?" I wondered. Then, as my deductive reasoning kicked in, I thought, "The chemo has taken the salt out of my tears." It took me a while to realize that the salt was still there. The chemo had taken away my ability to taste the salt and my deductive reasoning left a lot to be desired.

My hair had not yet started to abandon me so I held out hope that I would be that one person out of twenty million whose hair would not fall out from the chemotherapy. Every morning I got up, ran my fingers through and gave it a little tug just to see if any was loose. Repeating this ritual for thirteen days there was no such result. I wondered if somehow I might possibly be spared that dreaded indignity.

On day fourteen, I woke up, ran my fingers through my hair and thought "Wonderful! Day fourteen and it's still there and not falling out. Maybe this won't be so bad after all." Then I went into the shower and as I wrung the water from my hair, I looked down and stared at a handful of... reality.

It was at this point that reality struck full force: I WAS a cancer patient. No more denial, no more room for doubt. I slid down the side of the shower, arms hugging myself as that reality sunk in. I watched my tears, combined with my hair and the shower water, go down the drain and I broke into gut wrenching sobs.

*   *   *

My hair may have abandoned me, but my bike had not. I continued to train, coach and ride at some level throughout all my treatments. Going to the Velodrome and continuing what I loved to do was my much needed escape. This was now my new normal.

When Lance Armstrong announced that he had cancer the cycling community rallied behind him. The first LiveStrong bracelets were released to the market around the time that I was diagnosed and they started to be displayed in a few sporting goods stores and bike shops. Ken made sure I had one of the first bracelets and since it was for such a good cause, we bought a whole collection of those yellow rubber wristbands. We gave them to the riders we were coaching as well as our other friends.

It is amazing how seemingly small gestures can be so meaningful to those fighting for their lives. That small band of yellow rubber meant a lot to me. It was humbling to see the number of friends who chose to wear one in my honor. In my mind, this gesture was a real symbol of solidarity.

Pink ribbons had a similar meaning. When I noticed a pink ribbon magnet on a car or mailbox, I felt some connection with the occupants. They were supportive and invested in finding a cure. Were they a survivor themselves or had they lost a friend or loved one to breast cancer? I wanted to drive up to them, wave and hold a sign that said "Me Too!" or "Thank You."

Every yellow wristband, every pink wristband and ribbon made a statement. It said, "This person understands the horrors caused by cancer." and confirmed that people were there who supported the need for research and victims like me. To this day, I sometimes ask people who they honor by wearing their wristbands.

As my hair started to fall out, it became Madison's job to pick it off my jacket. It soon reached the point where I could lightly tug on a clump of hair and disconnect it from my scalp completely as if it had only been temporarily glued in place. At my mother's continued insistence, we went to a wig shop that specialized in wigs and hairpieces just for cancer patients. It was small, quiet and had an intimate feel.

None of the dozens of wigs that I tried really looked like me, but we did find one that was reasonably close. It did not fit well so the shop owner took a few stitches in the scalp to tighten it. I was still not sold on the whole idea of wearing a scratchy wig with a part that made it very obvious that it was one.

It was a warm summer, so I usually ended up wearing some sort of hat instead of a wig. Shopping became a constant quest to find a suitable hat. I didn't want a baseball style cap that had a hole in the back, as it didn't fit my rather small head and would be inappropriate for work.

Nina Edwards-Swain, a very special woman who worked with Ken, had gone through breast cancer a few years earlier. Before cancer, she had long blonde hair that cascaded all the way to the floor like a waterfall. She clearly understood what it was like to be associated with your hair. She surprised me with a package filled with several perfect hats that were comfortable, stylish and good for wearing in the summer. What a wonderful gift, gesture and all around good deed. With her help, I was able to wear a different hat just about every day at work.

When I went to the velodrome and would change into my cycling gear, my friends joked that they would never be able to see my head because I was always wearing a hat. It became a game for me to quick change from a hat to my helmet without ever exposing my head. I had a very sly way of sliding the hat off the back just as I slid my helmet on the front. Even though the helmet had open slots for ventilation, through which you could see my scalp, I didn't feel exposed and was not uncomfortable wearing it.

Hair continued to fall and I continued to ride, often becoming frustrated and angry at my situation because I felt I had no control over what was happening. The mixed emotions of frustration and anger and possibly a little self-pity sometimes became overwhelming. When I could no longer handle the situation and there was no possibility of riding my bike, I would go upstairs, turn on the television, run the shower, and then jump into my bed smothering myself with a pillow to muffle the tears and screams of outrage. "I JUST WANT MY LIFE BACK!"

I don't know if this was because I was too proud or because I was afraid of the effect that a meltdown in front of my family might have on them. I made it a point not to show any signs of weakness, especially in front of Madison and hid all the doubts and fears that I might not make it through to see her grow up and graduate. I hid them from her and from myself as well.

I sat in front of the mirror with a comb in my hand, looking at the clumps of hair that had so easily detached themselves from my head. I could not bring myself to throw any of it away. Although my hair was abandoning me, I was determined to save it and collected what little I had in a Ziploc bag. The hair itself looked dull and lifeless and as sick as I felt.

It is possible that vanity kept me from shaving my head. In hindsight, I should have done it when my hair first started to come out. It came out bit by bit, struggling to stay, but looking pitiful and diminished with a few stubborn patches that would not let go. I believe I ended up looking worse than if I had shaved my head. Like my hair, I too was stubborn and refused to let go.

Being the wonderful husband that he is, Ken told me he didn't marry me for my hair, but I knew that he liked my hair when it was long. I felt that he got the short end of the stick in our marriage. I was defective now and it was possible that my warranty might expire sooner than we expected. When you get married, you both fantasize about growing old together. The ultimate "Happily ever after" is being the elderly couple taking care of each other and fading into the sunset together, seeing their children grown with families of their own. He argued that he loved me regardless of my appearance and planned on living out his years with me, hair or no hair, breasts or no breasts.

*   *   *

Not long after my treatment started, Ken rolled a beautiful new aerodynamic time trial track bike out onto the track. He told me that I deserved a new bike. I had been secretly wondering whether I would live long enough to see Madison graduate from high school. Now here was my knight in shining armor showing me, by this amazing gesture that he had faith that I would not only live, but live to ride and race again. His faith in me boosted my spirits and gave me a goal. Since I am a very goal oriented person, the bike was the perfect medicine.

Ken is a world class bike mechanic and is like MacGyver with a bike wrench. He built the wheels and put the bike together to fit exactly like my other track bikes. When I got on the new one, it felt as though I had been riding it for years. My first thought was that I didn't deserve the bike, but I hadn't deserved cancer either. This gave me incredible strength and I silently vowed to make his investment count. I was going to take him to the winner's podium with me once again.

The Indiana state track cycling championships were coming up near the end of June and we wanted to make sure all our riders were ready to compete. I was very excited about some of the prospects for that year's racing season. Abby had been doing exceptionally well and David Kaplan had been showing a lot of improvement in his time trials.

The championships were just two days after my second infusion of Taxotere. I could feel my endurance beginning to wane, but could not resist testing myself. Sheer determination, along with a lot of support and encouragement from Ken, put me back on the track.

Getting on my time trial bike was like slipping into a favorite pair of blue jeans. I felt comfortable and at home. This was where I lived and planned to keep on living.

Like many times before, I found myself on the bike, held at the start line, waiting for the countdown to begin. Five… four… three, I looked down the track. Two, took a deep breath and stood up high on the pedals. One, I thought to myself "Hold it steady, listen for it, and go!" I pulled up on the pedals and just muscled it, using every bit of energy that remained in my legs to overcome inertia.

At that point, it was me, the bike, and the stopwatch. There was no cancer, not in this race! Then before I even realized it, the race was finished. It was not my best time, but it was not my worst either. Amazingly, I won the state championships. This proved to me that, with muscle memory and frequent training, I could continue to ride. I just needed to pace myself and pay attention to the side effects.

That day motivated me. When I won a race it wasn't just for me, I was racing for both Ken and Madison. We were a team and partners for life. I didn't want to disappoint, but simply needed to win my life back.

*   *   *

During one of my first visits with Dr. Miller, she told me that chemotherapy would wreak havoc with my ovaries. This made sense because my cancer was estrogen receptor positive which means that estrogen stimulates the growth of my type of cancer. Therefore, we would have to try to starve those nasty cancer cells to death by turning off their supply of estrogen.

Removing estrogen from the balance meant that hot flashes would become an issue. Never having had one, I was not certain what to expect. I had seen women at work, with flushed faces fanning themselves, while telling me what it was like, but I had never felt the flush they described. I will never forget my first hot flash, it did not build slowly but hit me like I had been doused in kerosene and someone had set my clothes on fire. The spark started around my belly button, and then the wildfire quickly went north. I started clawing at my clothing trying to shed them. My mother looked at me and said, "Been there, done that; it's a lot like menopause."

The night sweats were insufferable. In the middle of the night I often woke up soaked with beads of sweat across my chest. It didn't happen just once or twice a night, but more like once an hour throughout the night. Getting a complete night's sleep was impossible. I also noticed that turning onto my right side was like turning on the heat. As if my body had some sort of trip mechanism that fired the coals in my personal furnace.

My pillow was no help at all because it seemed to retain heat and reflect it back at me. After doing some research, I found a device called the Chillow which helped a lot. This was a vinyl bladder that held three cups of water inserted into the pillow. It was nice and cool; at least until my body heat would raise the temperature to unbearable again. At that point, I would turn the pillow over and allow it to cool down.

With my next hot flash I repeated the process. There were a lot of restless nights that usually started as soon as I got into bed. I would rush to get under the covers because I was freezing and pull the sheets up around my neck, shivering uncontrollably, then without notice or reason, it suddenly felt as if my body was on fire and I would kick the sheets off only to go searching for them moments later when the cold returned. Ken was very tolerant of my pancake flipping, sheet clutching, and pillow tossing nights.

My family got used to my constant on, off, on routines with sweaters and jackets and I learned to dress in layers. The bottom layer was always a sleeveless V-neck so that I could get down to it and ventilate if I needed to. I noticed an odd trend. It seemed that the cold flashes happened just before the hot one hit me. I bundled up and froze, shivering and asking Ken to turn the heat up. Without warning there would be a complete reversal with heat enveloping me as though I must be standing on the rim of an active volcano.

One evening Madison had an after school function and Ken was late coming home from work. While sitting and working at the computer a wicked hot flash hit me. I started to shed layers and did not stop at the sleeveless V-neck layer. As I became completely disrobed from the waist up, Ken walked in the door just in time to see me shed the last layer. He walked toward me as he started to remove his own shirt. "Okay, I'm game," he said with a big smile on his face and gleam in his eyes. I looked back at him with a scowl and exclaimed, "It's not what you think. Don't even come close to me or I will melt you!" Ken's shirt went back on and he began buttoning it back up. "Just let me know when you want to do that again."

*　　*　　*

The women's team, that had been at our house for training just before I had my mammogram, was preparing for a 20 Kilometer team time trial in Ohio. There were enough riders on our team that we could enter two teams in the competition. They asked if I would like to race with them and I was hesitant at first. I explained that, if I rode I needed to be on the slower team because my endurance was getting worse as my blood count plummeted. "No problem" JoMay told me. "I recently bought a house and both my spare time and money have gone into it, not training or racing. We can ride together and focus on providing a good experience for Abby and Brooke." Just knowing Abby and Brooke were on the team with JoMay made me feel much better.

The time trial was scheduled three days after the third intravenous infusion of Taxotere and I was very concerned about my body's ability to transport oxygen due to the declining red blood cell count. I was starting to get breathless walking up and down stairs and knew that the lack of endurance left me far from race ready.

In team time trialing each member of the team takes short turns at the front pulling into the wind while the others sit in the slipstream behind them to rest. JoMay was very strong and took great pulls at the front. Abby and Brooke were both very well synchronized and strong. Ken drove behind us in the support vehicle. It wasn't at all like the experience at the Tour of Texas with Tracy and Sally screaming at each other to work harder. This group worked smoothly together and communicated like we had been riding together for years. It was a joy to be back in a team time trial, especially with such great friends. We assumed that our other, stronger team was destined to win the gold medal so we were just there to ride for the experience.

When we finished, the men's team gathered at the finish line to welcome us. Earlier along the road, we heard voices yelling and screaming, "You're up! You're up!" We didn't quite understand what that meant at the time, but after finishing we looked at the leader board and realized that our team was at the top and stayed there as the other teams finished. Our time had been faster than we realized and we ended up winning the time trial! Sometimes riding relaxed with no pressure is a greater advantage than riding with high expectations. I never heard anything like that in any motivational tapes.

*   *   *

Surgery was delayed to be scheduled after all the chemotherapy treatments were completed and my red blood cell count had a chance to return to a point where the operation was survivable. As the cancer killing effects started to accumulate in my system, I began to experience more and more fatigue and soon I didn't even have enough energy to change out of my pajamas.

Ken came home early from officiating a bike race, on an absolutely gorgeous August afternoon, but I was too tired to even get dressed. I had been sitting all day on the couch staring out the window gazing at the blue sky and longing to be with the riders passing by our house all day. I kept thinking "I should go for a ride," but couldn't get up enough momentum to get off the couch.

Mom had been home with me all day and when Ken arrived she told him, "You need to take her out somewhere. Maybe out to eat." He turned to me and asked, "Where would you like to go?" "I don't know." I replied. "Do you want to get something to eat?" "I don't know," I repeated. He then rattled off a bunch of destinations, but I found it hard to respond. Wanting to go out, but too exhausted to care, I didn't know where I wanted to eat. Why did it matter, since I couldn't taste anything?

Decision making was difficult because that took energy. Dragging my feet I opted for the closest restaurant to home, Bob Evans. "I can go, but do I have to change out of my pajamas?" I asked. "No, you don't have to change anything. You look fine to me." Ken assured me.

Coincidentally, that day happened to be the Sunday of the Brickyard 400, a huge NASCAR race in Indianapolis. When we got to the restaurant I noticed that it was almost empty and the few people that were there appeared to be lobster red. They had been baking all day in the scorching hot sun at the Indianapolis Motor Speedway. I was a little conspicuous being pale faced, wearing pajamas and sporting a hat in a futile attempt to hide my hairless head. Thankfully, everyone else was too toasted to even notice or care.

Fatigue was becoming all-consuming, leaving me breathless with the slightest activity. The next day I called my oncologist's office to tell the nurse that I was getting out of breath just walking up one flight of stairs. When the nurse heard this, it seemed to trigger a red flag. "You need to come in immediately for a CAT scan. It's possible that you might have a pulmonary embolism which could be life threatening." That was enough to get my heart racing without a bike, so I got to the hospital as quickly as I could.

They did the scan with an IV contrast, along with some blood tests. The good news was no pulmonary embolism. The bad news was they detected a very low red blood cell count. Even though I became breathless with the slightest bit of exertion and had low hemoglobin, they did not give me a transfusion nor did they give me EPO to help boost my red cell production. They said, in no uncertain terms, that I was just going to have to tough it out and rest. For me, being idle is like being in prison.

Time passed slowly while I waited to see how much worse I could feel. Ken mentioned that a little more than two weeks after my last scheduled chemo the National Cycling Championships for track racing would be held in Kenosha, Wisconsin which was close enough for us to drive there. Part of me wanted to go, yet another part didn't want to see what I had been missing.

I doubted that it would be worth the time, money and effort it would take to go. With such a low red blood cell count, it was very questionable whether I could make it at all. Once again Ken stepped in with a voice of encouragement and suggested that we should go to coach and support Abby. She had been blossoming, as a track rider and was a joy to coach. Ken then pointed out that if we were going, I might as well ride while we were there, if nothing else but to play with my new track bike.

Getting on that bike turned out to be great medicine, I was moving my body in a way that felt natural and familiar and I didn't have to think. The bike and my muscles were united and I was just along for the ride. Off the bike I felt like a fish out of the water, gasping for air, but back on, I was in my natural environment and swimming again.

When we arrived for registration I recognized several of the names on the list and was a little nervous, wondering how my performance would be under my particular circumstances. It was decided that I would not advertise the fact that I had cancer. Many of the riders hadn't seen me all summer because I had not been competing in national events for obvious reasons. I didn't want to talk about having cancer or see the, "Oh, I'm so sorry" looks of pity on people's faces.

I chose to enjoy the escape back into competition on the track. Keeping my head covered and staying mostly to myself in our camp in the infield I felt more comfortable. So much of racing is psychological strategy and if others knew I had impaired endurance they would not hesitate to take advantage. My goal was to submerge myself in riding and feel like "the old Cindi" if only for a brief period of time and not have to answer questions and deal with cancer. This was my party and cancer was not invited.

The American Bicycle Racing National Championships we were attending was an omnium. That means there was not one race, but many races of different distances and the person with the top score at the end of all the races combined, was the champion. They consisted of a 200 meter time trial, a 500 meter time trial, a 2000 meter time trial, match sprints, and a point's race. Three of these events were very short. My focus would be on shorter races since I had not done a pursuit or a points race all summer, but had a lot of experience with them before cancer came into my life.

Warming up on the track felt so comfortable because I had low expectations for myself and was relaxed enjoying just being there. The 200 meter race was first. I had a stationary trainer set up with my road bike on it, so I was able to get in a very good warm-up just before the race. In the 200 meters there is a lap and a half in which to build up speed culminating in a full sprint. Timing starts as soon as the rider crosses the 200 meter line on the back stretch and stops when the rider crosses the finish line. This was the shortest of all the races.

Relying solely on muscle strength I had inherited from my father and years of training, I asked Ken to give me a big gear. My thinking was that I could push the gear with muscle and not rely on my aerobic system which was far from recharged. He set up my bike with a fixed gear that was 104 inches around. Translated, that means one complete rotation of the pedals causes the bike to move forward as if you were riding a wheel 104 inches in diameter. Most women race with a gear between 85 and 90 inches.

The hardest part would be winding up the gear. Within a lap and a half I had to bring my bike up to speed and keep riding high on the banking. This way I could take advantage of gravity as I dove down to the start of the 200 meter line. After reaching top speed I was driven to maintain that speed until crossing the finish line. This race was all muscle and not red blood cell dependent and I had done it many times before and was hoping to do it again. And I did. I had the fastest time and won the race. Unbelievable! This single personal victory strengthened my resolve. I was NOT going to let cancer take my passion away.

The win in the 200 meter race gave me confidence and qualified me as top seed for the upcoming Match Sprints; all the more reason to keep my diagnosis quiet.

There is an area in the infield where riders preparing for the upcoming race can ride around in the small circle to get physically warmed up and mentally prepared. A woman rode up next to me while we circled like sharks in the warm-up area and started talking. She asked me where I was from and how long I had been riding, and then surprised me by saying, "I hear that one of the riders here this weekend has cancer." I thought, "Are you kidding me?" However, my reply was simply, "Really?" and I didn't say anything more.

Abby was racing in the Junior Women's competition and it was great to put my focus on her. Riding exceptionally well, she was a dream to coach because she not only listened to our instructions and advice but also applied what we taught her. This young lady, a natural on the track, was winning.

The next race was the 500 meter time trial. It was a lap and a half around the track from a standing start. This was my specialty and favorite race. You don't hold anything back in the 500; you just go. I was ready to let all the anger and frustration I had felt towards cancer come out in this race and I did. There was enough adrenaline accumulated that I tore it up and won the 500 meter time trial.

Since I was the top seed in the 200 meters, I was the last competitor to race the 500 meters. When I saw my time after I finished, I burst into tears while gasping for air in the cool down area. Ken came walking toward me and I nearly dropped the bike to hug him. I had won! This was our victory, and no one could take that away from us. We were living in that moment. I had won races before, I had won Nationals before, but this one was different. This meant that I was reclaiming my life.

I knew that the 2000 meter pursuit would be the most difficult race for me. It was hard even when I was in good shape, complete with a full set of red blood cells. There is a real skill in racing a pursuit related to pacing yourself. It is said that one second too fast at the start will cost you three seconds in the finish. This race, completely determined in fractions of a second, drains every bit of strength and endurance a rider has. I was hesitant to do it because I knew it would hurt and was not sure how much strength I had left.

Ken talked me into it. "Just ride so you will get omnium points. Don't worry about winning. Just pace yourself and ride." Because I like to ride and push myself, I usually go out way too fast feeling just fine in the first several laps, but ending up paying for the effort in the last two. With no energy to waste this time, I went out slower than usual, but ran out of gas toward the end, gasping for air and feeling like I couldn't breathe. The woman I rode against was faster, but much to my surprise, I managed to take third place overall.

The next day I would be facing the Match Sprints and the Points Race. Lying in bed that night I began visualizing exactly what I would do in different situations in the race, thinking through scenarios and imagining ways to counter and handle them. This made my heart race as if I were still on my bike. Evidently Ken could not sleep either and he threw even more fuel on the flames. His voice, cool and analytical as always, said what I could not bring myself to consider. "If you do really well in the match sprints, you could make the podium for the overall final." After that, how could I possibly sleep?

My plan for the Match Sprints was to make sure I was completely sheltered in the draft of the wheel of my competition for a lead out to preserve enough energy for the finish or try to catch the other rider totally off guard. Looking at the results from my competitor's 200 meter times gave me an idea how she would try to run the sprints. I remembered what Mike Walden had told me so long ago. "Never make it easy for the other guy. Make them play your game." And that is exactly what I did. I so very much wished that Mike and Clair could have been there to see it.

The only race remaining was the Points Race; a long race with sprints every few laps to earn points. The rider with the most accumulated points at the finish wins. Ken calculated that, if I sat in the field, not taking any sprints and making sure to come in second or third place in each sprint, I could actually win the overall championships.

There is a real advantage having years of experience combined with no pressure to win. When your head knows what to do and performance anxiety is removed, things just flow. Astonishingly, eighteen days after finishing chemotherapy for breast cancer, I raced at the National Championships and won.

When I stepped up on the podium to receive my medals and flowers, the presenters were flanked by photographers. I had been on the podium before, but it was never as special as that moment. I was given the champions jersey. I still had my cap on to conceal my hairless state, when they reached up to put the medal around my neck. "Take your cap off" one of them urged me. "No, I don't think so," I replied sheepishly. We still managed to get the medals on and the photos taken, cap and all.

Winning the National Championship was quite surreal considering the recent debilitating weakness and fatigue. Perhaps everything before this was a nightmare and I was just now waking up. I thought about unveiling my diagnosis to let people know and to tell them that the rumor going around the infield was true. I wanted to shout to the world, "TAKE THAT CANCER, I just won gold at Nationals and you couldn't stop me."

* * *

Dr. Goulet was considerate enough to schedule my surgery after the Championships were over. My decision was to have a double mastectomy. "Why do you want to have a double mastectomy?" he questioned. "There is really only a 10% chance that you will get breast cancer in the other breast." He reassured. "I never again want to go through this nightmare of treatment and fear of survival again." I explained. He appeared to understand and didn't question my decision again.

My reconstructive surgeon's name was Dr. Rajiv Sood, a very tall man with dark eyes and thick dark hair. We discussed all the different types of procedures available to help restore my self-image and sense of normality. He told me that skin flap reconstruction would not be recommended as an option for someone my size. This was not in reference to my breast size but to the fact that I did not have enough fatty tissue to work with. He agreed that it was not advisable to move my abdominal muscles, which would have been necessary in that procedure, because I needed abs for cycling and skating. His understanding was very much appreciated since he was taking into consideration my quality of life after cancer.

After some research, I opted for saline implants because at the time, there had been so much controversy concerning silicone. I believed that saline would be safer and more reliable in the long run. One interesting conversation we had concerned the size of the implants I selected. It seems that saline implants did not come in my size and I would have to move up to a size larger than what God had given me. I told him I did not want to go very large because of my passion for riding and skating.

The thought of my knees bouncing off my breasts as I rode was not very appealing. When I was speed skating I didn't want them to interfere with the way I needed to swing my arms. In cycling, people spend big money to buy the lightest equipment. "Why would I want to invest in something that was not going to make me any faster and would just be more grams of added weight to pull up a hill?" I asked. He began laughing and said, "You are the first." Perplexed and a bit concerned, I asked "The first what?" "The first patient to tell me that she didn't want to go bigger," he replied with a broad smile.

The plan was for Dr. Goulet to do the mastectomy and if all went well and there was no sign that the cancer has spread, Dr. Sood would come in and insert tissue expanders underneath the pectoralis muscles to stretch them in preparation for the implants. Once the muscles had stretched over a few months' time, creating a pouch beneath them, he would go back in and exchange the expanders for implants.

In preparation, Dr. Goulet explained that he would inject blue dye into the area where the tumors were located the night before surgery. The dye would collect in the sentinel lymph nodes to make it easier for the surgeon to locate nodes the tumor drained into. During surgery, they would locate the blue nodules, remove them and put them under a microscope to see if there were any cancer cells collected inside. If there were, the surgeon would remove more lymph nodes. If they were clear, no more nodes would need to be extracted, radiation would no longer be necessary and the expanders could be inserted right away.

We arrived at the hospital at 5:00 am to check in and take care of paperwork. We sat in the waiting area looking at the others sitting in anticipation of surgery of some kind, most wore no makeup but had on very comfortable clothing. When my name was called we were taken to a small alcove where a drawn curtain acted as a door. The smell of institutional sanitizer hovered like an invisible fog as we walked through the corridors.

A nurse handed me another hospital gown and informed me that I could not be wearing makeup or fingernail polish. I almost laughed because the chemo had already stolen my fingernails and there was no makeup to remove. Next I was given some very attractive white compression stockings, a pair of "one size fits nobody" blue non-skid slippers and a blue bouffant cap to confine the patient's hair during surgery. This was the crowning touch. I had no hair because we had decided the day before surgery to shave off what little scruffs remained. My mother did the honors and I have to say, it looked much better. Since then, I had worn a soft cap to cover my bare head and keep warm.

Each of the main players on my surgical team came to check in with us in that little alcove of a room. I was very impressed with them all. The anesthesiologist, a tall woman with dark hair and very lively eyes for that time of the morning, told me her name but having heard so many names that morning, I couldn't remember it. Stickers were placed on my chest for the EKG and other monitors then Dr. Sood came in with a black marker and drew all over my skin, placing dashes and lines following natural contours as guidelines. I am sure it was to create a reference where everything was before, so he could match things up during surgery; However, I looked very much like a sewing pattern when he finished.

When the time came to say goodbye to my mother, to Ken and to my breasts, I shared one last hug, and attempted to joke with Ken, "This is your last chance to see them before they are gone, your last chance to kiss them goodbye." He grinned, a small Ken style grin then took my hand and pulled it to his lips and said, "I don't need them. I only need you. I love you, don't you know that?" "Thank you," I whispered with tears in my eyes. "I love you too." There was just enough time to hug my mom before a nurse in blue scrubs led me out into the hallway where I shuffled along the cold linoleum tiled floors to the restricted doorway.

The images of all that I was leaving behind faded as I entered the sterile zone. The large operating room was cluttered with equipment of all shapes and sizes, and quite a few people were milling around in preparation. With assistance I was hoisted up onto the firm and narrow surgical table with my arms positioned out to the side on extensions.

Faces darted in and out of my visual field as an IV was started and large blood pressure-like cuffs were placed on my calves, inflating and deflating periodically to prevent blood clots from forming while I lay motionless for hours on the table. All the members of the orchestra were entering the room and warming up their instruments. At last the conductor entered the stage and the players took their places. Dr. Goulet's masked face was a welcomed sight as he entered my ever narrowing view of the room. "We are going to take good care of you," he said with warmth and confidence. The anesthesiologist appeared over my head and in a soothing voice, gave me instructions to start counting. The curtains came down quickly and the symphony began.

The next thing I remembered was waking up in recovery, looking at the world through narrowed slits. My mouth was dry with a metallic taste hovering over my tongue. Hopeful, I looked down at my chest. If there were mounds on the landscape, I would instantly know that the news was good. If flat, it meant more cancer than was expected. How relieved I was to look down and see two mounds, the tissue expanders, where my breasts had been. I closed my eyes again in thankful relief.

My surgical bed was wheeled into a room where Mom and Ken were nervously waiting. Still groggy, thinking and moving in slow motion, the shock of immense pain was startling when I was moved quite swiftly from one bed to another. My chest was firmly wrapped in bandages and an IV and urinary catheter were in place. There were four drains suspended from my sides with small avocado shaped clear bulbs filling with red fluid. I drifted in and out of sleep. Ken was there and saw that I was in good hands, but was called back to work while my mother stayed at my bed-side. She made sure everything was taken care of and my pain medications were administered on schedule. If I moved or opened my eyes at any time during the night, she appeared. I don't think she slept a moment while we were in the hospital.

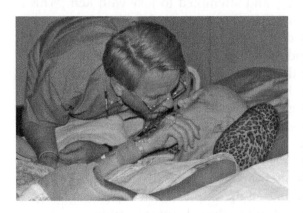

I was not prepared for the intensity of the pain. It was difficult to move my arms for any reason; even lifting my hand to point for my water glass was extremely painful. Insurance had authorized a twenty three hour hospital stay for a double mastectomy, so we were told that I would be charged as an inpatient for any time spent after that. As I was being prepared for discharge, the catheter and IV were removed. The nurse informed me that I must prove that I could use the bathroom on my own before I could leave. This was quite a challenge since I definitely couldn't use my arms to deal with the drainage tubes hanging from my sides.

Between the waves of nausea and vomiting I experienced just before leaving the hospital, a physical therapist came in and gave me five minutes of instruction. She demonstrated a few simple exercises and stretches that were required to be repeated on a daily basis to avoid any long term loss of mobility in my arms and shoulders. I questioned the logic of why they sent a PT in to teach a patient on narcotics for five minutes before they were to leave. To my disappointment, all the moving around made me very nauseous and I threw up a few times just before they sent me off in the wheelchair to the car.

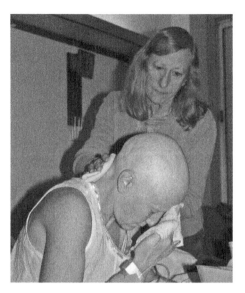

When I got home to sleep in my own bed, mom had everything set up at my bedside and came in to check on me often. We propped my arms up with squishy bean bag pillows on all sides and I slept fairly well, much better than in the hospital. There really is no place like home!

It didn't take long for me to fight taking the prescribed narcotics for pain relief. Although the pain was difficult to handle, as a control oriented person, I could not tolerate the fuzzy, stuporous side effects created by the narcotics. Much to my mother's dismay, I decided to manage my pain with Tylenol.

I could not sit around waiting to heal without worrying about how much my level of fitness was depreciating. Awkward drains remained in place and were difficult to deal with. Mom milked them and measured their output daily. It was very difficult to be mobile with four bulbs on a string dangling from your sides as if they could fall out at any moment. To deal with the situation, I took action and donned one of my cycling jerseys turned inside out, and put the bulbs in the back pockets. Not very fashionable, but it worked well for me.

"The fact that I can't move my arms does not mean that I can't use my legs," I thought. I asked Ken to set up my bike on a stationary trainer in the living room. He did while my mother watched nervously. He helped me put on cycling shoes and stabilized the bike while I climbed up on the saddle with a step stool. My mother stood very close by to do whatever she could to make sure I was not in pain. Then I clicked my cleats into the pedals and began to ride sitting upright, thinking, "There's no place like home." With Ken's help to mount and dismounting the bike, I did not need my arms to ride. This was my way of spitting in the face of cancer.

The bathroom mirror was cruel and honest. There I was alone with my reflection and viewing the ravages of chemo and the surgery. I decided that I looked like a member of the Borg Collective from Star Trek, bald and bandaged with tubes sticking out in awkward locations. I felt much more comfortable going out in public, once the drains were removed. My energy level was low, but I kept trying to push myself. Mom, however, was always hovering at my side trying to make sure that I was not going to do anything that might rip out stitches or cause additional pain.

After two weeks of wrestling with the drains, finally the appointment with Dr. Sood came to remove the drains. I sat on the exam table when Dr. Sood walked in to appraise his work. The incisions were healing well, and three of the four drains had markedly diminished their output. One kept producing a transparent pink fluid.

He decided that it was time to pull them out. Each drain was held in place with one small suture. The sutures were clipped and then the time came. With one continuous pull an additional foot of tubing was yanked out of my body and fluid started streaming out of the holes in my sides. Alarmed that I had copious amounts of gushing fluid pouring out, I placed my hand under where the drain had been and said, "Um, can I have a towel here?" He didn't seem to think this was unusual at all and I was given a 4x4 bandage and told I could go home.

*   *   *

Even with all the wonderful support I had from my friends at work, the people I coached and my family, there were still times when I felt absolutely lost and alone. People frequently reminded me to, "Take it easy and rest; save your strength to fight the cancer." While I appreciated the love, encouragement and support, waiting and resting was driving me completely bonkers.

What I really, absolutely, positively needed, was to talk to someone who was an athlete that had been through similar cancer treatment. I needed to know how chemotherapy had affected their lives long term, as well as their athletic performance. This was a major preoccupation dwelling constantly in the back of my mind.

I searched the Internet looking for someone, somewhere to connect with. A person or group that I could identify with and that would understand what I was going through. I looked at numerous sites and found a chat room on a major breast cancer website. I was hoping I might find at least one person to talk to that had been through treatment for breast cancer and understood an athlete's need to train.

Timid at first, I read every posting I could in an attempt to learn the etiquette of the site. There were definitely some dominating conversations going on. I kept seeing the postings and discussions peppered with the words "mets" and "rads" which were foreign and frightening to me.

Regrettably, I learned that the majority of people in the chat room were dealing with recurrences, metastases, and terrible disabling side effects. The term "mets" was used to refer to metastasis and "rads" represented the units of radiation they had received. Their discussions became addictive, disturbing and depressing. I felt that I was adrift at sea, clinging to a life preserver, searching the horizon for the appearance of a ship that could save me. Instead, I realized that all the other swimmers around me were floundering, pulling me under and completely obscuring my view of the horizon.

The participants in the chat room could see I was logged in and monitoring their discussions. "I see we have a lurker. Introduce yourself." Came a text from Pink Mamma. "I was diagnosed with ductal carcinoma in May and have had a summer of chemo and then a bilateral mastectomy. I am looking for information about how chemo affects athletic performance." I typed, trying to introduce myself as simply as possible. Then I got a flurry of questions: "What stage were you?" "What was your treatment protocol?" "Are you Her2/Neu positive?" "ER/PR negative or positive?" they asked. I was overwhelmed by the unfamiliar terms thrown around casually like a beach ball over my head.

I went to get my mother's notes and my biopsy results to find the answers they were demanding. "I'm stage 2B, Her2/Neu negative and estrogen receptor positive." I answered. "That's good news. You don't want to be Her2/Neu positive. ER positive can be managed. Are you pre or post-menopausal?" came a post from 'Darling Darla'.

I was not quite certain how much I was ready to divulge. "My primary question is how chemo affects athletic performance long term. I am a competitive bike racer and skater who finished chemo in August, but I feel even worse after surgery. Is there anyone on this chat who is an athlete?" One woman piped up and said that she was a tennis player and had played tennis a week after her double mastectomy. I found that very hard to believe, considering the difficulties I had experienced. I was going to ask if she had expanders or reconstructive surgery in addition to her mastectomy, but before I could, the tone of the chat turned dark and got quite vicious and angry. Out of the blue the dominant chatter demanded to know if I was a nurse researcher and questioned if I was a patient at all. I must have used a term like "palpable" again. They were insistent that if I was a nurse researcher or any type of researcher, I needed to get off *THEIR* chat room.

This was NOT a healthy environment and not what I needed. They were hostile and dwelled on the depressing side of breast cancer. How was I ever going to find someone who understood? Was I that much of a freak? Again, I was set adrift looking for security and answers from someone who could relate.

*   *   *

Mirrors continued to plague me and many times I wished that they had been removed or at least turned to face the wall. I was pale with dull eyes and skin. Even my eyebrows and eyelashes had abandoned me. I looked like a withered ghost of the person I had been. On the up side, I hadn't had to shave my legs or underarms all summer. What other feminine traits could chemo and surgery possibly take away?

Just when I thought things could not get any worse, my fingernails and toenails began to desert me. They didn't just break off, oh no, they completely fell off. Trying to pick up a dime when you have no fingernails is truly a challenge. I looked at myself one day and thought, "If you throw in the fact that I now have no boobs, I could be a stand-in for Gollum in the Lord of the Rings."

Mom insisted that I get out of the house, so she took me to the mall where there was a small makeup store. She decided that I needed a makeover to lift my spirits. Quick to understand, the older woman behind the counter took it upon herself to take me on as a challenge. After she looked at my skin tone and eye color—because that was all there was to work with—— she powdered, brushed and sketched her way around my face. Then, with a smile of accomplishment, she turned me to the mirror to reveal her work. I don't think anyone expected my reaction. Not even me.

It took a full moment for the face looking back at me to register. I blinked and smiled faintly at seeing myself with eyebrows again. The makeup had restored the appearance of a glow to my cheeks but my sunken, chocolate brown eyes were still there, hiding the pain, knowing that this was all just a temporary mask. I missed my eyebrows and hair and this experience just confirmed how much.

Tears pricked at the corner of my eyes and started to spill over and down the makeup she had so painstakingly worked to perfect. Looking as if she was going to cry as well she ran to get me a tissue and instructed me to "Blot, don't wipe." I told her that I was just so happy to look normal again as I forced a smile of gratitude. In reality, this look was not me at all. Never having worn that much makeup in my life I felt clownish, but I suppose clownish was more acceptable than looking like a walking corpse. It was hard to sort out my feelings, and in some way I was a little frightened.

I was happy to see myself look more alive, but at the same time I mourned the realization of how far from alive I looked, and sometimes felt.

*   *   *

The first speed skating session of the season was approaching and I felt I owed it to my skaters to at least make an appearance. They were part of my family and had been so very supportive through my treatment. I wanted to be there and watch them train and to let them know I was still alive and kicking. I watched through the warm up room window and what I saw made me very proud. I felt my strength growing just seeing them again, skating and running the practice with precision, just as I had taught them.

Abby had taken on a leadership role and was working with several beginners. One of the skaters left the ice to take a break and came up to me to show me what they had been working on. "Coach Cindi," he said. "I was able to do some crossovers today and it is all because of what Abby showed me." Then he demonstrated the drill that she had shown him and I immediately recognized it as the same training skill I had invented especially for Abby to help her master her crossovers. I felt comforted in the knowledge that if I were to leave the earth that day, part of what I did would be carried on.

*   *   *

I dream a lot; I dream in color, and usually remember them. I often think I dream simply to entertain myself. I don't like to be bored, and what could be more boring than sleeping? The night of the speed skating practice, I had a very vivid dream. I saw myself rushing into a theater, because I had been entered in a beauty contest—which was unbelievable. However, the believable part was that I arrived late!

Breathlessly, I ran up an old wooden staircase to the dressing room. Upon opening the doors I could see that I was so late that all the other contestants had already left for the stage. In a panic, I turned to the clothing racks and was shocked to find the only clothing left hanging on the rack was an excessively ruffled purple blouse, a long, tight, paisley skirt and to top off the ensemble; army boots!

I assumed that was my punishment for being late. I decided I would just get dressed, go out on stage and give it my best- despite my wardrobe. As I walked onto the stage, the lights were so intense that I could see very little beyond the edge of the stage. I continued my walk as the announcer introduced me to the audience as "Cynthia Louisa Hart"— which definitely is not my name. Hart was correct, but I have never been a Cynthia, and Louisa is a twist on my middle name.

I thought to myself, "Just keep smiling and you can get through this. You know who you are." At exactly that moment, through the glare of the lights, I saw Mike Walden's wife, Harriet stand up in the second row and proclaim, "That is not her name! Her name is Cindi Hart, and she is a cyclist and a speed skater." Then Abby stood up and said, "And she helped me with my crossovers!" Another stood and announced, "She taught me how to do a time trial start!" and then one by one, each person in the audience stood up and shared how I had somehow touched their lives.

At that point I was pulled from the dream with the realization that I did not need to be judged by the way I look, but by the lives that I have touched. We may not know our purpose, or who might someday benefit from the small part we have played in their lives. However, I am certain of one thing; eyebrows have nothing to do with it.

*   *   *

The Hilly Hundred is a huge cycling tour that travels through the scenic, and excessively hilly, countryside of Brown County, Indiana. Over five thousand cyclists flock to this event annually to ride the steep hills of picturesque Brown County Indiana. The cyclists struggle up hills with a grade of nineteen percent, and a total of five thousand feet of climbing in one hundred miles over two days. I had enjoyed riding the Hilly Hundred for many years. The Hilly has always been in October, which was —just a month after my surgery in 2004.

The atmosphere is festive and there are tents of food and music, with riders of all shapes, sizes and ages from around the world collected to take on the climbs. The hilly hundred is not a race; it is a celebration, an adventure and a challenge for many riders.

I desperately wanted to ride this event, but knew that hill climbing involved a lot of upper body strength, as I would be pulling on the handlebars to counter the downward drive of my legs. I was feeling better, but moving my arms still caused a lot of pain.

Joe Niccum was a good friend and cycling buddy who was engaged to my teammate, JoMay. Joe rode with us on the track and helped me train for Nationals. I trusted his smooth, steady wheel and bike handling. He was a very skilled and intelligent rider. Ken and I had a tandem and asked Joe if he would mind piloting the tandem so I could ride on the back and not have to worry about pulling on the handlebars during the climbs. Joe said that he would be happy to ride with me. I was both thrilled and a little scared.

Very early on that chilly October morning, I got on the back of the tandem with Joe and took the first pedal strokes on the road since my surgery. It felt incredible—much better than I had expected— as the two of us worked very well together. Once more I was reminded of how thankful I was and how great it was to feel alive and on the bike again.

Before long, I had completely forgotten about my surgery and just wanted to go fast. It was fun passing all the riders on the hills and leading the front of several pace lines. Joe didn't seem to mind a bit as he had the same need for speed that is ingrained in many racers. His smile, mischievous laugh and raised eyebrows were my assurance that I was not holding him back. I was back, and this was my coming out party!

Knowing that I could ride again motivated me to start training again. Feeling that I could move forward in accepting the fact that my body was no longer harboring cancer and chemo was finished, I was free to set my sights on strengthening my body and rebuilding my legs as much as possible.

Going to the gym became a regular event. Determined to regain my strength and get my life back on track as soon as possible, I lived on the incline leg press, starting around 400 pounds and eventually maxing around 700. There was a lot of catching up to do and I was set on reaching my goals.

*   *   *

A few months after surgery my hair began to grow back, but I continued to wear a hat in public. One afternoon, I was having lunch with Ken at a restaurant that had a salad bar. I had always loved fruits and vegetables, but after chemo, I could only tell what things were by their appearance and texture as my sense of taste had been absent for the past six months. Returning to the table with my favorite colorful assortment of crunchy, texture rich foods, a large red strawberry beckoned to me from my plate. Upon taking a bite I was struck with a sudden shock of flavor. I thought it must have been my imagination so I took another bite. Yes, that big red juicy thing really was a strawberry, and I could certainly taste it.

The realization hit me: I recalled all that I had been through and all that had been taken away, but now my life was slowly returning. Tears started to flow as I excitedly took another bite of strawberry. Ken returned to the table to see me chewing with tears falling around my huge grin. "Are you OK?" he inquired with concern. The tears continued as I nodded an enthusiastic yes and continued to embrace the flavor. "You can taste it, can't you?" he said, putting all the clues together. "Yes!" I replied, mouth still partially full, "Try the strawberries." I told him. He took a bite and made an unpleasant face, "Man, those are sour!" he said. "I know." I gulped, "Isn't it wonderful?" Ken then suggested, "You know, if those sour strawberries made you happy, maybe you should try the lemons." I tried a slice and found that I could taste them too. We determined sour was one of the first tastes to return. Look out pickles here I come!

*   *   *

Even though my hair and taste were slowly returning, there didn't seem to be any relief in sight for the hot flashes and night sweats. On the bright side, when I awoke in the middle of the night with my chest damp with perspiration, I found that I could remember my dreams. In them, I could race, I could fly, I could dance, and best of all: there was no cancer. But not all dreams were that liberating. Sometimes the dreams were very strange.

One in particular started with our house; I dreamt that it was full of people, all there, talking about skating and cycling, which is not far from our everyday reality. A knock at the door pulled me from my coaching and I turned to open it. A seven foot tall, bald man stood wordlessly in my doorway. He loomed over me and reminded me of Lurch from the Addams Family, with his sallow eyes and gaunt cheeks. Without a word, he pressed his way around me into the room.

Startled and upset by his rude entry, I turned and said "Excuse me, I don't know you. Who are you? What are you doing here?" He completely ignored me and continued to invade my home. Flustered, not knowing what to do, I rushed upstairs to my mother and told her about the intruder who was making me very uncomfortable. "I want him out of my house!" I demanded.

"Your father is outside talking with some motorcycle police officers," she said. I ran out to where he stood, wearing a kilt at the end of our very long driveway. Dreaming about my father in a kilt may seem strange, but he actually does wear one when marching with the Hamilton County, Ohio Sheriff's Department Bagpipe and Drum Corp in parades and in ceremonies honoring fallen police officers or military personnel at gravesites.

I rushed to my father and said, "There's a seven foot bald guy who just invaded my home. He's walking around looking at all of my things and making me very uncomfortable. I want him out of my home, now!" At that point the intruder walked out the front door, got on a recumbent bicycle, pedaled down the driveway and turned right in front of the police officers. I burst out, "That's him!" and pointed as he pedaled away. "Remember what he looks like because he has been in my home, He has been looking through all my stuff and I am afraid he is going to come back."

When I woke up I thought about the bald man in my dream. I was startled to realize what he represented in my reality. He was my cancer. He had come into my home uninvited, been through all my things, then disappeared, leaving me feeling violated and afraid that he might return.

Cancer is a thief that silently sneaks into our lives and takes many things. In talking to more and more cancer survivors, I have found that we all share this very common fear. It is not always what cancer had done to us, but the threat that it could come back at any moment, do more damage and take more from us the next time. The fear or recurrence seems to loom above the heads of all survivors, including myself.

This reminded me of a Greek legend called The Sword of Damocles: a very wealthy ruler named Dionysius whose court flatterers constantly told him how wonderful his life was. One of them, Damocles, was very envious of the ruler's luxuriously wealthy lifestyle. Dionysius asked him if he would like to sit in his place and experience his life first hand. Damocles eagerly agreed and was surrounded by opulence: beautiful women and servants, embroidered rugs, jewels, and rich food and drink. He was enjoying himself until he noticed a sharp and heavy sword hanging above his head, suspended merely by a thin, single strand of horse's hair.

Damocles was unable to enjoy the luxuries of his position as he could think of nothing else but the sword falling and ending his life. He asked to return to his previous status. The ruler told Damocles that was what HIS life was like all the time— with the constant threat that someone might kill him to steal his wealth.

This is the curse of a cancer veteran: we continue to live our lives and appear to be happy and healthy, enjoying life with a heightened sense of appreciation because our lives have been threatened, but the constant sword hovering over our heads is CANCER. Even when told there is no longer evidence of disease in our bodies, the sword of cancer continues to loom as an evil threat in the back of our minds. It may grow smaller over time, but it will always be there.

*   *   *

PART 4 – Back on Track

For a week in December 2004, Copper Mountain, Colorado, was headquarters and training camp for Special Olympics Team USA. The picturesque ski resort, with its European village ambiance and snowcapped mountains, felt far removed from the reality of the life we left behind in Indiana. The purpose of the camp was to bring all of team USA together before the World Games and evaluate the athletes' capability to travel overseas with minimal supervision.

Earlier in the summer I was told that, as head coach, I would review all the applications for assistant coach positions and have some say in their selection. Ken had applied and I learned that, because he was my spouse, he was not going to be approved as a first choice to be on my team. This was very disappointing, knowing that Ken had national and international experience and would be an exceptional technician to have on the team. He was passed over and we accepted that. However, due to circumstances of fate, two of the selected coaches were unable to attend the games and Ken was approved to join us. I could not have been happier with this news, both for the team and for myself.

As Head Coach, my duty was to leave a few days early for camp to get things prepared for the athletes' arrival. Ken traveled with the delegation from Indiana (Mandy, Wes and Katie) a few days after I left for Colorado. Katie was one of our speed skaters, but was selected for figure skating.

Since my very first experience with Special Olympians, I have treated everyone I have coached as athletes first and foremost; I believe they all deserve to be treated with respect and dignity. With self-esteem and respect comes the desire to achieve and maintain a level of respect. Yes, Special Olympians are intellectually challenged, but just like any competitive athlete they have a strong desire to compete, achieve, and be proud of their accomplishments. As coaches, it's our job to help make that happen.

It was exciting to see the athletes and coaches arriving from different States and then bond together as a team. There were a few challenges along the way to overcome, but I found that those made me think on my feet and dig into my creative bag for some solutions along the way. There was a moment during the camp when I realized my entire life had been leading up to that point, and my experiences as a nurse, coach, athlete, church camp counselor, and exercise physiologist all came together. Even acting in a play, getting hit by the car, then being declared mentally retarded, had a purpose. Each experience was a brick in the foundation of what we were trying to build with these athletes.

We were preparing them to race in Japan, as well as teaching them how to interact with athletes from other countries and ultimately, how to be leaders and contributing citizens in their communities at home. I decided to make it fun by conducting role-playing exercises to help reinforce what would be considered appropriate and inappropriate behavior at the games. The coaches pretended to be athletes with unacceptable behavior and the athletes would show us how they would act as good representatives of Team USA while interacting with the bad behavior coaches. The coaches would smack talk, "I'm going to win! Because I'm better than you! You don't have a chance!" Then the skater would try to suppress a grin and reply, without any prompting, "I'm happy for you. I wish you good luck." Everyone had a great time in this exercise. The coaches enjoyed playing the troublemakers and the athletes enjoyed laughing at our bad behavior and were thrilled with the idea that they were correcting us. I couldn't have been any more proud of them all, athletes and coaches alike. I think the rest of the world could learn a lot from their example.

On the last night of training camp the athletes were all looking forward to the big dance. When Ken was selected to be an assistant coach, I was told that we were not to behave like a couple at any time during the games. We made sure not to show any displays of affection or connection throughout the entire time we were coaching at training camp. This was not a problem for us, as we were very accustomed to training and coaching together in a professional manner and had done so for many years.

Special Olympians LOVE to dance. When the music started, I was prompted by several to come out and dance with them. It was refreshing to see the confident and joyful looks in their eyes while they expressed themselves on the dance floor. I could only dance for so long before I became thirsty. I found my way to one of the tables, where the speedskating team had set up camp, to take a break and get something to drink. I had only been sitting there for a few minutes when a slow song began to play and I looked up to see Ken walking straight toward me. He was flanked by all the guys from our speedskating team. It reminded me of a scene from "The Right Stuff." Their eyes were focused on me as they giggled and urged Ken on with glances and nudges.

Ken approached me and bent over with a very formal bow. The girls next to me giggled. He took my hand in his and said, "I have been requested by the skaters to ask you to join me in a dance." The excited giggles around us grew more noticeable as I stood and Ken took my hand. He walked me, escorted by all our skaters, to the middle of the dance floor. I placed my hand on his shoulder and his hand went to my waist as we began to dance completely surrounded by our family of speed skaters.

Cameras flashed all around as if we were celebrities. Dancing in a small circle, we were enveloped by their beaming faces. I realized that our athletes wanted us to have our moment together. Seeing us dancing appeared to give them great joy, more than I would have expected, and it felt absolutely magical.

Special Olympics training camp proved to me that I was meant to be there and I was fulfilling my purpose. It was hard to believe, but that entire week, no one asked me how I was feeling, what happened to my hair, or why I was always wearing a hat. They accepted me as I was without question or judgment. It was only appropriate that we should do the same for them.

*   *   *

The week after we returned home from training camp, I was scheduled for reconstructive surgery. The expanders had ports that allowed them to be injected with increasing amounts of saline every couple of weeks to gradually expand the size of the pockets under the muscles where the implants would be inserted.

It would be nice to be able to say that this was a simple and painless experience, but it wasn't. The needles did not hurt at all because the nerves in that area had been severed during surgery. What caused the intense pain was the sudden expansion of the inserts, with the increased volume of saline solution, forcing the muscles to stretch. The abrupt change in size, even though it was only milliliters, was enough to cause pain within minutes of the injection. I wondered if the reason it hurt so much was because I was "fit" and the muscles might have been tighter and more resistant to stretching, similar to the round ligament pain that I had experienced when I was pregnant.

Not long after my double mastectomy, I noticed something strange happening to my body. Just beneath the skin, radiating from the surgical site down both arms and my sides were small lines of string-like fiber that I could see and feel. They were tight and limited my range of motion. I was later informed that this condition was called cording.

The cords were painful and restricting, but I discovered that if stretched enough, they would snap or break and bring relief after the momentary pain of stretching and breaking. It was worth the pain because left alone, they would grow thicker and even more restrictive. It felt like Spiderman was shooting webs under my skin and they were literally binding me from within. When I mentioned this to my doctors, they didn't appear to know how to deal with it.

After my chest muscles were stretched to a size that would accommodate the insertion of the implants, I asked Dr. Sood if he could cut the cords and release me from their hold and he agreed to do so. After the surgery, I was sore again, but no drains were required and the tissue was less damaged than that from the mastectomy. Recovery time was faster and I resumed skating as soon as I could swing my arms. Some cording returned after the implants, but knowing what to do, I snapped them myself, as soon as they were noticed, so they would not have a chance to thicken.

Trying to research cording online, I found little to nothing published about this phenomenon, but I did learn that it is more prevalent after surgery in women with little body fat and is common in Asian women. The doctors have absolutely no idea what causes this condition, but there is discussion that it might have something to do with damage to the lymph system. From my experience, I have the distinct opinion that it has to do with the proximity in time of surgery in relation to administration of chemo. I believe that the smaller the amount of chemo in your system at the time of surgery, the less likely cording will occur.

By January I was back on my speed skates. The Long Track pack style National Championships were going to be in Salt Lake City at the Olympic venue. Since we were in Salt Lake just before my treatment started, it seemed appropriate to return soon after it was completed.

After tripping over a course marker that had been frozen to the ice at the Olympic Training Center and spraining my neck, I had lost my confidence in skating short track. The long, gradual radius turns, no walls to hit, and padding around the rink made of breakaway mats, made Long Track speedskating much more comfortable. If a person hit the mats, they would move and absorb the impact. With that fear removed, I felt liberated on the ice once more.

Before going to Salt Lake City, I had considered the Pettit Center to be the best place to skate in the United States, but walking into the Utah Olympic oval completely changed my perception. The ice was crystal clear and fast because the rink used deionized and filtered water. The temperature in the building was warm enough that we could skate comfortably while wearing short sleeve T-shirts. I could feel the speed beneath my feet in the warm-up. Until this moment, I had not realized that I had been training on slow ice my entire life.

Although my strength had been maintained with frequent visits to the gym throughout treatment, my endurance was still not up to par. The pack style event distances were 500, 800, 1000, 1500, and 3000 meter races. I felt confident that I would do fine in the events that were 1000 meters and less, but not so confident for the longer ones. I dreaded even thinking about the 3000 meters and secretly wished they would cancel it.

Five hundred meters is the shortest and fastest of all the races. It is considered a sprint. It was highly contested and the race was filled with passes and counter passes. Unfortunately, I slipped at the finish and fell across the line taking fourth place. There were many of us crossing the line within a fraction of a second from each other.

I won a silver medal in both the 1000 and 1500 meter events and broke two national records in the process. The 3000 meter race is always the last and I had dreaded it all day. I stayed with the pack for the duration because I was able to draft the other skaters and stand up and rest occasionally. However, I didn't have enough energy left to sprint to the finish. I just had to keep reminding myself that it had only been one month since I had surgery and five months after my last chemotherapy treatment. It didn't matter where I finished because the real win had been my ability to even be there; winning the race was icing on the cake.

*　　*　　*

Not long before discovering I had breast cancer, David Breen had shared with me that his wife Lori was having severe episodes of dizziness and vomiting. Dave worked for Special Olympics Indiana and was supposed to go to Japan with us as part of the management team. He was a very tall, amiable, and animated character, whose eyes shone bright with a bit of mischief.

Lori learned she had a brain tumor around the same time that I received my diagnosis of breast cancer. They spent their summer flying back and forth from Indianapolis to North Carolina for her treatment at the Duke Cancer Center, which specializes in treating her type of cancer. When I occasionally stopped in at the office, Dave would ask how I was doing and give me updates on Lori's condition.

Unfortunately, while I was recovering from surgery and chemotherapy and getting stronger, Lori was losing her battle. A week before we were to depart for Japan in March 2005, Lori's fight ended. Her funeral was held in a large church filled to overflowing with people whose lives she had touched. As we sat watching a video that celebrated Lori's life in pictures and song, I felt an overwhelming rush of guilt. "Why has this wonderful person been taken by cancer and why am I still here?" The pictures displayed the obvious love and devotion Lori felt for Dave and their children and for life in general. It seemed cruel that she should be stolen away from so many who obviously loved her.

After the service, I was talking with Scott Mingle and Scott Furnish, who worked with Dave at Special Olympics. "Are you excited about leaving for Japan next week? Have you got everything packed?" they asked. Once again, I was struck with the painful guilt that not only had I survived cancer, but I was going to Japan and Dave was not. This was more than I could manage in public so we gave our condolences and excused ourselves quickly. I wanted to try to understand and deal with my feelings and cry in the privacy of my own home.

The feelings were very confusing. In an effort to help me, Ken searched for and discovered an online support group called "Cyclists

Combating Cancer." They referred to themselves as the CCC. I signed up and started following their posts. I soon realized the group was exactly what I had been searching for. It was composed of avid cyclists who were survivors battling all types and stages of cancer, as well as family members and healthcare providers.

There were many levels of cycling expertise within the group, including recreational riders, tri-athletes and a few racers like me. Our discussions ranged from subjects as diverse as ways to deal with chemo side effects to how to select the best saddle for long distance riding after prostate cancer. The CCC members were bright, uplifting and truly understood the need to ride as well as the power of a positive attitude.

One of my first posts to the group was regarding my experience at the funeral for Dave's wife Lori. I had felt so many conflicting emotions related to the fact that I lived, while she had not. This unfamiliar feeling haunted me. It was Will Swetnam, the moderator of the group, who fielded my question first. He explained to me that what I was feeling was survivor's guilt, a new side effect of cancer that I had not anticipated or prepared for.

I quickly found that being a member of the CCC was addictive. I looked forward to seeing stories shared every day through daily e-mail postings. I learned about their personal connections and battles with cancer, as well as their interests in cycling. I could not have found a better support group anywhere.

*   *   *

A few days after the funeral in early March, we were bound for Japan. During the first three days in Japan, we participated in something called "host town." This was an opportunity for athletes of visiting nations to acclimate to time changes, the climate, and the culture of Japan. Divided by sport we were assigned a "host town," and stayed with families there.

This gave us an opportunity to experience Japanese culture first hand. We landed at the Narita Air Force base and were taken by bus to our host town. Team USA Speed Skating was staying in Matsumoto where we were warmly received by a large crowd of people cheering and holding up signs of friendship and welcome. They were gracious and helpful as they took our bags and escorted us to a concert performed by the local children's violin school.

Walking from the concert to dinner, we met our host families for the first time. They stood holding signs bearing our names like the chauffeurs at the airport. Once we found our names, we found our Japanese host family. The athletes that were staying with me at our host's home were Mandy and Amy.

Asian food has been a favorite of mine for many years. My first official date with Ken had been at a Chinese restaurant where the use of chopsticks was mandatory. Since then, Ken and I have become quite proficient with chopsticks and very much prefer them when eating oriental food.

When my host mother noticed that I had no trouble eating sushi with them, she became very excited. "Oh, you eat with chopsticks." She said brightly. "Yes, I very much like to use them." I responded. She grinned broadly with relief. "I have been very nervous trying to find something you might eat during your stay. Seeing you like our food makes me very happy." "Arigato gozaimasu," I said, which is a polite way of saying thank you. Her face brightened even more. "You speak Japanese!" she exclaimed. "Sukoshi Des." Was my reply, which means "a little" "But I want to learn more." I told her.

On our first morning together, our host mother asked what we would like for breakfast. I requested a typical Japanese breakfast. Mandy and Amy agreed. She was bewildered because she had researched what an American breakfast consisted of and had purchased bacon, which was rather costly in Japan. Since she had no experience cooking bacon, she asked if I would do the cooking. I love to cook and felt honored to be asked, but was surprised when she presented me with a pair of very long cooking chopsticks to turn the bacon. They worked just fine.

Every day after breakfast, the speed skating team was reunited at the cultural center to be transported to practice at the outdoor long track oval. We traveled by bus for thirty minutes to get to the rink. Instead of sitting and staring out the windows during the ride, I saw that time as an opportunity to make announcements to the team. After the announcements, I walked down the aisle asking each athlete to share highlights of their experience from the night spent with their host families. Seeing Japan through their eyes was fascinating and certainly one of my favorite memories from the trip.

Row by row, I approached each of the twenty-seven skaters and made the same request. "Tell us what exceptional experience you had with your host family last night." I got very happy responses such as, "We slept on mattresses on the floor." "They have heated toilet seats!" or "They like baseball too!"

When I came to Howard, an autistic athlete from Hawaii, he smiled warmly and spoke very little. I wanted to be respectful and treat him the same as everyone else. Each time I asked him a question, he would smile, bow his head, start to tap his hair lightly and rock back and forth in his seat. This was the way he would 'stim', a very common trait in people who are autistic. This is generally a repetitive physical gesture to help deal with overstimulation. Howard patted his hair above his right eye as he bowed his head slightly, smiling. I have seen others athletes rotate their wristbands, pull on their ear, or make snapping motions with their fingers, among other repetitive motion activities, in an effort to help during times of sensory overload. This movement occurred not only in stressful situations, but during happy times as well, as was demonstrated by many of the athletes standing on the awards podium waiting to receive their medals.

Each day I asked him if he wanted to tell us something and Howard became a little more at ease with the questions each time I asked. As he grew more comfortable with the team, he began to tap his head a little less and smile a little more. I believe that hearing the others answer enthusiastically helped him realize that no one was judging him. He was accepted completely for who he was: a valued member of our team.

The long track oval where we were skating during "host town" was the training location for the Japanese Olympic gold medalist Hiroyasu Shimizu. I had brought my long track ice skates with me to Japan, as they were the most comfortable to wear while coaching on the ice. After long hours sitting on an airplane, then on multiple buses for days, being able to get back on the track and skate felt like home, regardless of the country we happened to be in.

The city of Matsumoto had many cultural events planned. These included a tour of the castle, a dance with Kabuki Drums, and rice pounding demonstrations where Team USA speed skaters met the local Matsumoto Special Olympians. I was pleasantly surprised to see how animated our Japanese hosts were when the song 'YMCA' was played and everyone was united in the gestures and fun, while dancing to the song.

The last evening with our host family, Mandy, Amy and I were in for a unique treat because they took us to their favorite restaurant. We walked in to see a conveyor belt that snaked its way past all the tables, presenting diners with a constant parade of sushi. When something looked good, we could simply pick it up from the belt and claim it as our own.

Mandy was very interested in trying sushi, but every time she selected something she didn't like the taste of, I ended up eating it in an effort to keep from offending our hosts and creating waste. At last, Mandy found her perfect sushi. It was a small hand formed cylinder of rice with a miniature grilled hamburger patty on top. After she tasted it, she enthusiastically proclaimed to all, "I love sushi!" and happily looked for more hamburger sushi as it paraded by.

After dinner, I gave our host mother a LiveStrong bracelet. She had lost her husband to cancer and her daughter was an oncology nurse. They had not heard of LiveStrong, so I explained to them what the bracelet represented. I'm not certain if they understood, but they were very gracious while accepting my gift.

They surprised us with a Kimono ceremony, another astounding experience to top off our immersion in Japanese culture. Several women in the neighborhood came to help dress us in traditional kimonos as this was not something that could be done alone. They taught us about the layers of clothing and their meaning as they wrapped a wide sash and a stiff board with a pre-made bow around our waists. These new friends placed special stockings on our feet, showed us how to sit and then took our pictures. This was a special moment for me and I shared the story with everyone on the bus the following morning.

Saying a final goodbye to our families was difficult as we boarded the buses to depart. There were tears from many and we knew that all of our lives, mine included, had been changed forever. I definitely wasn't ready for this moment in time to be over. I could not thank our hosts enough for the amazing experience they had given us. However, it was time to move on and prepare for the opening ceremonies and competition.

Countries from all over the world came together in Nagano. The opening ceremonies were held at the M-Wave, the Long Track Speed Skating venue for the 1998 Olympic Games. All the Nations delegations were lined up in alphabetic order, waiting to make an entrance for the parade of nations.

I was honored to be allowed to lead Team USA into the arena behind the uniformed woman carrying the sign proclaiming the United States' entrance into the games. We stood waiting in a quiet, dark hallway, but once we entered the stadium, we were bombarded by bright lights and colors. Hearing the music and the roar of the crowd was overwhelming and the lights and colorful displays were spectacular. We waved to the huge crowd of people in the stands and were able to see American flags waving in one section, identifying several groups of parents. This was as impressive as any Olympic Games procession I had ever seen.

We were seated in chairs placed on carpet covering the ice we would be skating on in the days to come. After the grand procession for the entrance of the Special Olympics torch, the raising of the flag, and the reciting of the Athlete's and the Official's Oaths, Eunice Kennedy Shriver took the podium. A hush came over the crowd as the frail elderly woman gave a powerful, yet beautiful speech. The Prince and Princess of Japan were present, warmly embraced by all the spectators. This was an incredible beginning of an event that would change so many lives.

Since our competition location was used for the Opening Ceremonies, speed skating was delayed by one day to allow the stadium to be transformed back into a speed skating arena. This gave us an opportunity to sightsee around downtown Nagano and Olympic Town. Because all the other sports were competing at their venues that day, we felt relatively certain that anyone we might encounter wearing a Special Olympics uniform would be a speed skater.

We saw several skaters from other countries exploring as well, taking advantage of their day off. We posed for photos with the Canadian team and saw a coach and two athletes from Venezuela. One of the two skaters was in a wheelchair with a broken leg. The coach did not speak much English, but one of our athletes spoke Spanish and interpreted for us. We learned that the Venezuelan skater had fallen and broken his leg at his skating practice in his host town. We adopted their small team and helped with the injured athlete in an effort to free the coach to focus on his lone competitor.

Another part of the World Games experience for Special Olympics is called Healthy Athletes. This was a free service that brings health care of all kinds to the athletes gathered at the games. Complete health care was provided for athletes in a fun and educational environment. This was especially important for athletes who have very limited access to health care in their own countries. Services include ophthalmology, audiology, podiatry and dental, to mention a few. One of our athletes didn't realize that she needed glasses, until she was tested and they made her a pair on the spot. Another skater had needed hearing aids for over a year, but could not afford them. Custom-made hearing aides were ready that day, free of charge. These were incredibly generous gifts for those in need and I was humbled by the outpouring of support all the athletes received.

Each country was granted an official practice time on the rink where the competition would be held. This was essential to help the skaters to get acclimatized to the rink size and the conditions of the ice. I ran the skaters through the same warm-up that I had during training camp. I had intentionally trained them in a structured manner so that no matter where they were, they would know what to expect and be familiar and comfortable with the routine; this helped them adapt both mentally and physically to new environments.

The M-Wave bleachers were filled with Japanese school children who were cheering by using various school chants. As our group warmed up on the ice, we could hear the children's voices chattering excitedly. However, each time I blew my whistle to signal my skaters, there was a sudden hush and the students became totally quiet. I learned later that the Japanese teachers routinely used whistles with the same pitch to direct their students.

Later at the competition, one of the volunteers approached me. They had a message that was a request to meet with someone who had noticed me coaching on the ice. It was Mr. Shimizu, the Japanese Olympic Long Track Gold Medalist. He proceeded to compliment me on my coaching and said that he had spent some time in the United States. I was honored and pleased to meet him, especially since we had been given the privilege of skating on his home ice.

In Special Olympics, athletes are placed in divisions by age, gender, and skill level. The first few days are dedicated to grouping skaters by skill and speed through the use of preliminary time trials. After divisioning was completed, we received the official start list announcing the names of the other athletes who would be in my athlete's division and heats. Every day on the bus ride en route to the rink, I would stand at the front of the bus and read the list to my skaters. In this way, I could help them learn which athletes were in each heat and what country they would be skating with. Every evening as we rode back to our hotel after the competition, I announced the skaters who had performed so well that they had set their own personal records. Each one received a huge cheer from everyone on the bus. I put emphasis on personal records and downplayed the color of any medals won. It was rewarding to see the skaters faces light up when they heard that they had set a new personal record. Their pride was genuine and the group bonded even closer as a team as they cheered for each other's accomplishments.

In Mandy's first competitive distance race, she won a silver medal. As she coasted across the finish line, her arms shot up in a victorious celebration and her eyes scanned the watching crowd searching for her mother. Mandy's mother, Debbie, was easy to spot. She was the woman screaming, jumping up and down, and hugging the people near her. Across the rink I could see eyes wet with pride and knew her heart was bursting with joy.

Debbie had always been Mandy's number one fan and the connection between them was obvious as they shared that special moment. She told me later that her daughter had competed in figure skating at the world games in Alaska, but had never won a medal. Mandy was so very proud of that shining silver medal, but the competition was not yet finished. She later won two more medals: both of them gold.

Howard was an interesting skater to watch as he shuffled his skates on the ice moving forward a few inches at a time, consistent and determined. Occasionally, as he skated, I saw his hand tapping his helmet in an effort to overcome all the noise and excitement of competition. I am happy to report that his effort paid off. He also won a gold medal.

The pomp and circumstance of the awards ceremony rivaled many of those I had seen in the regular Olympics. The athletes were queued up to take the podium and as the music began to play, the officials paraded in. They presented the medals with great ceremony and honor, after which the athletes posed for photos on the podium.

When Howard stepped up to accept his coveted award, he was tapping his head with his fingertips as he had done so many times before. I positioned myself beside the other photographers to capture the moment with my camera. To my left stood a dark haired woman who appeared to excitedly share my goal. When Howard stepped up, she moved nearer to me, touched my shoulder and very proudly announced, "That's my son." I looked at her. She had pride and love spilling down her cheeks when I replied, "He's mine too."

She beamed as the presenters paraded forward with a velvet-lined tray on which was placed a gold medal destined for Howard. He lowered his arms to his side and bowed at the waist to receive the award around his neck. The dignitary shook his hand and then Howard straightened himself up tall and beamed proudly. He lifted his head, put his shoulders back and stood as the music played. After it was all done, he lifted his arms triumphantly.

Seeing him standing there and not tapping his head meant the world to his mother, as well as to me. After the games were over, Howard's parents sent me an email informing us that he had continued to talk nonstop about the things he had experienced in Japan. "Howard keeps reminding us that Coach Cindi says to drink a lot of water," they wrote. What a blessing it was for me to get to witness this experience with Howard and so many others since that time.

I love coaching. It is not just paying it forward, it's a way I am challenged to use the sum of all of my experiences. And I love a good challenge. Coaching stimulates me to think outside the box and to create methods that work best for individual needs and goals. I have to ask myself, "How do they learn? What is the best method to use in my attempt to get my message through to those who do not always learn or understand the world in the usual way?"

Many of the athletes came from group homes, jobs, or schools, where they had been treated as second-class citizens, seen for their disabilities and not for their abilities. In the Special Olympics World Games, they are the leaders, the champions, the focus, and the reason that we were all there. To witness everyone celebrating and acknowledging these extraordinary athletes and their accomplishments was an astounding and magical moment that I will never forget.

As the games progressed, we could see the change in the coaches from different countries as well. Initially they focused solely on their own athletes. However, as we all began to witness the struggles and the triumphs of the individual athletes, attitudes and focus changed and it was no longer country versus country. The coaches started cheering for everyone, regardless of the uniform they were wearing. The athletes were experiencing moments that they would relive for the rest of their lives and we were blessed to be there to help make it happen.

*   *   *

After returning from Japan, the week before my first Susan G. Komen Race for the Cure, the Indianapolis Star created a "Unique Lives and Experiences" series. To my surprise, I was nominated and recognized as a "Woman of Character" as part of the series. The award was to honor a woman in the community who demonstrated personal strength, courage, compassion, and was committed to changing the world around them.

It was to be presented at Clowes Hall on the campus of Butler University, just prior to a Lily Tomlin one-woman show. I invited my mother as my backstage guest and they instructed us to arrive early to practice the timing of the presentation. Rehearsal was over quickly and we watched as Lily Tomlin took the stage to check the lights and sound. She was absolutely delightful, even when she wasn't in the spotlight, she was a star. After stepping off the stage we were briefly introduced to her.

Over a thousand people had packed the hall that night to see Lily Tomlin's performance. Once everyone was seated the awards presentation began. I was given a beautiful crystal award and the presenters read the story of my battle with cancer and the leadership responsibilities I had assumed over the years, including that I was Head Coach for Team USA.

The audience was very welcoming and their applause heartwarming. I was surprised to find that Lily Tomlin had been standing in the wings listening to the presentation. As I exited the stage, she stopped me, took my hand, and looked straight into my eyes. "You are an incredible inspiration." she said, "Your work and story should be shared with everyone. I admire your strength." I was stunned. "Thank you," I replied, awestruck that she would take the time to listen to my story. "My daughter was the driving force behind my fight," I explained. "My doctor told me that if I wanted to live to see her graduate from high school, I needed to take chemotherapy."

"What's your daughter's name?" she asked, "Madison." I replied, "Oh that is a wonderful name. If you would write down her name, along with your mailing address, I will send her something in the mail," she said. Her very anxious stage assistant then reminded her that she needed to take the stage. She excused herself, rushed out into the spotlight and gave a dynamic performance.

I tried to sneak out and join my family as they watched from premium seats near the front of the theater. In an attempt to be as inconspicuous as possible, I walked down the stairs from the stage into the audience. My family was seated in the middle of the row and I had to excuse myself as I climbed gingerly over and in front of several people seated in aisle seats. Thankfully, they didn't seem annoyed. After hearing my story, they were actually very friendly and several congratulated me. People from the surrounding rows reached out to touch me and shared words of hope and encouragement as I made my way past them.

I sat between my daughter and mother, watching the portrayal of the memorable characters I grew up watching on television. Her energy and honest portrayal of life was exhilarating. Now this was a true 'Woman of Character.'

After the show, we were invited backstage to a reception where the rest of my family was introduced to Ms. Tomlin. I was impressed by her genuine warmth and caring. If I hadn't been a big fan before, I certainly became one that night.

A week or two later, Madison received a surprise package in the mail. She was very excited because she rarely got packages addressed to her. Tearing it open, she found an autographed Edith Ann doll and a DVD collection of Edith Ann cartoons inside. To this day, Edith Ann sits in a place of honor in our home and our hearts are touched by Miss Tomlin's generosity and warmth.

On April 22nd the Indianapolis Komen affiliate held its Race for the Cure. I had heard about this race, but had never found an opportunity in the past to participate and I was uncertain what to expect. It had been almost a year since I had discovered the lumps in my breast and I was ready to join the fight.

My coworkers and friends, Anne Belsito, Sandy Poremba, Silvia Moore, Amanda Smiley, and Theda Miller had supported me through my cancer. Each of their lives had been affected by breast cancer. This year they created a Regenstrief Race for the Cure team. They were devoted to doing all they could to help fund researchers who might someday find a way to eradicate this devastating disease.

Anne was team captain and just happened to work in the cubicle next to mine. For nearly a year she had checked on me daily regarding my treatment. Sandy was a bright and shining pick-me-up whenever I saw her. She always had a great attitude and I never saw pity in her eyes. "Who needs hair anyway," she would say, "It's totally overrated." There was no way I would miss being a member of the Regenstrief Institute team.

The festivities started very early on a Saturday morning with unusually dense traffic on the interstate. It appeared that all of Indianapolis was funneling into downtown to walk or run to raise money to support those affected by breast cancer. Ken dropped me off early near the survivor's tent. While he parked the car I followed the stream of pink shirts into the large white tent marked "Survivor's Tent." I waited outside in line, unsure of what I was going to find inside.

I made my way in, surrounded by many survivors who looked like they had been there before. We were greeted by volunteers handing out long pink feather boas. This was a fun and frilly addition to the pink that symbolized the femininity that breast cancer tried to steal from us.

After donning the boa, I was led to a woman standing with a race medal suspended on a pink ribbon that she held out expectantly in preparation to place around my neck. Much to my surprise, a year's worth of emotion boiled up in my chest at the sight of the medal. I was absolutely speechless, which is rare for me. Tears flooded and blurred my vision. Although I had won many medals in my racing career, I realized this was a medal given to symbolize that I had won the race for my life.

Conflicting emotions filled me in that moment. This was a celebration, yet I felt anger and grief for all the things I had experienced and lost over the past year. I felt guilt and shame that I had cancer at all. The presenter of the medal hugged me and I embraced her on behalf of all the survivors who had gone through the torture of diagnosis and treatment. I embraced her for the elation I felt just knowing I was still there and on behalf of the multitude of the women who had not survived breast cancer.

Another line led me to a different volunteer who had pink ribbon stickers to place on our caps to commemorate the number of years since we had been diagnosed. I told her that I had not yet met my one year mark. "That's okay, honey," she said. "That means you are with the one year survivors." Then she handed me a single pink ribbon to stick to my cap as she told me, "Wear it proudly until next year when you will get another one." "How many would not make it to next year?" I thought.

Survivors were lined up in order of years of survivorship. Since it was my first year, I stood under the one year banner. While waiting, I heard someone shouting my name. I turned in the direction of the voice and saw a woman in pink frantically waving over her head. It was Nina

Edwards-Swain and her niece. Nina had given me the box full of hats that I had worn all through treatment. She was a five year survivor and was walking with her niece, Kimmie Jane, who had also endured breast cancer.

Nina told me that I should stay and walk with them through the pink parade, as she did not want me to be alone for my first experience at the Race for the Cure. The parade of pink started to move through arches of pink balloons; the route was completely packed with supporters.

Entering the colorful arches, I looked ahead into the sea of faces crowded along the parade route. Everyone was cheering and clapping and I was engulfed by their love and support. Another flood of emotions rushed through me as I waved and I tried to wipe away the abundant tears as I struggled to smile in appreciation.

Looking into the eyes of other survivors, I saw a palpable energy and diverse emotions. Some were quite jovial wearing funny hats or holding balloons, seemingly elated as they waved at the spectators, while others, like me, had tear stained cheeks as they walked on in amazement. I hugged women I had never met and we shared a moment of celebration. It was astonishing to see the sheer number of people affected by cancer. We had all gone through some of the most terrifying and painful experiences of our lives and were now being honored by over forty thousand friends, family and strangers.

With every step of the five kilometer walk, I felt overwhelmed by the support and the love of family and friends, and the quiet understanding from the other survivors in pink. Many people have been turned off by the color pink and feel that it has been over commercialized. To me and the multitude of breast cancer survivors walking that day, it meant that we were not lost, forgotten, or alone, feelings that are all too common when fighting cancer on a daily basis.

*   *   *

In late autumn of 2004, an article published in Indianapolis about my cancer and life afterwards happened to catch the eye of a medical student attending the IU School of Medicine. The article mentioned the Indy Speed Sports Club and stated that Ken and I coached cycling and speed skating. Todd Bertrand, an exceptional young man with curly blond hair and an infectious smile, contacted us and joined our team. We essentially adopted him.

Todd had never speedskated before, as he came from southern Indiana where there were few ice rinks. Because he was new to the sport, there were no bad habits to unlearn. We found him to be friendly, intelligent, outgoing, and eager, so he responded to coaching extremely well. The best kind of person to coach is one who listens and applies the principles he is taught. His previous experience in other sports brought him to us in reasonably good shape and it was a bonus that he was also a cyclist.

He was dedicated and focused and soon became a wonderful training partner. We were on a year round training program and he partnered to help me meet my training goals. We often rode long sessions on stationary bikes, doing intervals while watching movies in our basement. Weather permitting, we did hill repetitions on cold mornings and sometimes climbed long, arduous hills on road bikes. Todd was the best training partner I could have asked for.

My good friend and neighbor Fred McKee talked us into doing the 'Ride across Indiana' (otherwise known as RAIN) ride that year. The predetermined route literally goes across the state. Starting in the very dark, early morning hours on the Illinois border in Terre Haute, the ride went east on State Route 40 to Earlham College in Richmond, Indiana on the Ohio border.

The ride is 159 miles in one day and I was not certain how well I would hold up after all I had been through. However, Ken had great confidence that I could do it and offered to be my support person. There was a large mass start at the Illinois / Indiana state line in the glow of the predawn light. Announcements were made, cautions were given, acknowledgements and thanks were made, and then the official start was declared.

"Click, click, scrape, click," was the sound of hundreds of cleated bike shoes as they were snapped into pedals and the adventure began. The pace picked up right away to burn off some of the slow riders. The experience of knowing how to move from wheel to wheel kept me solidly in the pack. I often positioned my bike behind another rider's wheel, taking advantage of the hospitality of their draft. If they started to fade off the back of the group, I swiftly jumped over to the wheel of the strongest rider nearby.

We only stopped briefly at major intersections in Indianapolis when there were no police to escort us across busy roads. The rest of the ride was pretty much nonstop. I was having a fantastic ride and holding my own, sitting in and talking with the men in the pack. Oh my goodness, it was ever so good to be back again!

We did not stop for food or drink, and that's where Ken came into play. Before the ride I had prepared my own recipe for smoothies. They contained the standard ingredients of bananas, strawberries, orange juice and blueberries, plus protein powder and royal jelly. I had decided that if royal jelly was good enough for the queen bee, it was good enough for me. I had funneled the mixture into disposable water bottles and placed them in the freezer the night before.

Ken kept an ample supply of both smoothies and regular water bottles in a cooler in the support van and drove ahead attempting to predict when I would need food and water. He had a great deal of experience supporting teams on both national and international levels and did it for me over the years during races at national events. Ken knew my quirks, especially the fact that I needed to eat at least every four hours to prevent low blood sugar grumpiness and fatigue.

My insightful husband seemed to know exactly when and where to meet me for a hand-up. He wore his yellow Cyclists Combating Cancer team uniform and a brightly colored hat so I could easily spot him ahead on the road. I wore my CCC uniform so he could identify me in the field of cyclists barreling down the road. He parked uphill along the route, knowing the field would slow down on an incline and I could move over to the right side of the road and head straight for his outstretched arm. When I got within striking distance, Ken would start moving by running backwards up the hill with the items in his hand. With this strategy, when I made a connection with him at 20 MPH, the item was not likely to be slapped out of his hand so quickly that it could not be recovered. We didn't need musettes at this event because Ken was skilled and polished at handing-up the bottles directly to me. It was cycling support poetry in motion.

Some of the other riders noticed how synchronized we were. Most did not have trained support people to give them food and drink. Many relied on wives and mothers who were trying their best, but didn't understand the mechanics of a hand-up. There were many failed hand-ups and many curse words were exchanged as adrenaline clouded communication and food and water went flying out of reach. Others had not expected to see a woman stay in the field of riders, let alone take a hand-up so professionally. I made sure they knew it was all because of Ken. It was clear to me that I was just the rider, while he was the magic that made it all happen.

By the time I got a smoothie, it was half thawed and the perfect consistency. I squeezed the bottle to take the nutrition into my mouth. It was a cold slushy liquid and had all the components I needed to keep riding at a vigorous pace. One of the other riders gave me a questioning look and said, "What do you have in there?" "A smoothie," I replied. He then sat up in the middle of the field and shouted, "Hey guys, she's got smoothies!" Much joking and teasing followed and it helped pass the long miles as we continued pressing toward the finish.

One of the most fantastic hand-ups during the 159 miles was when I asked Ken to give me an aspirin. What made this incredible was that, on the next hand-up, he passed the aspirin from his hand to mine while I was going nearly 20 MPH and neither of us dropped it. I am blessed to have Ken in my life. He has been my support and my rock in more ways that I can count and I am grateful for his love and faith in me.

At one point I looked down at my bike computer and realized that we had just completed 100 miles in less than four hours. That meant we were averaging over 25 MPH. I knew, without a shadow of a doubt, that I was only able to stay at that pace for such a long distance because of his amazing support and the extensive training I had done in preparation. As a coach, I have said very many times to my athletes that the true mark of fitness is not the ability to go, but the ability to recover and go again. This you can only get from doing intervals.

The main field started to dwindle after 125 miles and we began to enter the more hilly sections of State Route 40 as we approached our final destination. Each rider poured heart and soul into this effort even though there was no cash prize, no championship title, or glory, only bragging rights.

We rode up the final hill at almost a sprint pace. When we arrived at Earlham College, our ride was over and they directed us into a finishing chute much like they would with cattle. Our group arrived first and we were all forced to stop suddenly to enable the officials to record our names, numbers and finish times. Out of breath after having ridden our bikes nonstop and sprinting uphill the last half mile, being forced into a sudden stop did not seem to be the best way to end our ride. Our muscles started to rebel as we stood in long lines waiting to have our numbers recorded. My time was documented at six hours and forty-four minutes. Relieved and exhausted, we were finally free to go.

Trying to walk after riding that long was quite a challenge. It felt like my leg muscles had developed total amnesia and didn't seem to remember how to do anything other than ride. I had to physically force myself to keep walking because I knew if I stopped, my muscles would not recover and they would seize up in painful cramps. It took some time to recover enough to get into the van for the long ride home.

Was this worth it? Absolutely! I was riding, I was breathing and I was living life on my terms. Cancer did not enter my mind for a single moment while I was riding across the state. I had survived cancer and I survived the RAIN ride. What a great feeling it was to know I could do them both. I felt so alive, even though my legs wanted to kill me.

*   *   *

During the summer of my chemotherapy treatment, I escaped from my reality of cancer by watching the Tour de France on television with my family. I couldn't wait for the evening summaries of the races, so I watched them when they were televised live in the mornings. As I watched, I remembered how I had gasped the year before when the world witnessed a race up a huge mountain in which a spectator, who stood cheering on the side of the road during a climb knocked Lance down. He was riding close to the spectators when one of the straps of a musette held in the hand of a spectator snagged Lance's handlebars and instantly threw him and the rider directly behind him to the ground. It was something else Lance and I had in common. We had both been knocked down by musettes during bike races. My heart raced for him as he got back on his bike and pounded on the pedals to make up the time he had lost. It was endearing to watch, as the gentlemen of the tour actually waited for him, instead of taking advantage of his misfortune. As amazing as all that was to see, it seemed a miracle that he actually won the stage.

Watching him race, while I was going through treatment, felt like a surge of lightening, sparking hope inside me. The fact that he won was a bonus. What was truly touching was that he was able to overcome disaster, both on his bike and off. I felt like doing cartwheels in my living room when he won his sixth tour. Not only was he an American cyclist, but also he had stared cancer in the face, called it out and triumphed over it. I had heard of the 'Make-A-Wish Foundation', an organization that grants wishes and sets up experiences for children with terminal illness. I thought to myself, "If there were a 'Make-A-Wish Foundation' for grownups with cancer, my wish would be that I could take my family to see the Tour de France."

In late spring of 2005, I received a phone call from a film producer. He was working on a documentary that would follow several cancer survivors on their way to Paris to see Lance Armstrong compete in the Tour. He said he had read about me and wanted to know if I was interested in being part of the documentary. I said yes… but I had to find a way to get to France. Then I found out how much it would cost and I was very doubtful that we would be able to do it. I shared my news with a friend at work, and somehow, through the magic and generosity of my fairy godfather, part of our trip was funded. We were going to Paris to watch the Tour!

*   *   *

On the second of July, our friends Joe Niccum and JoMay Chow were married in Columbus, Ohio, and Ken and I had the honor of being in their wedding party. It was a perfect day to witness two wonderful souls starting a new life together.

At the reception, we sat at the main table with the rest of the wedding party, while Madison sat with Brooke Crum and her mother Laura at a table nearby. JoMay gave Joe the most exceptional wedding gift: a new track bike. Joe not only got a gorgeous bride, but also a new bike all in the same day. Champagne was served and glasses rose to toast the happiness of the new couple. I watched closely as Madison, who had never been around alcohol before, discovered that she did not like the smell of the Champagne. We laughed when we saw her turn her nose away and make a "That stinks!" face. She was not at all shy about letting people know her opinions.

Time passed very quickly after the wedding and before we realized it, we were boarding a flight to Paris to watch the final stage of the Tour de France. The most recent Harry Potter book had been released, so Madison was engrossed in the world of wizardry for most of the trip, while I tried to brush up on my French. Sleeping was out of the question for the two of us. Madison was too excited and had her book to keep her entertained, while I could never sleep well on planes. Ken, on the other hand, can fall asleep instantly just about anywhere. To say I am envious of this ability would be an understatement.

Ken arranged to rent a car instead of taking a bus or taxi from the airport to Paris, because he likes to drive. The rental agency had a nice new car ready for us and asked if we wanted additional insurance. Ken is a good driver, so he said, "No." We drove through the beautiful rolling countryside, blanketed by different crops, with an occasional hint of civilization scattered in here and there. Madison and I watched through weary jet lagged eyes as we passed picturesque villages and vast farmlands. There were quaint bread shops on every corner of the small villages we traveled through, with artfully manicured flower gardens everywhere, and stone-walls separating fields and outlining properties. If we had not been so exhausted, I'm sure it would have been breathtaking.

Madison had fallen asleep in the back seat by the time we got to Paris. The traffic was thick and aggressive, similar to what I had seen in New York. By the time we arrived, we were spent and very hungry. When I asked Madison what she would like to eat, she quickly piped up and decidedly announced, "Sushi!" But I insisted that we were going to eat real French food since we were in France.

We decided on a crêperie that was little more than a hole in the wall restaurant, where we were the only customers in the shop. We sat at a table and looked at the menu. When the waitress came to take our drink order, I was trying to be a good mother and encourage Madison to drink milk, because I knew she had not had any in over 24 hours.

Ken ordered a Coke Light, which is the translation for Diet Coke. I ordered milk and Madison noticed that they had apple cider on the menu. She loved apple cider, so Ken ordered it for her. The waitress returned with our drinks and placed the milk in front of me, the Coke Light in front of Ken, and for Madison a bubbling carafe of amber liquid. She looked at the sparkling liquid and sniffed at it, "It smells like the wedding," she grumbled in a low tone.

I was amazed that the waitress gave a ten year old girl hard cider without blinking an eye, while giving the adults the soda and milk.

Needless to say, I traded drinks with Madison and she drank milk and I drank the cider.

We stayed in the fashion district at a very old hotel in the heart of Paris, the Hotel Castiglione. The only elevator in the hotel was so small that we had to sit on top of our luggage to get to our floor. The room was long and narrow. Madison had a bed that pulled down sideways from the wall and the room had a screen-less window that overlooked a courtyard below. We turned on the television briefly and were quite entertained to see Sponge Bob Square Pants speaking French.

The man standing at the front desk in the small lobby said, "American's, huh?" as we passed. "Yes, how could you tell?" I responded as I turned to look at him. He replied, "You are all wearing Crocs." We laughed as we looked down at our feet. We were indeed all wearing the rubber shoes called Crocs. I had packed them because I knew many of the parks in Paris were covered in dusty crushed limestone and we were going to be doing a lot of walking. I was certain that they would be comfortable and easy to wash.

He asked if we were in Paris for the Tour and Ken replied that we were. We introduced ourselves to our fellow American. Ken explained in more depth what brought us to Paris. He told him that I was a cancer survivor and cyclist and how much our trip meant to me. The man revealed that he was from Colorado and was a major sponsor of one of the teams, as his company made Rudy Project sunglasses. He then told us about his friend, Jim Owens, who was also a cancer survivor and cyclist. I was stunned when I realized that he was talking about THE Jim Owens, one of the many outstanding members of the CCC group that had become part of my online family and I communicated with almost daily via e-mail.

Jim, a true hero, battled brain cancer while continuing to fight and advocate for others. We learned that earlier that morning, he had dropped his new prescription Rudy Project sunglasses on the sidewalk and was out searching for them. With nothing on our schedule, we decided to help him search. We walked out the door of the hotel and turned left. Looking down at the sidewalk, our eyes scanned left and right. The sidewalk came to a stop at an intersection and we started to cross the street. Halfway across the street, I stopped, noticing Jim walking towards us doing the same thing, scanning the pavement for his lost sunglasses. I recognized him immediately from the photos that had been posted on the group website and said, "Jim Owens?" he paused and looked at me. "It's Cindi from Indy!" I announced. You could see the recognition brighten his eyes. A smile spread across his pale face. He gave me a big hug in the middle of the street and then we realized that we should move out of traffic.

We walked back to the curb together and began talking about how great it was to finally meet in person. While basking in the glory of the morning sun and my amazement in finding Jim in Paris, I happened to look over to my right. I was startled to see a pair of Ruby Project sunglasses sitting on top of a green metal trash can and realized they must be his. Obviously someone had found them and kindly placed them there to be recovered. If we had not stopped to talk at that moment, raising our gazes from the sidewalk, he might never have gotten them back. Things do happen for a reason.

We spent the rest of the week touring the city, steeped in history and romance, in our American made Crocs. In our exploration, we found the Paris velodrome, which had once been the final destination of the Tour de France. When we walked up to that landmark, there was a race in progress. Some of the officials noticed us and asked about our interest. We told them who we were and Ken told them that I was the current US National Track Champion. They were very excited to have us there and asked me to present the awards for the races that day. While on the podium, I learned that the French now kiss back and forth, four times on the cheek, not just two or three times.

We walked around the city instead of driving because the condition of the cars on the streets was alarming. We were afraid the brand new rental car would get terribly scraped up if parked on the street. All the cars parked on the narrow streets had long scrapes down their doors. Everywhere we looked, it was as if someone had driven a large truck down the narrow street, gouging the sides of every car along the way and bending or breaking side mirrors off the vehicles. Since we had not taken out extra insurance on the rental we were careful and kept it parked in a guarded garage.

Our family went to Sacre Coeur in Montmartre and walked up over 300 steps to see the breathtaking view of the city. Visiting the Paris Opera House was one of Madison's quests, as she loved the Phantom of the Opera musical. Entering the ornately decorated building, we imagined all the different parts of the musical that could have taken place there. On the right bank of the Seine, I argued with a street vendor, who tried to charge us too much for printed artwork, and we posed for pictures with Rollerblade clad Gendarmes in front of the Louvre.

Beneath the majestic shadow of Notre Dame Cathedral, we held little cakes called Madeleines up in the air as birds would fly up and eat from our hands. We relished gelato that tasted like fresh ripe mangos as we walked under and around the Eiffel Tower during the day, and then watched the sparkling lights dance on the tower at night. Ken made a point to visit every bike shop we could find in Paris. Walking through the stone streets we could not help but notice the distinct smell of urine, both fresh and old, on the walls of many of the stone and brick buildings we passed along the way.

The entrance to the Louvre was a large glass pyramid that descended into an incredible world of sculpted figures and paintings. The first great artwork we encountered was the Winged Victory statue standing over all who entered. As we turned, I saw the room ahead was full of angels and I stopped in my tracks. It was very difficult for me to accept that we were standing in the Louvre. It was a place I never dreamed I would get to see. I fought back tears that were attempting to emerge. At that moment I felt fully alive and astounded. I was surrounded by ageless artwork that had been created by lives long gone from this earth and admired by many. Madison did not understand why looking at painted and sculpted angels would cause me to cry. I was now surrounded by angels, both in art and in life. A year before, I had wondered if I would live. At that moment, it was hard to believe I was not in heaven.

*   *   *

Our last day in Paris was also the final day of the Tour de France. Jerry Kelly, a very active member of the Cyclists Combating Cancer group, had posted an invitation online for CCC'rs to join him and his wife Angie on the Champs-Élysées for the final stage of the tour. He had reserved an area for us to gather and enjoy the race at a strategic location on the course: the turnaround at the Arch de Triumph.

It was there that I first met Phyllis O'Grady, a beautiful breast cancer sister and CCC'r from Colorado, Andy Anderson from Ireland, Crawford Ingles from Scotland, Jeffery DalPoggetto from San Francisco, and so many others whose words I had read online over the last year. We shared the joys of cycling and the agony of cancer in our online communications, but we had never met in person until that day in France. We stood for hours in drizzling rain waiting for the Tour parade to arrive, the harbinger of the race's arrival. Excitement was building. The shared camaraderie and love of life in the moment bound us all together and kept us warm despite the chill of the morning drizzle.

We were witnessing a great moment in bike racing: an American winning a grueling month long race of strength, endurance and strategy. But to us, it meant more than the fact that he was an American. He had won his personal race against cancer and was now charging ahead and clearing the path for others to win theirs. He was our Champion.

At the podium, they played the National Anthem of the United States, and to my amazement, a hush washed over us like a wave as the music started in the distance. A murmur at first, but then gaining in strength and pride, a chorus of voices from the crowds packing the streets began building in volume, singing the words of our national anthem and no one objected.

On the way back to the hotel that night, we passed the hotel where Lance and his team were staying. The flag of France no longer flew above the building. It had been replaced with the flag of Texas. It was very unusual for a US state flag to be flown in France, but this exception was to honor his victory.

While we watched the conclusion of the race and cheered Lance on to his seventh win, we saw photographers everywhere capturing the moment. As soon as we landed back in the United States, we called to tell my parents that we were safe at home. They told us that we had already been home for a while. We were on the front page of USA Today, celebrating the day and the victory on the Champs-Élysées.

*　　*　　*

A few weeks after returning from Paris, the National Track Championships were to be held on our home track in Indianapolis. In anticipation, I had trained hard for many months in an effort to polish my 500 meter time trial and trim off some time. I found that riding behind a motorcycle, drafting in its slipstream, definitely goes a long way in the effort to bring a rider to an elite level.

The night of my event, the local news media came to the track while I was warming up in the infield. They interviewed me and had a photographer with his video camera follow me in my preparation. I was bothered by a slight headache and I didn't want to have any distraction in my competition, so I took a couple of aspirins. I did not realize that they were actually Excedrin and contained caffeine. I don't drink any caffeinated drinks, including coffee, tea or soft drinks and I never have.

Feeling jumpy, excited, and nervous after taking the aspirin was unusual for me. I had done this race many times before and won many times, but this time I had cameras following me. They were recording everything I did and I had to carry on as if they were invisible. It was just the bike, the clock, the cameras, and me. Once again, Ken was working as an official and was not in my preparation area. My mom was helping me, while my brother and Madison were there to watch the race and be there for me when I won.

The time came to take my place on the line. I went through my starting routine just as I had so many times before. I followed the way Mike Walden had trained me: "Do it by the numbers." First, I placed the bike on the track and positioned the pedals. Next, I circled around to the top side of the track to mount my bike from the high side of the track. Locking my cleats onto the pedals and tightening the extra straps, I tried to relax and breathe slowly while the official held my bike steady. I listened to the countdown. On two I stood on the pedals. On one, I focused up the track and listened to the clock ticks. On the final click I took off, pulling up on the rear pedal as hard as possible and bringing the bike up to speed.

The 500 meter race is all about getting up to and maintaining speed and the start is extremely important. I was off the line and a few pedal strokes away when I heard the "BANG! BANG!" of the starter's pistol. Realizing that the two shots meant there had been a false start, I thought, "It must have been the woman on the other side of the track. It couldn't have been me." As I slowed the bike down to turn back to the starting gate, the official approached and said, "You have one false start." I was completely amazed. "It wasn't me. No way!" my thoughts yelled. I didn't think I had jumped the start at all.

I was a bit concerned because two false starts would be a disqualification. But I still had a second chance. Intent on a good start, I listened to the starting "Tick, tick" as the numbers flipped on the counter. I heard the final tick of the clock and saw the numbers change. I leapt into action and there it was again, a double shot! It HAD to be the person on the other side this time. The official approached again, "That was your second false start," he stated as he waved me off the track. I was in denial. It felt like he was speaking a language that I didn't understand. I wanted to go back to the start and ride the race that I had been preparing for, but unfortunately, I was disqualified, disheartened, and disappointed. "How could this have happened?" I wondered. I had been preparing nearly a year for that moment and had somehow blown it. I had been so focused on the timer that I wasn't listening to the tones.

Ken was unavailable for quite a while during the competition because he is a dedicated, by the book, rule follower and was committed to upholding his role in the competition. During a break between events, I asked him what had happened. He told me in plain, straightforward terms that I clearly jumped the gun. I argued that I was listening to the tick, tick, tick of the start clock below me as the numbers on the clock changed. He then explained that the official time began with the beeps and not the numbers on the display. I was so frustrated with myself, and so furious that I just wanted to ride away as hard and fast as possible.

To help me get over this jump start problem, Ken later recorded the sound of the beeps from the official timing system and put them on my phone. This gave me an audible signal to recognize that would help train my brain and enable me to surge off the line without false starting. This is one case where it was not *"Watch and Learn"* but "listen and learn."

* * *

In the late fall of 2005, Mary Jayne, my survivor go-to person from Regenstrief, sent me an email communication she had gotten from Komen. They were looking for an Honorary Survivor for their upcoming

2006 Race for the Cure and she thought I would be a perfect candidate.

I questioned whether I should apply, but with relentless urging from Mary Jayne, I finally submitted my application. Later, Komen's administrative assistant Ginger Moore contacted me and announced that I had been named as a finalist for the position. She then scheduled my interview with the selection committee.

One of the roles of the Honorary Survivor was to attend various functions and give speeches. This person needed the ability to share their cancer story with others in clear, relatable terms. I was told that some at Komen were a bit reluctant to select me because I was an athlete and not everyone who gets breast cancer could relate to many of the things I had accomplished. However, they did decide to select me.

The Indianapolis Woman magazine was doing a cover story featuring me as the Honorary Survivor. My hair had grown back curly and long enough that the curls evolved into ringlets. When I reported to hair and makeup, the art director instructed the stylist to slick my hair back and pull it into a bun. When I questioned his plan, he stated that the style was designed to represent speed.

I brought my bike, CCC cycling jersey, speed skates, and skating uniform with me to the photo shoot. I was surprised that it took them so long to apply the cosmetics. The makeup artist was a young man with a slight build, dark shoulder length hair, wearing a black velvet blazer with a black flower on the lapel. I could smell his cologne as he leaned over to apply his artistry. The only makeovers I had ever had in my life were just before my wedding and after chemo. Normally I wear little to no cosmetics, so this would be a real change for me.

I set the bike on the trainer as usual, with the back wheel spinning and

the front wheel stationary, but the photographer thought the pictures would look better if the action was reversed. Using what we had, we put the front wheel on the trainer and had it spinning. I had to put all my weight forward and I was told not to smile. As awkward as it felt, when the magazine came out, the cover looked great.

The Race for the Cure was in April and the organizers were very active in the cool pre-dawn hours on that Saturday morning at Military Park. TV crews were interviewing people arriving and preparing for the explosion of pink.

Standing on the stage overlooking the record setting crowd waiting for the event to begin, I was told that there were 40,000 people participating that day. As I stood on the stage waiting to be introduced, I realized that about that same number of people die every year from breast cancer. I saw a multitude of lives physically present before me and realized that they could easily represent each life that would be taken in the following year by breast cancer. The sight was staggering.

I had the honor of starting the race from a perch overlooking the seemingly endless sea of pink, as runners, joggers, walkers, and survivors passed over the starting line. I joined my family after the start, and walked the distance with them, again enjoying the feeling of solidarity in the fight.

Upon returning home after the race, Ken checked the mailbox and discovered a letter from the Olympic committee with my name on it. I opened the letter with some curiosity. It was informing me that I was one of the top five candidates for the US Olympic coach of the year award. It was an honor just to have been named coach of the year for speed skating, but being named as one of the top five out of all the sports was unbelievable.

A few weeks later, during a seemingly normal morning at work in May, my cell phone rang. I was standing in Jill Warvel's cubicle, discussing user requirements related to the Regenstrief electronic medical record computer system. When I looked at my phone, it was a long distance number that I didn't recognize. I apologized for the interruption and answered. The caller identified herself as Kathy Sellers, from the United States Olympic Committee. She had my full attention.

In February, US Speed Skating had named me volunteer coach of the year. This made me a candidate, along with all the other coaches in their respective Olympic sports, to be recognized as the overall coach of the year. I was honored to be nominated, because it meant that my skaters appreciated what I had done and what I had given them and US Speedskating also thought I was doing a good job.

When Kathy Sellers identified herself I could almost hear the words, "We wanted to let you know that you are a runner up for the overall coach of the year. We would like to send you a plaque acknowledging..." but that was not the case. Instead, she congratulated me, as I had been named THE US Olympic Coach of the year. I dropped down in the chair next to Jill's desk, my heart beating like a hummingbird's. She continued to talk, but once again, I couldn't hear the details. My mind was still focused on the unbelievable fact that I was receiving this incredible honor.

Stunned in disbelief as the realization soaked in, I floated, no, bounced through the hallways at work, telling my co-workers, Anne Belsito, Bruce Williams, Marc Overhage, and Sandy Poremba my news. After that, I was basically worthless for the rest of the day.

It took all the strength and restraint I could muster to not call Ken and blurt the news out to him. When I met him for lunch, I ran straight into his arms and hugged him. His response was, "Good news?" I cried and laughed and jumped up and down trying to find the words. After lunch I did not return to work, but went on a bike ride instead. How could I better celebrate and process it all?

Upon returning home, I discovered the message light flashing on the answering machine. I listened as the woman on the machine stated that she was from IU Cancer Center. There had been a drawing of cancer patients' names and five names were drawn to win two tickets to a black tie dinner / fundraiser with Lance Armstrong as featured speaker.

I returned the call and discovered that my name had been the first one drawn for the event to be held on May 27th, which happened to be our 16th wedding anniversary. I called my mother and shared the events of my unbelievable day. She told me I should buy a lottery ticket and circle the date on the calendar, remembering the date as a lucky day. When I did look at the calendar, it struck me that the date had already been circled. Not only was it my sister-in-law Linda's birthday, it was exactly two years to the day since I received another call from my friend and physician telling me that I had cancer. Then I was asking, "Lord, what did I do wrong to deserve this?" Now I asked, "Lord, what did I do right?"

The black tie dinner was held at the Indianapolis Colts sports complex. Cyclists from Indianapolis lined the red carpet, welcoming guests and waiting for Lance to arrive. Many of my friends were there and it felt surreal to be walking down the red carpet, dressed in a beaded evening gown, while my friends in Lycra cheered from the sides. As we walked through the gauntlet of jersey-clad friends, I stopped several times along the way to hug people and to smile, laugh, and celebrate. Madison was there with our friends Gary Schmitt, Fred Evans, Jeannie Neal, and Sue Nuyda lining the red carpet and I was so happy and proud to share this with all of them.

Once Inside, I was surprised to find that we were seated at a table with my good friend Mary Hardin and her husband of twenty years, Jeffrey Hammond. He had been diagnosed in January of 1996 with non-Hodgkin's lymphoma and was in remission for about a year, followed by several more years where they had to play the game of watch and wait since his was a slow growing form of cancer. Unfortunately, it had returned with a vengeance just a few months before the dinner. We felt it was quite an honor to spend that evening with them, while listening to Lance's speech. Even more special was to see the love that Mary and Jeffrey had for one another, so very evident in their eyes and their hearts. Sadly, he lost his battle the following year.

In June, Ken, Madison and I flew to San Diego to attend the awards presentation for the US Olympic Committee Coach of the Year award. Of all the Olympic sports combined, both summer and winter, I had been selected for this award. I felt this was greater than any gold medal I had ever won.

After landing in San Diego, we were walking toward the baggage claim where people stood holding signs to connect for transportation. Madison tugged on my sleeve and pointed, "Mom, that man is holding a sign with your name on it." She was right. There stood a limo driver waiting to take us to the resort hotel where we were spoiled with gifts in our room, as well as spa packages.

The Award presentation was part of the US Olympic Congress Annual Meeting. At the dinner, I saw a lot of people that I hadn't seen in quite a while from both Speed Skating and Cycling.

My Aunt Janet drove in from Phoenix to join us and one of the members of the Cyclists Combating Cancer group that I had connected with online, Keli Ann Lawton, drove up with her three year old daughter, Kamryn, to meet us. I was delighted to get to share the experience with them all. What good is a memory if you cannot share it? Madison and Kamryn enchanted members of the Olympic congress as they skipped from booth to booth, collecting souvenirs and giggling about all the treasure they had found.

Of course, while we were in San Diego, we had to check out the zoo and the velodrome. We were able to rent bikes and ride a training session at the track. That is where I discovered another cyclist familiar with Mike Walden's techniques and we actually did a little coaching together. Once a coach, always a coach; it's hard not to help when you see people who could benefit from your advice. Janet also joined us in some California sightseeing and we turned into the ultimate tourists for the rest of the trip.

Not long after our return, Special Olympics International (SOI) contacted me and asked if I could fly to Washington, DC, to shoot a video that would help teach coaches how to coach cycling. It turned out to be a very humid 97 degree July day and we shot the video in the middle of an open parking lot. I was hot, sweaty and tired. When we finished, the director asked if I would be willing to go to their office to meet Timothy Shriver, the Chairman and CEO of Special Olympics.

How could I refuse? When I found out that I would be in DC, I contacted a good friend who lived there and had been one of my co-counselors at church camp in Ohio many years before. Patrick Fee was a lifelong friend and was like a snake charmer with the campers in the backwoods. I will always remember him in the early '80's wearing a Greek fisherman's cap, black T-shirt and blue jeans. Now we were all grown up and he wore business suits, shined shoes and a tie, but still had the same grin and radio-ready voice. We had previously arranged for him to pick me up at the Special Olympics' office after my meeting so we could enjoy lunch together and get caught up.

When I arrived at the SOI office, I was taken into Mr. Shriver's office. He was involved in another meeting, so they asked me to make myself comfortable and wait there. I sat on a couch along one of the long walls in the room and marveled at all the memorabilia. There were banners, photos and posters, as well as framed Special Olympics medals on display. I was a little nervous, but he was so casual and relaxed when he entered the room that I soon felt quite comfortable. Mr. Shriver took a chair and moved next to me on the couch. We discussed many things, ranging from coaching to my recent award.

I talked to him about my cancer experience and about Howard and Mandy in Japan. I expressed to him just how proud and honored I was to be part of an organization that was truly changing lives. He asked what I thought could be done to make Special Olympics more of a true athletic competition.

After we discussed a few thoughts on that point, he inquired about my availability to meet his daughter Rose and his mother. His secretary called his daughter who was unfortunately unavailable. I was still flabbergasted and thrilled to have the opportunity to meet Mrs. Eunice Kennedy Shriver, founder of Special Olympics. They asked if I had a way to get there. I immediately thought of my friend Pat and called him to see if he would be free to drive me there instead of our planned lunch date. He said he would be honored. Pat met me in the office, got the directions to camp Shriver, and away we went.

Excited to catch up with all that had been going on with our lives since we had last seen one another, we exchanged stories and updates as

Pat drove out to the suburbs of Maryland. The closer we got to our address for Camp Shriver, the more Pat became suspicious of our actual destination. As he looked around at the evolving terrain he said, "I don't think this is a normal camp like those we attended when you and I were counselors."

We arrived at the given address to discover that it was the Shriver Estate and that Camp Shriver was run from Mrs. Shriver's home. We called the phone number we had been given and a gentleman told us to come around back. Her personal assistant met us there and gave us a tour of the camp. At the pool, Mrs. Shriver, wearing her swimsuit and white flowered swim cap, was busy teaching a Down's syndrome woman how to blow bubbles in the water. During the tour of the camp, we saw one group playing tennis and another playing bocce ball.

When we returned from the tour, Mrs. Shriver was just getting out of the pool and was draped in a large beach towel. Thin and frail, she still had a look of power about her. I said "Hello Mrs. Shriver. It is an honor to meet you. My name is Cindi Hart and this is Pat Fee. Timothy Shriver suggested that we come and meet you here today." "Let's go sit over here and we can talk," she said, pointing to the patio with umbrella covered tables next to the pool. We escorted her to the table as she wrapped the towel tightly around her body. She seemed to know who I was. She asked, "Do you have a pamphlet?" "A pamphlet?" I asked. "About cycling, I am interested in learning more about cycling," she explained. I told her that Ken and I were in the process of writing an instructional manual for track cyclists, to which she promptly replied, "Well, send me your book and I will buy it." We looked at each other and smiled.

I wasn't certain how much time we would have with her, so I wanted to make sure I thanked her on behalf of all the lives she had changed. She was very modest and brushing past my praise. "My doctor told me I should not spend so much time in my suit," she said, referring to her swimsuit, "so I need to go change." I thought she was tactfully telling us that this was the end of our conversation and our visit. To our surprise, she then said, "Why don't you go inside the house and wait for me there. I can change and we can continue our discussion." I could see the childlike excitement flash in Pat's eyes. This was the most unexpected lunch date either of us could ever have.

We were directed to enter the house through the side door to the kitchen and then go to the main foyer. There we stared with wide eyes at walls decorated with paintings and other memorabilia. Pat called me over to see the handwritten letters framed on the wall and said, "These are actual letters written by President Kennedy when he was at boarding school." A sculpture with a photo next to it of Nelson Mandela presenting the sculpture to Mrs. Shriver, birth announcements, family photos and presidential documents were all displayed before our eyes. It was very surreal to be standing in the midst of all the history of this world changing family.

Shortly, Mrs. Shriver walked down the stairs and took us on a tour. She pointed out a photo of President Kennedy presenting her with a copy of legislation he had passed regarding Maternal Child Health and Welfare. "And I made him include Mental Retardation," she proudly proclaimed. She was such a beautiful woman and so animated in the crisp black and white photograph. One look at that picture and you could see how proud she was. I noticed just how beautiful and strong she remained.

She continued the tour and directed us to a family photo on the other side of the doorway. "This is Bobby and Jack, and this is my sister Rose and that's Teddy on the floor," she beamed with each new picture she pointed out.

We settled in the living room as she asked questions about cycling. I told her that I had recently been named head coach for Team USA cycling for the upcoming World Games in Shanghai. Mrs. Shriver then told me about the Best Buddies cycling program and suggested that perhaps I could help Maria (Shriver) with her riding. She talked about Anthony, her son who had been inspired to start the Best Buddies program. When he was in school, a classmate with an intellectual disability really impacted him because the boy had no one to play with. She said that Anthony had befriended this young man and vowed to make sure that people like his new friend would always have someone they could call their "best buddy." I shared the story with her about Madison's experience at school that led her to befriend many of her special needs classmates.

After two hours of fascinating conversation with Mrs. Shriver, her assistant entered the room to announce that it was nearly time for her to leave for her appointment. I somehow came up with enough courage to ask if she would mind if we took a photo with her. She smiled and agreed. Pat said he would take my photo if I took his. She looked around for an area that she thought would be a good background. Then she said, "How about we stand in front of my brother's inaugural speech." and we happily agreed.

We walked together to the waiting car and helped her to get in the back seat. We thanked her once again for the afternoon and all that she had done for intellectually disabled athletes and their families. The door closed and they drove out of sight. Pat turned to me and said, "You know that if the United States had royalty, we just had tea with the Queen."

We walked to his car without saying a word. Opened the doors and climbed inside and without hesitation we were both on our cell phones. The first words that spontaneously poured out of our mouths in synchronization were, "Hello, Mom? You will never believe…"

A couple of months later, I was standing in the kitchen with my mother making dinner. The phone rang and I answered it. The voice coming from the phone asked in a New England accent, "May I speak with Cindi Hart?" "This is Cindi Hart," I replied. "You are Cindi Hart?" the voice asked. When I replied "Yes," she said "Please hold."

Thinking this was a caller trying to sell me something, I was tempted to hang up. But I was in a good mood, cooking side by side with my mother, so I placed the phone on the counter and turned the speaker on so I could continue cooking. Soon a new voice came on the speaker, "Cindi. This is Eunice Kennedy Shriver." Needless to say my mother and I stopped what we were doing and gave her our full attention, staring open mouthed at the phone. "I'm having a black tie event at my house for Best Buddies. It's a fundraiser for Best Buddies of Israel and I would very much like you to be there. Do you think you can attend? You can bring a friend." Stunned, I replied, "Thank you very much. I am very honored and I would be delighted to attend." "Good." She said. "I will have my assistant send you the details." And then she hung up.

After hanging up and looking at the date, I was crushed to realize that I had previously committed to go to the LiveStrong summit in Austin on that very same weekend. I racked my brain looking at flight schedules and arrangements to try to do both, but alas it was not to be. It devastated me to be forced to call back and tell her assistant that I could not make it. I hoped she was not offended and understood that I had already made a firm commitment and was trying to think of any way possible to do both, but it was not going to happen. To this day, I wonder what I missed and how things would have been different if I had gone there instead of Austin.

* * *

Every day since Ken first discovered the Cyclists Combating Cancer (CCC) online group, I eagerly read the posts that were shared. People

---

discussed topics ranging from their most recent bike ride to diagnostic scan results. We learned much about one another and trusted people with details that, at times, we did not even share with our families. This was a very close group of warriors and I yearned to meet each one in person. In Paris, we had a small sampling of what it was like to meet some of them. Those moments we shared on the Champs-Élysées will linger in my heart forever.

Every time I met another CCC'r the magic returned. It was like going on a blind date, but knowing a great deal about each other before you ever physically meet. Enthusiasm boiled over, as we were finally able to give real hugs and speak to one another face to face.

When I went to the LiveStrong Summit, the previous commitment that kept me from attending the Best Buddies black-tie event, I got to meet even more of the group. Now I was able to put faces and voices together with the people I had been reading about and communicating with, and it escalated my desire to make a difference. Some of these people were fighting wicked battles with cancer, and yet remained optimistic.

We were placed in workgroups based on geographic regions. By doing this, we could network and come together to create plans to fight cancer more effectively in our respective areas. In the evenings, everyone gathered for huge celebrations. The people in attendance had either lost family members to the disease, were fighting cancer personally, had survived it, or were healthcare workers. Everyone was there for the same purpose: to find ways in which we could help eradicate cancer in our lifetime.

My room at the Austin Summit was shared with Keli Ann, who met us at the Olympic Congress, and Holly Ganote from DC. We had a great time jumping up and down on our beds, sharing our life stories and the moments of this summit together. We had all fought cancer and were now there to make a difference in other people's battles. Holly was able to network at the summit to get support for her plan to help survivors run a 5K race in Washington DC. I believe she called it "Cancer to 5K."

I had to leave early so I could be home in time for the large Halloween birthday party that we planned for our daughter Madison. I got up in the wee hours of the morning before sunrise to get to the airport on time and tried to sneak out quietly so I wouldn't disturb my roommates. There were some impressive speakers lined up for the closing of the summit that I would miss hearing, including Elizabeth Edwards, but I wanted and needed to be home with my daughter for her birthday.

I boarded the plane without problems, but partway through our flight the pilot made an announcement. "Ladies and gentleman, it appears that we are going to be forced to make an emergency stop in Oklahoma City." There was a general buzz of conversation as people responded to the announcement, wondering if there was something technically wrong with the plane that would cause such an emergency detour. Once we landed, we were given more information. "Ladies and gentlemen, please plan to deplane. You are to leave all your luggage and belongings on the plane, take your tickets and identification with you." This was very disturbing and people stood up and filed out of the plane.

Once outside the plane, we were all held in a holding area. A man in a uniform addressed us. "The smoke detector in the lavatory on your plane has been tampered with, which is a federal offense." There were looks back and forth as the passengers tried to identify the guilty party. "The plane and all its contents will be searched with bomb sniffing dogs. You will all be required to stay in this holding area until everything is cleared." Angry chatter from the passengers increased. "Each of you will have to walk through a security check with your ticket and ID and there will be dogs at this checkpoint as well," he concluded. Someone behind me muttered, "Are they cigarette smoke sniffing dogs?"

No one confessed to tampering with or disabling the smoke detector; therefore, we all had to sit in the terminal and wait while drug/bomb sniffing dogs investigated every inch of the plane. After that, we were all interrogated. We sat for hours in a special holding area and could not leave, but we saw our flight crew leave, pulling their bags behind them. As they passed us, they kept their faces turned away to avoid eye contact.

I called Ken, and with a pain in my heart that felt like I had just swallowed a stone, I said, "I'm going to miss Madison's birthday," the realization hitting me hard. "I've never missed her birthday before." "Your mother is here and we will have it all under control. It will be alright." He attempted to reassure me, but still my heart ached; I wanted to be there. We were forced to wait until another flight crew arrived before we were safely on our way home. I did not reach home until after midnight.

When I got home, Madison had happily stayed up to share all the exciting details of her party. "Megan was here and so were Caleb and James Nelson," she said. "Were they the only boys?" I asked. "Yes and my favorite part was wrapping them in toilet paper like mummies and having them chase us around the basement." I could see it in my mind's eye, and she didn't seem very disappointed that I couldn't be there. My mother had taken my place to make sure everything went smoothly and Ken didn't have to deal with all the 11-year-olds in the house by himself. I was very disappointed, but Madison's birthday party was a huge success and that was what mattered most.

* * *

When I was in Paris, I met and bonded with Phyllis O'Grady in person. Her dark hair and eyes were accented well by the dark red lipstick she wore. We shared her bottle of pink champagne near the Champs-Elysees in celebration of our sisterhood. She invited me to be her guest at the "Ride for the Roses" in Austin, Texas, just two weeks after the summit.

Since I had such an unpleasant experience with the plane coming home from the summit, Ken decided that we should drive to Texas. This was not a big problem because Ken loves to drive and we could be together. In the past, he had driven all the way to Salt Lake City, so going to Austin wasn't a problem.

Arriving there, we met even more members of the Cyclists Combating Cancer family. Many had been at the summit before and some were new encounters. It was like eating potato chips, the more you eat, the more you want. I realized that with every new CCC'r I got to meet, I wanted to meet more. The group was addictive.

Phyllis O'Grady was one of the top fundraisers for the LiveStrong Challenge that year. I felt honored to know her and have her invite me to attend as her guest. One of the privileges earned by her fundraising was a private meeting with Lance Armstrong and she asked me to go with her. She had brought some posters for him to sign so she could auction them off for her next fundraiser.

Phyllis and I were ushered into the area where Lance was waiting. He recognized her right away and she greeted him with a hug and a kiss on the cheek. He was prepared with a Sharpie to sign just about anything that was placed before him. I had brought a few copies of the magazine where I was on the front cover in my CCC cycling jersey. I gave one to Phyllis and one to Lance. He reflexively picked up the Sharpie and started to sign it. I said to him, "No, that's for you to keep. It's just a little light reading for the bathroom." He grinned at me and accepted the magazine.

In the hotel lobby, we had a glorious reunion. Seeing all the cyclists we had met either online or at the summit was very heartwarming and uplifting. As more arrived, there were an increasing number of names that we were now able to match with faces. Scott Joy from New Hampshire; Steve Bartolucci from Thousand Oaks, California; Jim Owens from Minnesota; and Jerry and Angie Kelly, the couple we had met in Paris. Chris States from San Francisco, and Chris Brewer, Bryan Head, Fred Drewe, Chris Hornbeak and Will Swetnam, all from Texas, and so many more were in attendance. Working in the bike mechanics area, much to my surprise was Jose Alcala, a longtime friend from many years of bike camp in Florida.

The Saturday morning after our arrival, Will Swetnam and Chris Brewer had arranged a bike ride into the hills surrounding Austin past the Bee Cave. I was not sure what the Bee Cave was, other than a landmark outside of Austin, but we rode past it and had no problem with bees. Again, I was just happy to be riding, not sure what to expect with this group because I had only read their posts online.

The hills were reminiscent of the Tour of Texas stage races. The climbs were very long, surrounded by rock and cactus, with equally long descents. Chris Brewer, our tour guide, was very skilled at keeping the diverse group together after the climbs. Having been a coach and ride leader myself for many years, I appreciated his task. During this time I recognized that Chris States and I rode at a similar rhythm and pace. We also kept finding ourselves riding together on the climbs. He was just as happy as I was to be there, on our bikes, sharing the sun, life, and the road.

The main ride the following morning required everyone to get up before the sun rose. In the darkness of the morning, a very unwelcome cold rain fell while we gathered at the buses with our bikes. The light reflected off the wet pavement as the bikes were loaded and secured with blankets in the cargo hold beneath the buses. We filed onto the bus for the long ride to the start of the Ride for the Roses, still optimistic that this was going to be wonderful, no matter the conditions, because we were thousands of people coming together to support cancer survival.

Reaching our destination, we collected our bikes and assembled at the start. We tried our best to collect all the CCC'rs we could find to take a group photo. People planned to ride the distance that was most likely to fit their skills and condition, however, our particular group of survivors wanted to start off together because we had become family. This was perhaps the one time of the year we could be together, but might also be the last time we would see one another again.

Lance appeared at the starting area and gave a speech projected on large overhead screens for all to see. He led out the start of the ride and everyone jumped to catch up with him. It was raining and the water splashed up from the surrounding wheels into our faces and up our backsides.

Regardless of the rain, I still felt a great sense of joy in my heart. Before long the group had thinned and I found myself once again riding with Chris States. His pace and style, very strong and smooth, made him a good riding partner. It was as though we had been riding together for most of our lives.

When we came to a fork in the road where the ride distances separated, Chris pointed out that Lance was just ahead of us and was taking the same route that we were. So we worked together and bridged the gap up to his group of about fifteen riders.

Sitting in the peloton felt very natural. From my years of racing, I was very accustomed to sitting on wheels and enjoying the luxury of a good draft. Again, joy bubbled up so much that I started to sing to myself and it was a complete shock when I looked down to see that we were going 30 MPH. I felt perfectly comfortable sitting in this peloton, the French term relating to the main group of riders in a bike race.

Chris seemed to know everyone in the pack. I'm not sure if he knew them by their jerseys or had memorized their statistics from races, but he easily pointed out that the rider to my diagonal right was Lance and just next to him was Jake. He was the smooth, strong rider who I had been drafting most often and I had no problem sitting on his wheel. Chris was very excited that I was doing this. I probably should have known who he was, but I didn't recognize him. He looked like all the other pro riders in the group, same cycling jersey and shorts, same helmet and sunglasses. Even though I had been riding behind him for several miles, all I could really see was his back side. I must confess that it wasn't a bad view at all. The name Jake was not familiar to me from any of Lance's team rosters, but then I wasn't very good with names.

Later, after the ride was completed, I heard that the actor, Jake Gyllenhaal was preparing for an acting role potentially portraying Lance in a movie. He was the "Jake" in the group that I had been following, and he rode very well.

In the peloton, Lance was telling jokes and laughing, completely in his element. He was even pointing out snakes on the side of the road. He seemed happy and content where he rode in the field, but it wasn't too long before the pace started to pick up, as the route got hillier. In one area the field of riders stretched out and I found myself riding next to him. He looked over at me, realizing I was the only woman in the group, and asked, "Are we going fast enough for you? Are we holding you back?" I laughed and told him I was, "Just fine, thank you." Then he inquired, "Is that the same bike that is in the magazine? You know I hate that bike!" I was surprised that he had even looked at the magazine, let alone remembered me and my bike.

He said he read it the night before. I was even more impressed when told me he noticed that my bike was the same model, an Orbea Starship team issue from Spain, that had passed him in the Pyrenees and that was why he didn't like it. I had to laugh because Ken had procured this bike from team Euskaltel, from the Basque region of Spain that competed in the Tour de France. They were extraordinary mountain climbers and Iban Mayo rode a bike just like mine to beat Lance in the Pyrenees stage of the Tour one year.

I started to look around for my friend Chris States and saw that he was struggling at the back of the pack. So I sat up and drifted back to where he was. He was a two-time cancer survivor and because of his cancer, he had only half of his lung capacity. He was an astounding survivor and an amazing friend. The choice had been clear; I was there to ride with him.

We agreed to relax a bit and let Lance's pack ride off into the distance. As we were riding and sharing our experience, we noticed a man ahead on the right with the wheel removed from his bike. He stood there with wheel in hand, looking at it. Chris knew who he was immediately. I swear he should work for the CIA as he can recognize anyone in cycling clothing. He said, "That's Och!" a name that rhymes with coach. His real name was Jim Ochowicz and he had been the team manager for the Motorola team when Lance was racing for them in the Tour de France. Och was also the son-in-law of Clair Young, my team manager, when I raced in the Tour of Texas. It truly is a small world when you ride a bike, especially in events like this.

When we stopped to help him, I looked at the tire and discovered that he had, in his haste, placed the inner tube on the wrong side of the tire that was on the rim. I went ahead and changed the tire for him. Jim thanked us for stopping to help and offered to pull us back up to the group. When we got back on the road, he went into time trial mode. I sat on his steady wheel; his very strong legs, accentuated by well sculpted calf muscles, pumping like pistons. He may not have known how to change a tire, but he sure knew how to ride a bike.

After a while, sitting in Och's draft, I could see that Chris was having difficulty hanging on. He hadn't had a great amount of time to train and he was having trouble breathing. I realized that I needed to decide whether to keep riding at this pace or hang back with Chris. He told me to go ahead and ride with Jim because he didn't want to hold me back. However, from my perspective, I came to ride with my CCC brothers, so I thanked Jim for the draft and told him that I was going to sit up and ride in with Chris. I have never regretted my decision for a moment. Chris continues to be a great rider and an even better friend.

When we approached the finish I wanted us to ride across together in celebration. I knew that Chris was very experienced and could ride his bike without using his hands, so I reached over and grabbed Chris's hand and we held them up together in victory as we crossed the finish line. We shared a great feeling of unity and celebration, as if we were a team and had won that race together. Determined to reclaim our lives from cancer, we celebrated the joy of that moment. Members of the CCC team were standing at the finish waiting and ready to hand each of us a yellow rose, a tribute which only survivors received as a memento of this very special time together.

Participating in the Ride for the Roses did not satisfy my hunger to meet more survivors, but it definitely intensified my desire to bring them all together. Therefore, in the spring of 2007 I planned to host a bike camp for CCC'rs out of my home. I sent an invitation out to the group for any of them who wanted to stay with us in Indianapolis, where we could coach them for a three-day weekend. I was delighted when we had an excellent group who responded.

Phyllis O'Grady came and brought Kathleen Carrico with her. Kathleen was a metastatic breast cancer survivor who lived in the Denver area near Phyllis and part of Kathleen's bucket list was to ride to the top of every peak in the Rocky Mountains. Our group continued to grow as Dennis DeAtley from Texas, Mike Terry from Arkansas, Mary Trufant from Alabama and David Mitchell and his lovely wife Anne, from Pittsburgh joined us. We had local riders as well, including Tom DeBaun from Shelbyville, Sue Nuyda, Gary Schmitt and Marta Diaz from Indianapolis.

When everyone gathered at our house, very few introductions needed to be made. It lifted my spirit to see them milling about with an excitement that was infectious. In the past, the only time that members of the CCC came together were for LiveStrong fundraiser events and those were often very brief encounters.

I believed that our three-day camp would not only help improve riding skills, but provide a lot more quality time to share our lives and discuss our experiences in an intimate environment with no time limitations. Everyone bonded the moment they met. Of all the training camps I have coached in my life, I had never seen that many people with such positive outlooks, open minds and hearts come together as a team so instantly.

I never had to worry about entertaining them. We spent every spare moment sharing some part of our lives. David and Ann Mitchell, both survivors, were the sweetest couple you could ever hope to meet and their love for one another was obvious as we watched them interact. Mike Terry, a stage four kidney cancer survivor, was a strong advocate with an inspiring story to share, along with a heartfelt hug or two. He had gone through so much and it was a miracle that he was able to be with us at all. He never lost his warm smile and sparkling attitude toward life.

Riding with the group was an absolute joy. It was almost like all my favorite cousins had come to visit and play in my backyard.

Mary Trufant was a kindred spirit and shared my love of life and riding. We had an awesome time sprinting, chasing people down, and riding in rotating pacelines. I would love to have been able to train with her on a regular basis, had she lived closer.

Several years ago at the Hilly Hundred, I purchased a pink bike saddle that had an embroidered ribbon on it. We kept that saddle a few years before Ken crafted a bike around it. When he did, Ken built a perfect pink fixed gear bike with brakes. It was my new commuter bike to ride to work. "Pink" pretty much sums up the first impression people get when they see the bike; pink wheels, chain, chain rings, pedals, brakes, and handlebar tape all on a pink frame.

Because we live in Indianapolis, there are several places around town that paint race cars. Ken had taken the frame to one of those places and told them he wanted the frame painted the color of Pepto-Bismol. They asked why he wanted it that color and he told them his wife was a breast cancer survivor and he wanted to give her a pink bike. They said, "Oh, you don't want Pepto pink; you want Komen pink." He found out that they had painted the Komen Indy Race Car for the Indianapolis 500. When he presented the bike to me, I was tickled pink.

Mary is the founder of a fundraising bike ride in Bay Minette, Alabama. She had lost both of her parents and some very close friends to cancer. "I'm finished watching cancer take my family and friends away from me," she explained, "So I started this ride." It is called Ride Yellow and has become quite successful. Every year she donates a large portion of the funds to the LiveStrong Foundation and another portion to a children's camp and a local hospital. After she test rode my pink bike she asked Ken if he could build her an all yellow bike and he did.

Our camp happened to be scheduled the same weekend that Indiana had a huge community ride called the "Nite Ride." Five thousand of Indiana's cycling community gather annually and start the event at Major Taylor Velodrome. I had the pleasure of taking my CCC bike camp friends on a tour of the Velodrome and where we watched the races from the infield. I introduced them to both Abby and Brooke between their races. After racing ended at 11:00 pm., fireworks were launched into the night sky, and the huge parade of bikes adorned with glowing lights flooded the downtown streets with a police escort. We visited all the Indianapolis downtown landmarks before returning to the track, where Mary and Dave had their first 'on the track' experience. Sharing my love for the Velodrome with them and seeing them embrace the track made my heart feel like it was glowing. What could be better than sharing the things you love with people that you love?

*   *   *

A month after the CCC Camp, my mother came to visit. One evening after Madison had gone to bed; Mom invited me into her room and closed the door. "You know, Madison is twelve years old now. Have you had the sex talk with her yet?" She asked. I was a bit stunned. I wasn't expecting her to ask that question for some reason. "Uh…… No. She has had a lot of health classes at school and they have gone into detail regarding the anatomy, I have seen the curriculum." I replied. "I think you need to talk to her about the details that school missed." she responded. "I don't know." I stalled, "If you aren't comfortable talking to her, can I?" she piped up quickly. "Really, you want to have this talk with her?" I asked. "Definitely, I would be very happy to talk to her if you don't mind." Mom assured me. Then she proceeded to let me know that she had already prepared for the discussion, having gone to a Planned Parenthood clinic and picked up pamphlets and other visual aids.

I was still amazed, and a little amused that Mom was that enthusiastic about the opportunity. When I walked into my bedroom, shaking my head and suppressing a grin, Ken had already gone to bed but was not yet asleep. "What's up?" he asked, obviously noticing that I was chuckling to myself. "You will never believe what mom has volunteered to do." I said. "She wants to give Madison the 'SEX talk' and she brought props." His eyebrows went up.

The next day, Mom, Madison and I went shopping. As I was looking through the clothing racks, Madison popped her head out between the hanging blouses as if she were parting curtains. "Mom!" she whispered angrily, "I can't believe you said it would be okay for Nana to give me the talk!" "Well, you are twelve years old now and she felt it was time." I answered. "I didn't need her to talk to me; I've had it all in school." She argued. "Well, there are some details that may not have been covered in school that you should know. Do you want to hear them from Nana OR from me?" I offered. "This is so embarrassing!" she said as she rolled her eyes. "Who then?" I asked. "You!" she resigned.

Later that evening I was driving Madison to her best friend Kaitlyn's house. I thought that this time together might be a good opportunity to tackle the task at hand. It was just the two of us, no concern that anyone would overhear our discussion, and she couldn't run away. "Madison, I think this would be a good time to have that 'talk' you have been avoiding." I started. "Mom!" she exclaimed. "It's not what you think. I'm not going to talk about anatomy or how things work. You've already gotten all that in school." I said, glancing over to see her expression. "I'm going to talk to you more about how boys see sex." I had her attention. "This is not like anything you have heard before, but I want you to understand their perspective."

"Boys in high school look at sex like bumper cars at a carnival." I began. Her facial expression was screaming "My mother is nuts." But I continued anyway. "They want to bump into as many other bumper cars as they can. And they want to bump into them as much as they possibly can, without regard for anyone else's enjoyment or safety." "Really MOM?" She scoffed. I continued, "Then in college, boys are more like 'Speed Racer'. They want to go as fast and as far as they can." I paused to give her time to digest my analogy. "You need to wait. Wait for the guy who wants to go for a long, slow drive through the country, taking his time and making sure that everyone in the car is having a good time. AND he wears a seatbelt."

She burst, "Mom! Are you serious?" "Yes, I am. And that concludes my version of the sex talk. See, it wasn't as bad as you thought." I finished. "I will never be able to watch 'Speed Racer' without laughing now. You've ruined it for me," she laughed as we reached our destination. When I picked her up later she was in good spirits. "Did you have a good time?" I asked. "Yeah." she said. "I told Kaitlyn about 'Speed Racer' and she about died." I loved the fact that she shared the analogy. It assured me that she had gotten the message.

*   *   *

Jan Frandsen lives in Cleveland, Ohio, and is not only a palliative care Nurse Practitioner for the Cleveland Clinic, but also an extraordinary CCC'r. He nominated me as an honorary survivor for the Pan Ohio Hope Ride. Founded by the American Cancer Society of Ohio, it was to take place in early August 2007 and had been designed to connect two excellent facilities across the state, the Cleveland Hope Lodge and the Cincinnati Hope Lodge.

These American Cancer Society facilities were created to offer survivors and their caregivers a place to stay throughout cancer treatment, without charge. For the families forced to travel great distances for quality treatment, they provide a comfortable place to stay without the additional stress of accumulating debt. This helps with the many financial burdens that accompany cancer treatment. The Hope Lodges were more than a place to rest during the day and sleep at night; they were a refuge, free from scrutiny by those who did not know cancer or how to deal with it.

These were shelters where patients could feel free to let their hair down without eyes being cast upon them that would quickly dart away. Here they were free from pity or curiosity and could feel comfortable and supported while dealing with the side effects of treatment, including the emotional impact this disease has on patient and family alike.

The Hope Lodge in Cleveland was a new facility and Jan and I were given a tour to see how inviting it was. Each patient accompanied by a caregiver, had their own private room appropriately furnished. There was a common dining area for patients and family members where they could bring in food and cook in the kitchen. This was created to help facilitate social interaction between patients. The library was stocked with a multitude of books regarding cancer and survival, but also included an assortment of best-selling books to help entertain and distract.

When we stepped outside into the garden behind the building, we were greeted by a beautifully landscaped green space, complete with a barbecue grill and arbor that created a Zen Scape in the middle of the city that surrounded each hospital. It was a secret garden escape where one could relax, enjoy the living flora and fauna, and be removed from the sterility of clinical environments as well as the harsh reality of cancer treatment.

The Pan Ohio Hope ride started in the dark early hours of the morning. There was still a chill in the air as riders arrived and prepared their bikes for the long journey ahead. The start was in a lush park on top of a very steep hill, so the beginning of the multi-day event had a real kick with a screaming fast downhill start. John Anderson, a close personal friend of Jan's, was there giving his support to this event. John was a local sports broadcasting celebrity, who won my heart when he traded his microphone for a bike at the beginning of the ride. I was very proud to be standing at the start of the adventure with Jan, John, Madison and Ken and all of my new friends preparing to start the ride. This was the first time for this event, so it was uncharted territory.

There was a news helicopter hovering overhead to follow us as we descended quickly through the Cuyahoga Park. Next we entered the towpath leading out of Cleveland. This particular surface was not the best with my high pressure racing tires but I stifled my complaints. There was a lot of road shock riding over the crushed limestone that caused loss of traction and efficiency. We eventually left the path and entered the roadway. The road was much more comfortable and we collected again into groups of similar speed and ability.

During the first part of the ride John and Jan were my primary riding companions until we started to get to some large climbs that are common in northeastern Ohio. Starting with a large group has some distinct advantages, as it is much easier to find people who ride the same pace. We could alternate the work of pulling into the wind and getting rest along the way. This technique is not quite as effective when there are a number of large hills to climb, as was the case on that day. People attacked the hills at different paces and comfort levels and riders got strung out, resulting in a lot of solo riding.

The next day started out as hilly as the previous one had finished. Climbing through the hills, one after another, wore on a lot of the riders. Finally, the terrain started to level out as we drew ever closer to Columbus. That was the day we were joined by Brooke Crum, the young junior woman I had coached on the track. It was delightful to have Brooke with me, as she was not only a strong and competent rider; she was a good friend with a great attitude which made the ride even more special.

There had been a huge storm the night before and the ground and pavement were still wet when we rode through the Amish countryside. The route turned from open roads to a bike path that was frequented by the Amish horse drawn buggies. It was nice to have a path that we could use, but it was not so nice to have wet horse manure splatter and speckle us from head to toe as it shot up, thrown by our tires from the pavement.

This situation would have been miserable had we been alone, but as the saying goes, "misery loves company," and we shared the experience with some really great people who had a sense of adventure and fortunately, a sense of humor. We decided to leave the sense of smell out of the discussion altogether.

Brooke and I found ourselves riding with a couple of skilled riders who were moving at the perfect pace for us. We met them before we got to the horse traveled path and trusted their skills enough to invite them to join us in a rotating pace line. They were unfamiliar with the technique, so we taught them how to rotate and they caught on quickly and appreciated their ride all the more. We traveled like clockwork down the roads, chatting and joking as the miles flew by.

Along the path, at the designated rest area, Ken and Madison were waiting. Here we had our lunch stop and took the opportunity to clean up some of the horse splatter. They joined us for a brief time, riding together on the tandem. I was so happy to be riding with my family, even if it was not for very long. I wanted them to share the experience and the joy I felt while riding.

The following day, we entered central Ohio, where the terrain was much more hospitable as far as hills were concerned since the roads had flattened considerably.

The gentleman that Brooke and I had ridden with the day before eagerly approached me after breakfast. They had shared the joy of the previous day's ride with others who wanted to join us along with Jan to ride in a rotating paceline on the flat roads. This was my favorite part, not necessarily because it was flat, but because we were working so well together in a large group of about 15 riders. It was obvious that they loved it too, as the group joked and laughed as we rode along with a real sense of camaraderie.

Jan seemed to be having a fantastic ride and every time he came to the front of the line he picked up the pace a bit and I had to remind him to slow down after he finished his pull on the front. I didn't yell at him like Mike Walden had yelled at me when I had made the same mistake. The correct etiquette in a rotating paceline is to pull off from the working line into the resting line right away and rest, not continue at the same pace they had in the working line. All riders were supposed to keep the pace steady, even when they came to the front. So when Jan rode off the front I had to ride up to him and put my hand on his jersey then gently pull him back in an effort to slow him down. The first few times he did this I said "Hey there happy feet, not so fast." That day Jan earned the nickname of "Happy Feet."

Part of the joy of riding in a rotating pace line is the opportunity it gives to access more people while working together in a synchronized, mutually beneficial group. Because of the frequent rests during the rotation, we all rode faster and longer than a lone rider normally could. Riding with the group was so enjoyable that I was disappointed when it was over. When we reached our end destination for the day in Yellow Springs, we joked that we should go back and ride it again.

The final day of the ride stretched from Yellow Springs to Cincinnati. Most of the route was bike path and we encountered more and more local riders who were not part of our group as we approached our final destination. When we exited the bike path we were faced with many climbs through the hills of Cincinnati to get out of the valley and up to the Hope

Lodge. I realized that this difficult uphill somehow symbolized our struggle through treatment and the lodge was the rest and relief at the end of our journey.

My parents live in southwestern Ohio and my father, being a member of the Hamilton County Sheriff's Department Pipe and Drum Corps, had arranged to have the band, clad in kilts, welcome us to Cincinnati when we all arrived. They stood on the street in formation outside the Lodge, playing to welcome the weary riders. Three of the officers playing the bagpipes were cancer survivor themselves. Having them stand there in uniform jackets and kilts, with the soulful sound of the bagpipes floating in the air and reflecting off the brick buildings, made this a very special finish to our more than 300 mile journey.

*   *   *

Early in the summer of 2007, I won the Omnium Track Nationals on the same track where I had my first victory after my treatment in 2004. Later, individual track nationals were to be held in Trexlertown, Pennsylvania and they started on the Monday after the LiveStrong ride in Philadelphia. I had been training all summer and felt very prepared.

We traveled to Philadelphia a few days early so that we could meet the other CCC team members who were riding the LiveStrong Challenge. Scott Joy and Mary Trufant were a few of the first riders we ran into at the host hotel. Once we collect the team, we invaded a local restaurant to carb load for dinner. The next morning we awoke to rain soaked streets. As tempted as I was to join my fellow cancer warriors/riders to show our unity, I knew that doing so would interfere with my preparation for Nationals the next day. I wrestled with all the options and decided to try to have some of my cake and eat it too, but it would have to be a little nibble.

We rode into the LiveStrong Village to discover the easily identifiable yellow CCC jerseys gathering for photos. We joined them, having decided to ride the short loop at an easy pace just as a warm-up for the days of racing ahead. The wet roads glimmered as they reflected the lights around the starting gate and the team huddled together in a huge mass waiting for the start.

As soon as the speeches ended, there was a surge forward and we heard the popping and clicking sounds of hundreds of cleats snapping into the pedals. An immediate wild rush of bikes darted off the start. I hadn't expected such a violent start right out of the gate, since many of the riders rushing the pace were going to be riding one hundred miles of very hilly terrain that day. We suspected that the riders were trying to catch Lance since they rode with wild abandon to reach him after his rocket like start. The hills and roads on the route, still damp, proved more challenging than many could handle and we saw a number of casualties alongside the road with tangled bikes and fresh evidence of road rash.

Rider survival instinct set in and I once again sought the comfortable wheel of a steady cyclist. This time it was the wheel of Branan Cooper a CCC'r from Delaware who was there because of his father's cancer. He rode with a strong, smooth wheel and a cadence that reminded me of Chris States. His draft just beckoned me to sit in and enjoy the ride. My racing instincts were hard to ignore and I wanted to be able to go the full distance with him, but my higher brain kicked in and reason dictated that I turn off at the first course divide. The turn off came at the bottom of a hill, so I didn't even get to say goodbye to the wheel that promised such a confident ride. The day was reserved as a warm-up ride only, not a 100 mile challenge. I stood for a few moments watching the constant throng of riders pass by on the downhill as I searched for the familiar yellow team jerseys of the CCC riders and waved and cheered for them as they passed by us on the descent.

We drove to Trexlertown, where Ken and I went our separate ways. Ken was once again working as an official, so I hung out with the other riders from Indianapolis. I had ordered a special skin suit to represent the CCC at Nationals and thought it would be a tribute to my fellow cancer survivors to wear on the podium. But first I had to make it to the podium.

I had been training with Ken Nowakowski all summer in Indianapolis and he was there supporting his riders. David Mitchel, who had attended our CCC bike camp earlier in the year and ridden the Velodrome in Indy during the Nite Ride, drove in from Pittsburgh to cheer for me. He had never seen a bike Nationals before and I was able to get him into the infield with my coach's pass. He was very excited and seemed to be living in the moment.

Tall and lanky, with thick white hair crowning his head are the things one might first notice about Dave, combined with his soft blue eyes peering out into the world and a quiet voice that spoke no malice. The genuine heart of a puppy beat within his chest and he had the hands and feet to go with it. His personality filled any room he entered with joy and compassion and you would never, for a moment, imagine that he was fighting metastatic prostate cancer and going through some very wicked treatments. He was the perfect person to share the experience with at the track that day.

I was registered to compete in two events at this National Championships. Each race had its own medal event. This helped cater to the racers who specialize in specific events. I was competing against the World Champion in the 500 meters.

There was absolutely no chance whatsoever that I would false start this time. I focused on the beeps and not the clicking of the start clock. My start was excellent and the race was good. I put everything I had into the pedals. I was happy with my result and felt very confident until my race time was surpassed by 1/100th of a second. It was extremely close. I had been celebrating inside until the moment I realized that the color of my medal had been changed by a fraction of a second. It reminded me of the old adage, "Every second counts." and in my case that included micro-seconds.

Most people might think that I would be greatly disappointed, but much to my surprise, I only felt a little let down. I knew what disappointment in racing felt like. The previous year I felt crushed because of disqualification due to of my own stupidity. In this race I had performed to the best of my ability, but someone else finished a bit faster than I did. Sitting up and smiling to myself, I thought, "Good for her."

Many people know that I am a very competitive person, but they don't always realize that my drive and competitive spirit come from within. I am the most critical of and competitive with myself, I am my own greatest athletic opponent. To reach a new personal record means a victory. Therefore, knowing that I had done everything possible to win that day was good enough for me.

Since my diagnosis, I have realized that cancer is a part of me and will always be there, if only in my thoughts and fears. It shares my DNA and feeds off what I do. The greatest victory and defeat is the competition within, on all levels. The challenge to overcome doubt, fear, disappointment and complacency is paramount in my life.

That day, the real win did not come with a medal; it was the knowledge that I was there racing at the top of my game and privileged to share it with a very special friend. I was so happy that Dave could be there to see it all. There was a CCC jersey on the podium representing all my brothers and sisters who were or had been fighting cancer. The fact that I was able to wake up that morning and see the sun rise on the Velodrome was a glorious victory indeed.

*   *   *

One morning while Ken was preparing to take a shower, he removed his shirt and I noticed a small dark spot in the middle of his lower back. It caught my attention and pulled on my nursing experience. The more I looked at it, the more I was convinced that he needed to have it looked at by a doctor.

Every time I saw the angry dark shape it taunted me and I continued telling Ken that I didn't like the way it looked. After I could no longer take the uncertainty, I convinced him to get a referral to see a dermatologist. Distressingly it took over three months to get an appointment. That was after I had repeatedly called the referral coordinator to press for one. This was when I realized that I was obviously my mother's daughter; following my instincts that this was *something* and it had to be evaluated.

I was in the exam room with him when the dermatologist looked at his back. He turned on the table to show her his back and in an instant her gaze was captured. "Mr. Hart, do you mind if I take a photo of this and have my residents come in and look at it as well?" she asked as she continued to stare at the dark possessor of my attention for those many months. I knew this was not a good sign.

She left and returned with a camera and four residents. They all gathered around as she presented Ken's back to them. "This is a classic example of melanoma. It fits the ABC's of melanoma perfectly. Of course we will have to wait for the biopsy results before we can proceed with treatment." Her words bounced off my resolve. Even though I believe I already knew, hearing the words I hoped she would not say tightened my stomach with fear and dread.

Ken was immediately scheduled for an excisional biopsy. I was unprepared for this completely different side of cancer. He was the love of my life and had been my rock and now I felt completely helpless. The panic side of cancer hit me and I thought, "What can I do?" Most people feel the same when a family member is threatened with some form of life altering disease. I could handle it when it was me, but not someone I loved.

Ken once again appeared to be unscathed by this potential life alteration. He showed no sign of concern or worry. I battled internally, wondering if I should even ask him how he felt because I didn't necessarily like it when people had asked me that same question. I knew they were just concerned, but even their very kind and sympathetic voices asking, "How are you?" seemed to echo in my mind as, "You poor thing. I pity you." I needed to know exactly what we were dealing with.

"Was this how Ken felt when I had been diagnosed?" I wondered. Now I totally understood why my mother had said so many times during my cancer battle that she would gladly change places with me if only she could. That was exactly how I felt about Ken. I was already scarred and damaged, why him too? I can imagine how angry and helpless so many mothers feel when their children are diagnosed with cancer. This was likely even more difficult than being the actual patient.

The biopsy was done in the office and I asked to stay in the room while it was conducted. I wanted to be standing at Ken's head, supporting him, so he would know I was there for him no matter what. His doctor was reluctant to let me stay. "I can't tell you how many times we have allowed family members to stay and they have fainted. I don't want to have to pick you up off the floor. He is my patient and you are not," she firmly stated. "I am a registered nurse and can handle it." I assured her, but she was still reluctant. "Even if you are, it is different when it is family.

Sometimes seeing a family member sliced open can create a different reaction, even in trained professionals." She explained. I promised her I would be fine and would leave if I noticed the slightest inkling of lightheadedness, so she finally agreed to let me stay.

She numbed the site with a few injections, then with scalpel in hand, removed a patch of skin in the shape of a small football and the size of a large lemon. I was surprised at just how much she removed for a spot not much larger than a pencil eraser. I stood by Ken's side trying to distract and comfort him and neither of us had any problems at all tolerating the procedure.

When the results came back it was positive for malignant melanoma. Ken was now officially a cancer survivor too. The good news was that it was in-situ which meant that it had not spread beyond the margins of the biopsy. He did not require any other treatment, chemotherapy, radiation or further surgery. She said it was very close to the margin and if we had waited any longer the situation would have been different.

Great relief swept over me followed by a burning pressure in my chest. I had to excuse myself and I went to the restroom, locked the door and let open the floodgates of emotion. It was a combination of relief that Ken had escaped a deadly form of skin cancer and anger that cancer had once again threatened to wreak havoc in our lives.

This intensified my desire to deal with this thief that quietly sneaks into lives and steals security, dignity and potentially life itself. This invader needed to be called out with wanted posters and alerts displayed like those found on post office walls, identifying it by name, photo and description. If people could recognize cancer, they would lock their doors, get alarm systems installed, create neighborhood watches, and protect themselves from its treachery.

I am a nurse and educated regarding the ABC's of melanoma, but what if I had not been. Ken could have died within five years if that spot had been left alone and allowed to spread throughout his body. His doctor told us that his cancer was a narrow margin, just 0.1 millimeters away from entering his lymphatic system when she biopsied it. If I hadn't been so persistent regarding getting an appointment when we did, he would have had to go through miserable chemotherapy as well.

Ken is fair skinned and as a teenager, he worked as a lifeguard, spending long summers at the pool, in an era when a sunscreen SPF level of eight was considered more than adequate protection. As a young adult, he visited a few tanning booths to prepare for bike camp with the theory that a base tan might protect him from burning when he rode many miles each day under the piercing sun in Florida.

We now have a red haired daughter with alabaster skin. She did not understand why I totally blew up when she once came home from a pool party sunburned. I told her that I was angry because I had trusted her to have enough sense to take care of the largest organ of her body and she failed. So I grounded her for negligence. Some might consider this out of line and excessive, but I knew I had to get my point across. How many people realize that just one serious sunburn during childhood might end a life in the future, often long before old age. Tanning for vanity is unacceptable and everyone should know that as well. A tan is temporary, but the risk to health and life is permanent.

* * *

Earlier in the summer Ken and I attended a training camp for Team USA at Vanderbilt in Nashville in preparation for the summer games in Shanghai, China. It was there that we met our cyclists for the first time. Two of them were deaf, which was no problem for us, as Ken's mother had been deaf and we were comfortable with sign language.

As would be expected with any large group, there were a lot of "hurry up and wait" episodes. During one occasion when we were waiting for a bus I saw the opportunity to entertain our riders and designate sign names to each athlete. These names are often the first letter of the person's name combined with a gesture that describes a physical attribute or an interest in some way. To help teach them everyone's sign name I created a game where we would sit in a circle and sign our own name and then someone else's name. Once you recognize your name, it is then your turn to sign names back. It was like tossing an invisible ball around from person to person. The team LOVED the game and would play it for hours afterward. Anytime we had to wait for something they played the sign name game.

In September of 2007, we were slated to go to China for the Special Olympics Summer Games. Special Olympics Indiana had arranged a send off celebration for their representatives to the world games. The day before we were to depart for Los Angeles we were all gathered at a hotel and taken by limo to the NCAA Hall of Fame in downtown Indianapolis. Members of the Colts football team and a few cheerleaders joined us there. We toured the Hall of Fame, met with reporters then walked to dinner nearby at Don Shula's steakhouse where we were fed an outstanding meal with steak that seemed to melt as soon as it entered my mouth. It was one of those moments to stop and enjoy the flavor and the company. The next morning we boarded a plane from Indianapolis to Los Angeles. Once we arrived, our Indiana group joined the athletes and coaches from other states and we were divided by sport.

When the cycling team came together, I was surprised to be greeted with the sign game by the riders. They signed with such joy and affection that my heart was full of pride to see them enjoying each other and the game without prompting. That evening Team USA had a send off celebration with Peter Carruthers, the 1984 Olympic pairs figure skater who was our Master of Ceremonies. It was a spectacular presentation with a special address from President George W. Bush. Everyone got very pumped up and excited, only to be sent to bed and awakened at 3:00 am to board a bus that would transport us to the airport where we would board the plane to China, via Alaska.

As head coach of the cycling team, not only did I have to make sure all the athletes were safe and appropriately cared for, I had to make sure all their equipment made it to our destination. I did not get to see the bikes or packages containing our uniforms in Los Angeles. This was a constant nagging concern, especially when someone reported seeing one of the bike boxes and described it as having "a gaping hole in it."

Our flight to Alaska was an adventure in itself. Flying in a huge plane with Special Olympians is not like any normal flight you will ever take. Upon boarding, excited chatter filled the plane as we awaited takeoff. Then the athletes led a group count down until the wheels lifted up, and finally cheers and applause erupted with hands in the air as if they were riding a roller coaster during lift off. The flight crew was all smiles and couldn't help but adopt some of the athletes' enthusiasm.

We stopped in Anchorage to refuel and pick up the Alaskan delegates. Flying over Alaska and looking out the window was special for me, as I had never been there before and seeing the glaciers from above reminded me of how much life I had yet to experience. The landscape below was expansive and I was moved by the magnificent beauty the earth had to offer. After my diagnosis, I never expected to have the opportunity to see the glacier scarred terrain and it made me appreciate the gift of that moment and my life even more.

We all arrived in Shanghai exhausted, but very excited. There was so much to see and take in. Going through customs, I breathed a sigh of relief to see that our bikes had all arrived, along with packages containing the uniforms and donated Clif energy bars.

A long series of buses sat waiting for us at the terminal. Team USA had over 400 delegates and we were excited to see other nations arriving at the airport at the same time. The roads along the route to Shanghai were lined with flags and billboards announcing the Special Olympics World games and welcoming us at every turn. As the buses meandered through the streets of Shanghai, Ken and I were totally intrigued by the Chinese bike riders along the way, riding strong, heavy bikes often transporting an additional passenger or two or some sort of oversized cargo. At times the height and width of their cargo was overwhelming and it was hard to believe someone would even consider attempting to carry such a load on a bicycle. Bikes were not recreational here, but simply a way of life.

We arrived at our host hotel in the Pu Dong District of Shanghai. It was a Five-Star hotel and we were not the only nation staying there. It was filled, but there were only three elevators for fifteen floors of guests and the elevators were quite quirky. During busy hours they had operators that, we soon learned, would skip floors when the elevator was full. So you might find yourself waiting over fifteen minutes, if you were lucky, for an elevator to stop on your floor. One might think, like I did, that to save time you could take the stairs. In this situation, it was not a good solution, as the stairs had no access between the fourth floor and the lobby.

As head coach, I was assigned a fantastic suite. It was a corner room with a view of all the surrounding buildings. The room was big enough that we were able to use it for our cycling team meetings. There was a national holiday in China while we were there and we saw fireworks every night at the host town and they became part of the great view from my room.

We had to adjust to more than the time change and language. Even though we were staying in a five-star hotel, the tap water was still not suitable to drink and we had to train ourselves not to use water from the sink. If anyone accidentally rinsed their toothbrush in the running water, then put it into their mouth, they regretted it in the bathroom soon thereafter. Many of the athletes were finding it difficult to handle the water situation. So much so that I ran out of the Pepto-Bismol I had brought and had to venture out to find a drug store.

Drug stores in China are just that, drug stores and nothing else. After a long search I found a tiny pharmacy the size of a small bedroom. Every drug was on a shelf behind the counter, tended by workers clad in white lab coats. The medications were all in identical white boxes bearing only Chinese writing, so I had to figure out how to say, "Diarrhea" in Chinese. Even though I had tried to study Chinese before the trip, I didn't know how to say diarrhea, so I had to pantomime what I thought they would understand, which must have been very entertaining to any casual observer.

After looking through several packages, I discovered some small chewable tablets that were yellow with black flecks and the box had the word, "Bismuth" written on it. This had to be it. It was similar in size and displayed the primary ingredient in Pepto Bismol, so I purchased a box and took it back to some of my athletes that were having a rough time.

Brandan stood over six feet tall, was fair haired with blue eyes and weighed over 300 pounds and was very quiet, mild mannered and polite. I came to him first with the medication, as he seemed to be feeling the most miserable. I gave him two of the chewable tablets and he popped them into his mouth and started chewing. He then made a face and expressed that they tasted bad. Like a good substitute mom, I took one to prove to him that they were ok.

As soon as I bit into the tablet the taste hit my tongue. It was HOR-RIBLE! I immediately spat it out and tried to get any and all remnants of the tablet out of my mouth by pawing at my tongue. Brandan was a real trooper and continued to chew and swallow his. They appeared to work and he did feel better, but I can attest to the fact that they were very nasty tasting.

Team USA was grouped by sport to go to our host town experience. The sports of cycling and equestrian were combined and we were transported by bus to the section of town that was to adopt us. It was fun riding through town in motor coaches looking at all the sites and seeing people lining the streets and waving to us as we approached the community. "Welcome, welcome to our city." the children who were waving flowers chanted in rhythmic, well-practiced English.

The formal speeches were given and we were presented with large bouquets of flowers. The Chinese volunteers then split us into even smaller groups and escorted us around the community center where we saw locally created art, musicians playing American folk music like Old Susanna, Chinese opera, calligraphy, paper folding, and folk dancing. We loved everything we saw and very much enjoyed interacting with the local people.

My favorite parts of this experience were getting to practice my Chinese language skills and learning how to write in Chinese. It was a gift in itself to see how surprised and overjoyed our hosts appeared when I tried to communicate in their language. I know I wasn't very good, but I wanted to try. To me it seemed polite, when visiting another country to at least try to learn to speak some of their language.

We were invited into the apartments of our host town families, given tours and shown family photo albums. We learned to make Chinese dumplings and participated in a gift exchange. Each home had someone there to perform music for us and the Mayor of the town came and visited. I gave my host family a USA hat and explained our sign language name game, then gave each of them a sign name. Later on during a big farewell from the host town, I recognized my host family sitting in the audience and they signed to us as we stood on stage. That was very special and their faces lit up when we returned the signs. What a great connection across cultural and language barriers.

After our final evening in host town, we transitioned to opening ceremonies. All of Team USA was loaded on buses according to sport. It was a memorable experience, traveling through heavily trafficked streets with a police escort. In one part of Shanghai there was a huge spiraling exit ramp that circled around and around like a giant elongated slinky. We could see the long, long train of over twenty-five buses for Team USA rolling down the ramps.

Once we arrived at the location for the opening ceremonies, we filed off the buses and lined up in a staging area in preparation for the parade of nations. Anticipation was comparable to waiting to unwrap presents on Christmas. The athletes' excitement escalated even more when someone spotted the basketball player, Yao Ming, surrounded by many Chinese fans, sitting awkwardly in a small golf cart and ducking his head to keep it from hitting the canopy. The celebrity spotting continued as Arnold Schwarzenegger and Maria Shriver walked through the line of Team USA, mingling with the athletes just before our big entrance into the stadium. They cheerfully greeted the athletes, graciously posed for photos and were very hospitable and friendly to everyone they met.

We entered the stadium through a dark hallway and were suddenly greeted by lights, music and cheering from thousands of people coming from every direction. I was honored to enter the stadium holding the hand of Desi, one of my Down's syndrome athletes. She told me that she was afraid of being in big crowds, "Because short people get pushed and sometimes even got lost." She said, looking around at all the Team USA jackets that were taller than she was. Holding her hand as we joined the parade of nations was indeed an honor. To me the best part of the opening ceremonies was not all the fireworks and flashing lights or the dancing and singing, but being able to look into the eyes of this young woman. They sparkled well beyond the reflection in her glasses of the splendor going on around her. It was amazing to see and share that moment of sheer awe that I am sure she will NEVER forget, nor will I.

During our stay in the host town our bikes sat in their cases in the hotel lobby, lined up in an orderly fashion with orange netting thrown over the tops. I had been told that the bikes were supposed to be transported in advance of our arrival to Chongming Island, our competition venue, and mechanics would be there to take care of and assemble them for us so they would be complete when we arrived and we could ride the course in advance of the competition to enable us to make necessary adjustments. We had head coach meetings every evening when we were in host town and each one of the meetings I would ask about our bikes. No one seemed to know any details regarding their plans for the transport and assembly.

On our last day in Shanghai our interpreter asked me to oversee the transport of bikes and packages onto a bus going with us to Chongming Island. At that point, I was greatly concerned that our bikes would not arrive at the venue in time to be properly assembled, not only in time for our practice session, but more importantly in time for the competition the next morning.

Our two buses departed, one with the riders on board and the other loaded with a bike box in each bench seat. We traveled for forty-five minutes before we stopped in front of Olympic Town where everyone was unloaded and I was required to identify each of my athletes before any of them could be assigned a Chinese volunteer. This was the first time that I had heard that they were going to have assigned volunteers. I lined them up in order, as instructed, and each was issued a prison orange painter's cap with a number displayed boldly on the front. The volunteer with the matching number took their assigned charge by the hand and assisted them back onto the bus, as if the athlete was incapable of boarding by themselves.

The athletes who were very interactive prior to the stop now sat quietly with an unknown person sitting next to them. There was an uncomfortable silence hovering over us as we sat waiting for the bus to move. To pass the time and improve communication, I decided to assign all the volunteers sign names so they could play the sign game too.

The interpreter explained the sign names to all the college student volunteers and they appeared to be very enthusiastic to get their sign name. Once that was accomplished, they jumped right in and learned all the names of the athletes and vice versa. Talk about breaking the language barrier. We may have had difficulty pronouncing their Chinese names, but their sign names were very clear and memorable.

Once the buses started to move, we passed a long line of cars waiting for ferry boats. Specific boats were reserved for Special Olympic cyclists so the buses were *fast-passed* to the front of the line. Those carrying athletes from various countries were converging at the same time. It was at that moment I realized we were all literally, in the same boat. No country would arrive any earlier or later than another.

We arrived on the island and were taken directly to the hotel where all the cyclists would be staying: one hundred eighty athletes from forty countries all in a twenty story hotel. Again, there were only three elevators and with all the athletes and volunteers in one hotel the number of people traveling up and down the elevators doubled. We were on the eighth floor, but I must say I felt a bit sorry for the German team that was housed on the seventeenth floor.

The orange shirted volunteers relieved us of our luggage and we were ushered into the dining area for lunch. At that time the athletes realized the volunteer assistants were not just there for the bus ride and luggage, but were leading them around by the hand like children inside the hotel. One of the main goals of Special Olympics is to promote independence and all of my cyclists were adults. For them this was a huge step backwards and they were clearly not happy.

One of my Down's syndrome athletes was heard yelling, "I am thirty-six years old! I am not a baby!" at her volunteer, who of course did not understand, they only heard the yelling. At one point a volunteer could not locate her charge because she had intentionally slipped away to dinner without her escort. When she finally found her assigned charge, safe in the dining hall with the other athletes, she almost broke into tears. I decided I needed to step in and make it clear to my interpreter that this was not necessary and was offensive to our athletes. They were insulted being treated like children. It was decided that the volunteers would no longer come to our rooms, now to be considered private areas. The volunteers did continue to follow the riders everywhere for a few days and always held the bikes for them when they were in staging but respected our request to stay out of their bedrooms.

After lunch I was escorted to the first cycling head coaches meeting, where we were informed that all the bikes had been taken directly to the storage area on the racecourse. This was the good news. The bad news was that there were no mechanics available to assemble them. We were told that we must go to the bike barn and assemble the bicycles ourselves. I found Ken and gave him a heads up. He immediately took the few tools he had, grabbed a taxi to the bike barn and arrived before the head coaches meeting was over.

After the meeting we took the riders to see the course. We found Ken with a bike stand surrounded by the carnage of bike parts and boxes. The United States was the second largest delegation, just behind China who had forty riders. All the Chinese bikes were already assembled and ready to ride before we even arrived on the island.

We had sixteen bikes to assemble with the heat near ninety degrees and mosquitos coming out at dusk. The sun may have been setting, but the heat was not easing off in the least. There was no cool evening breeze and being near the ocean increased the humidity. To see him at work, you could see that Ken is a master at his craft, wheels spun as he trued them to roll straight and made tweaks here and there. I rolled up my sleeves, grabbed a wrench and attempted to help put bikes together alongside him. With growing anxiety, my personal Chinese assistant informed me that it was time to leave to attend the special dinner they had planned for that evening. I told her that my two other coaches would take the cyclists to dinner as I was going to stay and help Ken. She was visibly uncomfortable with my declaration.

It was absolute chaos as Ken whipped the bikes together, which was not a simple task as each bike was a different type and brand. The chief technical delegate kept bringing bikes to Ken to work on from other countries: a derailleur here, a headset there. This continued even after the athletes and most of the other country's coaches had left. With sweat dripping from his brow, Ken did not slow his pace enough to even swat the mosquitoes buzzing around his head. He hardly broke rhythm to answer the questions from the 50+ locals who had circled around to watch him performing magic with his wrench.

My assistant grew more and more anxious as the time passed and absolutely insisted that I leave and attend the dinner. "As head coach you are expected to be at the dinner," she said imploring me to leave. Ken looked up at me with a wrench in one hand and a pedal in the other and said, "Go. I'm just fine here and they need YOU there." I knew that he would be fine, but he would miss the dinner, and ultimately it was my responsibility to ensure the bikes were completed. But most of all, Ken was the love of my life and I could not just leave him in this situation. Sensing my hesitance, he looked up at me with a forced grin, which is rare to see in itself, assuring me he was fine. So I left with the assistant/interpreter and reluctantly returned to the hotel.

As the last remnants of daylight faded and it grew very dark, all the other countries finished their assembly and left. Most of them only had three or four bikes to assemble. With the barn now empty except for Ken and his spectators. He worked ferociously into the night using a special light they brought in just for him so he could see what he was doing.

I was very late to the dinner and upon arriving I realized that I had not missed anything special. There was entertainment, but the stage was completely blocked by a wide pillar in the middle of the room. When I saw that the riders were well taken care of, I took a taxi back to the bike barn. Of course Ken was still there, surrounded by local onlookers. He had just finished assembling the last of the sixteen bikes and I helped clean up and put them away. He had missed dinner, but the volunteers arranged to bring him food from Kentucky Fried Chicken.

What an absolutely exhausting, stressful day and the games had not even begun. Although the competition may not have started, in my eyes, Ken earned a gold medal that night and I don't know what Team USA or I would have done without him.

The next day was the preliminary divisioning heats. The riders were grouped by age, gender and ability. Then the qualifying time trials helped place them into the proper category, according to the distance of their race. There is an honest effort rule that states if the athlete performs in the race at a speed faster than fifteen percent of their preliminary heat in the medal competition, they would be disqualified. This is intended to maintain a fair competition and prevent anyone from 'sand bagging' to get into an easier division and then win.

The course was a five-kilometer rectangle of smooth flat pavement. The only part that wasn't completely flat was a small rise over an irrigation canal. It had two very wide lanes with a wide bike path paralleling the course and the venue was meticulously landscaped with Yucca plants and flowers lining the boulevard median.

Suzanne Anderson was our additional staff member. She worked at Special Olympics Texas and was officially part of the team to help with SO rules and administration, but she was more than that. I was especially impressed with the way Suzanne stepped up and joined the team with the skill of a coach and worked so very well with the athletes. She was an accomplished cyclist and was very comfortable switching roles as needed. The petite, blue eyed blond had solid strength, skill and compassion in her tool kit. She was my roommate during the games and it really helped to have her there to bounce ideas off and work through issues together. Suzanne was more than an administrative Special Olympics staff member, she was willing to go the extra mile to do whatever it took to make the games a great experience for the riders and I considered it a blessing to have her on our team.

Desi Holland, one of my female cyclists had difficulty keeping a steady pace with the 5K distance. During practice, I rode alongside and had to remind her to keep pedaling because she frequently got distracted and would stop. I discovered that she loved TV theme songs and show tunes, so I started singing songs from the Brady Bunch and Gilligan's Island, and anything else that might keep her pedaling. Her father was waiting for her on the back of the course and was flabbergasted when he saw her coming around the corner singing and pedaling. "I've never seen her ride so well or so fast." He exclaimed. She broke her personal record by over three minutes in the preliminaries.

Kerry, one of my other riders, was obsessed with High School Musical and proclaimed she was in love with the main character named Zac. She told me he was her boyfriend, so I played along with her fantasy. The strategy was to tell her that Zac was at the finish line waiting for her. Then her eyes lit up, she let out a squeal of joy and with the countdown, she took off like a bullet. Suzanne was down the road yelling Zac's name to keep her going. She won the race and her prize was a gold medal.

All in all, our twelve riders won eight gold, eight silver and eight bronze medals. I saw every one of them break personal records and improve their self-confidence and esteem. During the awards ceremony I had parents hug me with tears of pride in their eyes, telling me how thankful they were for our coaching and more.

During our last dinner at the cycling venue, the orange shirted volunteers each gave their athletes a gift, and watching them hug the athletes and play the sign name game one last time was gratifying. I believe the volunteers gained a lot more than they ever expected from the experience, particularly the knowledge that people with intellectual disabilities are valuable members of every society.

The next day we took the ferry back to Shanghai, returned to our original host hotel and rejoined the rest of Team USA. Closing ceremonies were filled with fireworks and interactive participation with the audience. It was a fantastic show and celebration, but just like the regular Olympics, the athletes spent most of the closing ceremonies trading things, not just pins, but often uniforms. There were many people from other countries that approached, wanting to trade coats. We encouraged Team USA members to hold on to their uniform jackets. It would mean a lot more, long term, to be able to wear a jacket with "Team USA" across the back at home, rather than one with the name of another country.

The celebration went late into the evening and it was after 11: 00 o'clock when we got back to the hotel. There was a buffet dinner waiting for us, but the true star of the meal was brought out on a platter. The athletes swarmed the wait staff that held the tray of French fries. Servers never made it to the buffet table before they had to return with an empty tray to refill. I managed to get some of the crinkle cut fries myself. The taste was comforting and they tasted heavenly after a week of strictly Chinese food.

The late night turned quickly into morning for the coaching staff, as we had to make sure everyone's luggage was appropriately tagged for the trip home. We got up at 4:00 am, boarded the buses and headed to the airport. After saying our last goodbyes to the volunteers and shepherding our athletes, we made our way through customs and boarded the plane, looking forward to home. After leaving the ground in Shanghai at 10:00 am Friday, we watched 4-5 movies and ate four meals before landing at LAX at 6:00 am on the same Friday we left China.

A few months after the games were over I was contacted by Special Olympics International. They asked if I would be interested in being a technical delegate for the next Winter World Games. That would mean that I could not be a coach for Team USA and would not be able to directly coach the athletes. I thanked them, and after some consideration, I decided that I was not yet ready to give up my role as a coach.

*   *   *

Spring break 2008, Ken was unable to join us on vacation because of his commitment to work. I wanted to spend some quality time with Madison, as she was growing up so quickly before my eyes; I started to make travel plans for just the two of us. We didn't have any planned destination, but after a full season of speedskating, we wanted to go somewhere warm.

I turned to my CCC group for ideas. Bob Sega, a longtime member of the group and metastatic prostate cancer survivor lived in Boulder City, Nevada, just twenty minutes outside of Las Vegas. He piped up right away after seeing my post to the group, and invited us to come out and stay with him and his wife, Allis. I had never had the opportunity to meet Bob in person, but we had shared so much online that he felt like family. When I mentioned it to Madison, she said that she would really like to go out west.

Bob mentioned that Allis liked to knit, and Madison had been teaching herself to knit for the past three months. So it was arranged; when Madison didn't want to ride with us, she could stay at the house and keep Allis company while they knitted. I shipped my bike out so Madison and I could fly into Las Vegas and Bob agreed to pick us up at the airport.

As a coach and a mother, I always pack extra snacks in my bag for trips. You never know when someone will need an energy bar on a bike ride or be delayed on an airplane. The flight went well and when we landed, we were on the lookout for Bob. "Do you even know what he looks like?" Madison asked. "Not exactly," I replied. "But he said he would be wearing his CCC bike jersey."

When we got to the baggage claim, I saw him standing among a large group of people waiting for arrivals. He stood over six feet tall, wore a black baseball cap and his bright yellow jersey. He waived upon seeing us and I ran to him and we exchanged hugs. "It's so great getting to meet you in person!" I chirped. "I'm so very glad you could make it." He said in reply. "I'm looking forward to riding with you, but you will have to slow down for this old goat. I'm not as young as I am handsome ya know." He smiled.

Bob had retired from the mining industry in Minnesota and moved to Nevada with Allis to be closer to where their sons had settled. He had an olive complexion with a salt and pepper mustache to match his hair. Allis was a petite woman who had light brown hair and a Danish accent. Her glasses could not conceal the joy in her brown eyes whenever she saw Bob walk into the room. It was good to see a couple so perfect together.

When we arrived at their home it was already late evening. Allis made her personal secret recipe scrambled eggs for us since we'd had nothing to eat except peanuts on the plane. Bob showed us to our room and we went to bed looking forward to seeing Nevada in the daylight.

Like an experienced tour guide, Bob drove us around to see the natural wonders of the area. First, we visited the Valley of Fire to see the oldest petroglyphs in the United States. The three thousand year old markings on the sides of sandstone cliffs were made by Native Americans.

We hiked through the park, amazed at the red-orange-rust color that seemed to just explode in the middle of an otherwise beige desert. When we climbed onto one of the ledges, the surface felt warm from the sun, but also gritty, like sandpaper. The ebb and flow of the rock displayed years of carving from wind and water. Bob was very happy to share this expedition with us, as he had a passion for mineralogy.

Once my bike arrived, Bob found a bike for Madison and we rode on some of his favorite routes. The spring flowers were starting to bloom and the animals were very active in the morning, which made the ride more interesting for Madison. He took us to one of his biggest personal challenges, a hill that he called his "Come to Jesus" hill. The length of the climb was around two hundred meters, which wasn't a problem for us. The difficulty turned out to be the grade which was greater than twenty degrees. Bob told me that he had never been able to make it all the way to the top of this hill in the past. I took the challenge and climbed it. I returned to where he and Madison stood at the bottom. "There you go." I said to Bob. "Now it's your turn."

He attacked the hill with all the speed he could muster, but lost his momentum and slowed to a near stop about ten meters from the top. He turned around in defeat and joined us at the bottom. "I just can't seem to make it past that point." He complained as he tried to catch his breath. I spoke up and said, "I think I know what your problem is. You are not pulling up on the pedals you are only pushing down. If you pull up it's like gaining an extra gear and shifting into overdrive." I said. "Here, I'll show you." He watched as I demonstrated, then waited at the top for him to join me. He once again attacked the climb and when he stood out of the saddle I yelled, "Pull up on the pedals! Pull up on the back stroke! Pull yourself up the hill!" And he did.

Bob finally climbed his "Come to Jesus" hill. When he joined me at the top, he was breathless, sweating profusely and absolutely giddy. We yelled down to Madison and urged her to climb up and join us, but she quickly declined our invitation. All the way back to the house, Bob was shaking his head in disbelief that he had finally accomplished his goal and all it took was a little coaching.

Allis had lunch waiting for us. For Bob she had prepared a large salad while Madison and I shared a bowl of broth soup and some crackers with tea. So grateful for the opportunity to stay with them, we were hesitant to ask for more food, so we went back to our room and devoured the last of the snacks we had packed in our luggage.

Dinner that night was tuna salad on crackers with tea. Allis was trying to help Bob lose weight, but Madison and I still had appetites to feed.

After a breakfast of oatmeal and half a banana, Bob and I went on a fifty mile bike ride through the desert. Madison stayed at the house with

Allis and they spent the day knitting. The ride took us up huge gradual inclines with steep down hills on the other side. Bob often struggled up the hills, but would soar down them with great enthusiasm. We then returned to the house for a light lunch with Allis, followed by another ride.

One afternoon we went exploring Boulder City, and stopped at the Medical center where Bob was being treated with injections of Depot-Lupron, an agent to prevent his body from producing any more testosterone. Just as estrogen was the main source of energy for my cancer, testosterone was his. I joked, "We are just too sexy and cancer is trying to bring us down to normal sexy." He laughed and joked with all the nurses, as they knew him by name.

With growing hunger, I offered to take Bob and Allis out to dinner to thank them for their hospitality, with an ulterior motive that Madison and I could eat a large meal. They would not hear of it and insisted that we stay as their guests. On the third day I convinced them to at least let me cook for them. We went shopping at a small grocery store and I bought a salmon fillet, pecans, broccoli and a loaf of French bread and made my favorite grilled salmon recipe. Madison and I made sure that there were no leftovers. As the days continued, so did our appetites; I kept trying to find ways to get Bob and Allis to let us treat them to dinner, but they wouldn't hear of it.

My aunt Janet drove up from Phoenix to take us to Vegas for an overnight adventure before we returned to Indianapolis. When her car appeared in front of the house we ran out to greet her. After we introduced her to Bob and Allis we piled into her car and she asked me to drive since she had been driving for hours. As soon as we got in and shut the doors, she asked, "So what do you want to do first?" Madison and I both shouted in unison, "EAT!" Janet laughed and must have thought we were joking but we weren't. There was a casino at the edge of one of Bob's bike routes that had a flashing sign that had taunted me all week. "All you can eat Buffet! $6.99!" When we drove near with the flashing sign in sight I suggested that we stop to eat there, but Janet said, "You don't want to eat there. We will find something much better in Vegas."

We drove to our hotel and quickly checked into the room. "What would you like to do now?" Janet inquired. "We are starving. We want to go eat," was our immediate answer. So we walked to the closest casino, The Aladdin, and checked out their buffet. It was the largest and most culturally diverse buffet I had ever seen. We piled our plates high with sushi, crab legs, pasta, roast and potatoes. And that was just the first plate.

"My goodness," Janet laughed when she saw us devouring the food in front of us, barely pausing to speak. "I guess you were hungry after all." She said, and we grunted our response with mouths full and eyes happy.

Then we went for two more plates loaded with food. I called Ken mid meal and told him how wonderful everything tasted as I continued to eat while he spoke.

On the third plate we stacked cookies and cake. Madison spotted cotton candy on the dessert bar and asked if she could have some. "Honey, you can have anything and everything you want." I confirmed. Janet then, looking at the contents of our plates, said, "Well, at least you are almost done since you are eating dessert" She had finished much earlier and was sitting, watching us stuff ourselves in absolute amazement. "Oh, we aren't done." I said mid cookie, "Who said dessert had to come last? I want more crab legs after this. How about you, Madison?" Finally we were stuffed, happy and extremely grateful to Janet for taking us to dinner.

We walked through the colorfully lit streets lined with names of casinos that we had heard about in movies and on television. We walked through gaming rooms filled with the heavy odor of stale cigarette smoke and a cacophony of bells and alarms ringing as people sat, mesmerized, playing slot machines. Madison and I were enchanted by the indoor Venetian Gondola boats with singing oarsmen, the statues, the fountains, the replica Statue of Liberty, the Eiffel tower and the people everywhere dressed in everything imaginable, and then some. We visually devoured all the sites just as hungrily as we had the food. We walked until Janet's feet could no longer take it, then returned to the hotel and fell, giggling, into bed.

The next day we consumed another large buffet meal and set out to explore the roller coaster at Circus Circus, the Lion exhibit at the MGM, an aquarium exhibit at the Silverton Hotel, and one of my favorites, the Star Trek exhibit at the Hilton, which made me wish that my brother could have been there with us. I was absolutely delighted to get to share those moments, sights and tastes with Madison and Janet. Another moment that I could have missed, had cancer taken me off the planet, but I also realized that had if it not been for cancer and cycling, I would never have been able to meet Bob and Allis.

We returned to the Sega home the next day and brought them gifts of chocolates and cakes as well as restocking our supply of snacks and energy bars.

On the last morning the Sega's took us to the Red Rock Canyon, just 13 miles outside of Vegas. Bob and I rode our bikes and Allis drove the car behind us as Madison leaned out the window taking photos. Fearing that she might fall out the window, Allis drove with one hand on the steering wheel and the other clutching Madison's legs, trying desperately to keep her from being ejected.

At the peak of the highest climb over the canyon, the grade was almost as steep as Bob's "Come to Jesus" hill. We had climbed several times that day to get to the highest point and he was starting to fatigue. I stopped at the pinnacle of the climb to wait and cheer for him when suddenly he stalled and before he could clip out of his pedals he fell over in slow motion, spouting a few expletives along the way. Allis stopped the car and ran to his side to make sure that he was alright. He dusted himself off and pushed the bike to the top. The good news was that he was not hurt and the remainder of the ride was all downhill.

After the ride was finished we loaded the bikes on the car one last time, and then stopped at a casino on the outskirts of Vegas to meet their sons and have lunch. We talked them into letting me treat everyone to a buffet lunch. They seemed hesitant, but Madison and I insisted. It was not as glorious as the buffet we shared with Janet, but it was still all we could eat so we piled our plates high with food and joined them at the table. Bob looked over at our plates and then nudged Allis in the ribs with his elbow and said, "See Allis, I told you we weren't feeding them enough!"

Even though Madison and I had been hungry for food during our visit, Bob and Allis filled our hearts with affection while we were there. They had such an undeniable love for one another that it was evident in everything they did.

The kisses so freely given between them as well as the twinkle in their eyes after more than forty years of marriage spoke volumes. They took us into their home like family and we appreciated them for it. Ken and I got to see them both again at the LiveStrong ride for the roses in November of 2009. He was weak but determined to ride. Although his cancer had spread to his lungs and he was on oxygen, he was still determined to ride on.

Bob's ride through life ended in January of 2010, and he finally got to "Come to Jesus" and stay.

* * *

PART 5 – Recalculating

O n May 18, 2008, the four year anniversary of my breast cancer diagnosis, I had an annual visit with my oncologist, Kathy Miller. Since my original diagnosis, many things had happened in both of our lives. We often shared details during my annual visits regarding family. Dr. Miller had an addition to her family, which brought her great joy and as she was doing my physical exam, we exchanged stories about parenting.

Everything was going well until she stopped abruptly at my left armpit. As she focused on one particular area her tone drastically changed. "How long has this been here?" "How long has WHAT been there?" I responded. She had found something that concerned her. "This can't be anything." I thought. Then I recalled a few times over the past year that I had noticed a very small pea sized bump under my arm. I assumed that it was just an irritated hair follicle that itched and believed it had gone away. Apparently it had not.

The room that had only moments before been filled with light happy chatter seemed to turn dark and foreboding. My heart raced and my head could not fathom what I was hearing. She was ordering an ultrasound guided biopsy to be done as soon as possible.

I had not expected this routine visit to result in such a shocking discovery. But I had never expected my original diagnosis either. She was supposed to tell me that everything looked fine and I should return next year for my five year visit. She was supposed to tell me that in one year I could stop taking Tamoxifen and my life would be back to normal.

After my appointment, I shared Dr. Miller's finding with a few of my friends and family, they all assured me that it was probably nothing. I was amazed at how calm I felt and thanked them for their support, positive thoughts and prayers. Even though I was not distraught or panic stricken, I did not dismiss the possibilities for one second that it could be cancer again. I began preparing myself for war. I knew the drill and was ready to do battle. If the results told us that it was a false alarm, I could breathe easy and celebrate. However, until I heard differently, my guard was up.

A few days after the biopsy, I was shopping with Madison at our favorite locally owned tea shop, Tea Pots and Treasures, in downtown Indianapolis and we were surrounded by tea paraphernalia and hand-blended teas where the smell of Chai and Jasmine fought for our attention. My cell phone played my ringtone, Queen's *Bicycle Race* and I saw it was Dr. Miller calling on the caller ID. I almost heard the words before she spoke them and I was prepared. An appointment was made to discuss treatment options to handle the breast cancer that had returned.

This time it was much more serious, as this evil beast had invaded my lymph nodes.

Even though I thought I knew, it was still not enough to handle the inevitable flood of emotion that accompanied the reality of recurrence. After treatment for my original diagnosis, there had been a small whisper of hope or perhaps denial, telling me that it was all a mistake. I wanted to believe that my biopsy results had been mixed up with someone else's and I never really had cancer in the first place. *THIS* totally blew that whisper away. I was finally forced to look reality in the face and admit to myself that it was cancer, it was real and it was invading my body again. That "damn bald guy" was back, stealing my sense of security once more.

Dr. Miller explained to us that the chemotherapy I was to receive this time contained a different combination of drugs. But in addition to chemotherapy and surgery, I would be going through radiation.

Dr. Goulet entered the exam room with his eyes glazed with disappointment and concern as he surveyed my chart. Upon completion, he looked at me with remorse dripping from his words, and said softly, "They are going to tear you up."

I was told that Dr. Peter Johnstone, head of Radiation Oncology, would be my radiologist. I researched his bio and found that he was the best in the business. When I got a phone call informing me that they were going to change my doctor from Dr. Johnstone to a new doctor to relieve Johnstone's caseload, I immediately recoiled and insisted on staying with him.

During my first visit, he walked into the exam room and graciously introduced himself to my mother and me. He was jovial and upbeat and complimented us both in a humorous way, then looked at my chart. "So I hear you insisted on keeping me as your Radiologist. Whatever possessed you to do that?" He asked with a flicker of humor in his voice. "My new partner does *glowing* work. Radiology does that to a body." He finished with a smile, waiting to see if I appreciated his pun. I chuckled, "But I heard that you were the best, and I deserve the best, don't I?" I retorted. "How can I possibly argue with logic like that?" He agreed, smiling broadly.

He explained that my radiation would be started after the chemo and surgery were finished. Then I would come in every weekday for a little over a month, probably starting in late September. I felt much better knowing he was on my team and now I was ready to get it all over with.

Before treatment started, I was still working through issues in my head, trying to accept that I was facing this demon again and I felt like things were just out of my control. I don't respond well to circumstances that are forced upon me. If you were to set a bowl of chocolate almond ice cream on the table and say "You have to eat this!" I would probably bristle and push back.

There are moments when those who love us the most, try too hard to help. I could hear my mother and Ken discussing what was going to happen and what they were going to do as if I wasn't there or like I was incapable of making decisions on my own. This was a repeat of the over-whelming wave of emotion I felt when I was first diagnosed and I had nowhere to go in the house to deal with my emotions alone. Recognizing the pressure, I suddenly burst out, "I am not dead yet!" and rushed out to my bike to ride. My mother yelled after me, "Don't forget your helmet!" and all I could think was, "What good would a helmet do now?" A helmet would not make a difference in the fight against the monster inside that was trying to mess up my well planned life.

I was scheduled to go in for chemo in June, which was déjàvû. It had been almost exactly four years since I first walked through the doors for treatment. The faces and drugs had changed, but the situation was the same. The same cold blue vinyl recliners waited by the windows for patients to occupy them and the same mixed looks of anxiety and fatigue in the waiting area. I made the same attempt at being brave for my family and had the same dread, knowing that whatever they were going to give me would make me sick. I had to force myself to remember that it would also save my life.

This time the names of the drugs of choice were Adriamycin and Cytoxan, known as the "Red Death" in breast cancer circles. Dr. Miller told me these were cardio toxic drugs and would not only affect the blood vessels in my arm where they would be infused, but could have effects on my heart as well. She reassured me she would keep the dosage controlled in an effort to avoid damaging my heart. The Adriamycin was red, came in a very large syringe, and was pushed into the IV slowly and carefully in an effort to spare my veins and not overwhelm my body.

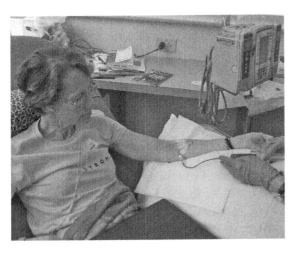

The side effects of this chemo were much like those that I had experienced before. Once again, my hair started to fall out on schedule, fourteen days after the first time the concentrated cancer killer entered my veins. I was prepared, but at the same time you are never truly ready or accepting of such a shock to the body and spirit.

Bike Nationals were to be held in Kentucky around the same time my hair began to appear on my pillow once again. This time they were earlier in the year and geographically closer to us. Madison had been away at camp and the day she was scheduled to come home, was the day my hair started shedding, the very day Ken was leaving to go to Nationals to officiate.

She was dropped off by her best friend's family in our driveway just minutes before Ken finished packing and was preparing to leave. I had decided not to go with him and opted to stay home with Madison instead. She had been gone a week and I missed her and felt I should spend some time with her instead of rushing off to race.

Saying goodbye to Ken was even more difficult this time because I knew that I would have so much less hair when he returned. His leaving for a week, not being there to see a slower transition from full head of hair to partial, would make my hair loss seem much more dramatic. Once again, he assured me that he loved me and had not married me for my hair. We kissed goodbye as Madison stood in the driveway, rolling her eyes, trying not to notice.

After watching the van go down the driveway and out of sight, I did not feel much like eating and definitely did not feel like cooking. I knew Madison must have been hungry and had so much to tell me about camp, so I asked if she would like to go out to eat. She eagerly accepted my offer and asked if we could go to one of her favorite restaurants.

The one she requested had a reputation with our family as having very slow service and that day was no exception. It took an exorbitant amount of time for the hostess to even acknowledge our presence, let alone seat us. In frustration I said, "Let's go someplace else." We decided to go to Red Lobster and left without notice.

We were seated very quickly and when we got the menus we contemplated the decision before us. I was not very hungry and Madison was a small eater to begin with, so we decided to get a couple of appetizers to share instead of a full meal. We sat and enjoyed our food together, basking in the delight and adventure of Madison's camp experience. When the check came and I paid with a credit card, Madison asked how credit cards worked for tipping. Taking this as a teaching moment, I started to explain how the process worked.

As we sat talking, I glanced over to my right and noticed an elderly gentleman seated with a younger man at his table. He suddenly stood up with the classic hands grasped around his throat in apparent distress. His companion remained seated at the table, frozen with his gaze fixed on the man standing before him. Instinctively, I stopped mid-sentence, stood up and walked over to the man in distress, then clicked into automatic nurse mode.

The frail, frightened gray haired man stood before me. I asked him quickly, but in a very calm voice, "Excuse me, sir, are you choking?" He anxiously nodded his head, eyes watery and full of panic. I said, "Do you want me to do the Heimlich maneuver?" He responded with a quick nod. I stepped behind him and placed my arms around his mid-section. "Ok, on the count of three," I said. He stood a bit taller than I did, but that was no problem. I placed my hands in the classic Heim-lich position, thumbs inward just above the navel, fists wrapped around each other, then thrust inward and upward three times trying to dislodge the item choking him using both my strength and positioning from behind.

The first several attempts were non-productive and an audience of waiters and waitresses appeared out of nowhere and gathered around us. The largest waiter, nicknamed Sven in my mind, was tall, tan and blonde with a very muscular build. This eager, pale-eyed waiter looked as if he could have been through training for choking class, but also appeared to have spent a lot more time in the gym than dislodging food from chok-ing elderly people. I was afraid his combination of inexperience and muscular prowess would crush the gentleman's fragile frame. The last thing, besides choking to death, we wanted for this gentleman was to break his ribs during the Heimlich maneuver. Doing so would likely puncture a lung and increase the risk of dying as a result. So when he offered to help, I assured him we were fine. Again, calmly and clearly, I braced the victim for the next three count and on the final thrust, I heard someone exclaim, "There it is!" and I could hear sucking air returning to his lungs.

I sat him down at his table with his companion. He looked up at me and asked in a shaky, weak voice, "What is your name?" "Cindi Hart," I told him. With his watery, yet appreciative eyes looking at me he said, "Thank you Cindi Hart. You saved my life." "I'm happy I was able to help," I assured him, taking his boney hand in mine.

The moment I stood up from kneeling beside him, the entire restau-rant erupted in applause and I turned and saw Madison, eyes as big as dinner plates, staring at me with an expression that said, "Who are you and what have you done with my mother?" Not expecting the clapping and feeling awkward about the attention, I took Madison's hand and we briskly exited the restaurant.

Once we got to the car, we sat going nowhere for a moment, trying to realize what had just happened. "What the heck, Mom, you just saved that man's life!" Then my phone rang and it was Chris States. I recounted the recent events and while telling him what had just transpired, I realized that, if I had gone to Nationals, that man might have choked to death or been severely damaged by Sven.

Before going to the restaurant I had felt disappointed and sad that I was not going to Nationals and had a mini pity party in my head. I no longer felt that sense of lost opportunity, knowing without a doubt that this was precisely where I was supposed to be at that moment. My purpose for that day.

*　　*　　*

PART SIX - Cancer isn't contagious, but hope can be

Ever since I met my first CCC'r, my desire to bring survivors and supporters together had grown. I wanted to bring them to an activity that did not dwell on fundraising and a single bike ride shared with thousands of others. The group had a wealth of energy and imagination and intense dedication to life. I kept wondering how we could harness all that passion and power and come together for a purpose.

I had been selected to attend the second LiveStrong Summit and it would be held in Columbus, Ohio near the end of my chemo that summer. There were many other CCC group members that were chosen to attend as well. On the internet I had shared my thoughts and ideas and several of the most respected members of the group suggested that we meet at the summit and brainstorm in person.

By that time, my hair had left me with only scattered strands remaining, die-hard phantom memories of what had once covered my head. My friends and co-workers at Regenstrief Institute had been truly supportive and even though wearing hats at work was not in the dress code, no one complained that I wore a hat every day. Many were complimentary of my creative headwear, but still I was very aware how odd it looked.

In fact, they were so supportive that unknown to me, my friend and co-worker, Sandy Poremba, along with a few of my other close friends at Regenstrief, had asked administration if they could wear hats to show their support. It was allowed company-wide and they officially declared a "Hat Day" on Fridays. All kinds of hats appeared, from baseball caps to a Panama hat and even one that looked like it might belong at the Kentucky Derby. This endearing gesture meant so very much to me. It was hard trying to remain professional when both my hair and energy had deserted me, but knowing that this compassionate group of people understood and showed their support without pity, helped me feel stronger and less alone in the fight.

Mary Trufant was attending the summit and had planned on driving up from Alabama to Indianapolis to pick me up on her way. She arrived with her "Ride Yellow" fixed gear bike that Ken made attached to the rack on top of her station wagon. It was essentially a twin to my pink fixie, except for the color.

Seeing her was a breath of fresh air. When she arrived, we hugged as though we were long lost sisters. The feeling reinforced the idea that we needed to ignite the fire everyone felt in the fight against cancer. Mary's attitude, when she saw me, with my hair all but gone and my pale lackluster skin, was precisely what I needed. She did not show even a glimmer of pity, but exuded joy, energy, humor and promise. We packed her car and headed across I-70 from Indianapolis to Columbus, Ohio and then I presented her with a hat that I had made to match the goofy LiveStrong one I was planning on wearing at the summit. I figured if I was going in nearly bald, we might as well make a statement.

Jan Frandsen, aka Happy Feet from Cleveland, had also been invited to be part of the summit and met us when we first arrived in Columbus. I had not seen him since my cancer had returned and seeing him again was energizing. Jan, a nurse practitioner specializing in palliative care, was one of the kindest and most compassionate souls I had ever met.

All three of us had arranged to bring bikes, in hopes of sneaking in a ride before the summit convened. When we got together to ride I realized that I had forgotten my helmet, but didn't want that to ruin the possibility of riding with Mary and Jan, so I broke a cardinal rule and rode wearing my baseball cap.

Mary had more strength and red blood cells than I did, so she followed her spirit and rode ahead of us on the path a couple of times. I encouraged her to follow her heart and ride on, as I did not want to hold her back. Jan insisted that he stay with me. As we were talking and riding side-by-side, the wind caught the bill of my cap and blew it off my head. Feeling exposed as if I had just been de-pantsed in public, I reflexively put my hand where my hat had once been. I was not comfortable bald and even Ken had rarely seen me with my head uncovered, so I was a bit distressed. Jan was such a gentleman, that as soon as the hat took flight, he circled back and rescued it. My head was bare for all to see and Jan rode back to me, eyes diverted and held out the hat for me to take. This was an act of kindness that showed his respect for my dignity and it warmed my heart. An incredibly endearing soul inhabited the six foot two inch Dane that I was honored to call my friend.

The Summit was housed on the campus of the Ohio State University and the opening event was a special LiveStrong Presidential Town Hall on Cancer. Senator John McCain, a cancer survivor himself, spoke at the meeting, which was co-moderated by Lance Armstrong and broadcast journalist Paula Zahn. Barack Obama had been invited to attend, but had declined the invitation. All the Summit delegates were given "Vote Yellow" shirts and Mary had given me a black pair of cycling socks that said Ride Yellow on the band just above the ankles.

As fate would have it, I was randomly selected to go on stage and sit in the first row behind Lance and Senator McCain. The senator spoke about improving access to health care and broadening clinical trials, then shared his cancer fighting plan and answered questions from the group gathered on stage.

The town-hall event was streamed live online and many people watched with interest from their homes around the country. There were two very large screens on each side of the stage with the camera's view of the discussions. After the deliberations were over I rejoined Mary and my CCC family in the audience. They were all excitedly talking about my socks. Evidently, when I crossed my legs, they were clearly in view just behind Mr. McCain's head. Mary said that her friends from Alabama were texting her non-stop about the "Ride Yellow" socks on display for the whole nation to see. They were a big hit.

The next day we divided into groups of interest. My interest was advocacy and Mary's was fundraising. Ken Youner, an active CCC member, physician and kidney cancer survivor, was in my advocacy group. He was from New Jersey and was not at all shy about speaking up on behalf of survivorship. He and his wife, Cecile, had co-created a foundation for kidney cancer research. Sadly, Ken lost his wife to complications related to her breast cancer treatment.

Jamie Lindsey, a very dynamic speaker and motivator, was the facilitator for the group discussions. He was a survivor who had a great sense of humor and tremendous enthusiasm and kept everyone energized and ready to fight cancer. I thought he would have made an excellent game show host.

We went through training and exercises in advocacy. We had mock meetings with lawmakers and competitions that made the experience helpful, motivational, informative and fun. The energy and devotion was high until someone walked into the room and announced that Randy Pausch had just passed away. The room flooded with the solemn reality that cancer was deadly, even in the strongest and brightest of lives. In the cancer community, hearing that news was like hearing that Kennedy had just been shot.

Randy was one of us, someone whose life had been cut short by cancer. He had authored _The Last Lecture_, which was his inspirational message to the world, but most pointedly to his children. It was his legacy after battling pancreatic cancer. This news hit everyone hard. Even though we never met him in person, he touched our lives.

During one of the lunch breaks, a few of my CCC friends and I decided to hold a meeting to discuss the potential birth of a new organization. Our plan would connect survivors and use their strength and desire to change the way that cancer was treated and perceived to make a difference in the world of cancer... Some in attendance had been very quiet on the on-line group, but meeting them in person exposed them as strong champions of change. They were true silent heroes.

Sharon Duncan was a fine example of this. Her steadfast determination, attention to detail and experience with creating a 501c3 charity gave me direction and hope that this really could be done. Steve Bartolucci, from California, was another bright leader and motivator with creative ideas and insights. Jan from Ohio was also completely dedicated to making a difference in lives affected by cancer. The passion of Ken Youner, whose every waking moment was a reminder of how cancer had changed his life since his beloved Cecile was taken from him, was evident

At this meeting we agreed that our mission would be to combine our passion for cycling and the desire to change the way cancer was perceived and treated.

This was the birth of Spokes of Hope.

The summit ended on an optimistic note. The ability to bring Cancer Warriors from around the country together to share their passions, ideas and experiences was a petri dish for positive change in the fight against cancer. What we made of it was our responsibility; what we took with us was hope, encouragement and inspiration.

Now it was time to go home and take care of my own cancer. A week after the conclusion of the summit, I went in for surgery to have the lymph nodes in my left arm removed. Going in at 5 o'clock in the morning felt like déjàvû. In the operating suite, after they started the IV and prepped me for surgery, Dr. Goulet walked up and looked me straight in the eyes, said a few words of encouragement and then bowed his head and silently said a prayer. I was very touched as I drifted off to sleep knowing I was in such caring hands.

My mother once again stayed for my short-term hospital stay. I had terrible reactions to the pain medication. They tried morphine this time and as soon as the syringe finished pushing the medication into my IV, I started vomiting. Note to self: "Stay away from morphine. It makes you puke."

Knowing the date of my surgery coincided with the Summer Olympic Games was the perfect excuse for Ken to go out and buy a flat screen high definition TV. He made sure that when I returned from the hospital, the Olympic Games were on 24/7 in HD. Due to the pain and the medications, my sleep schedule was erratic and it was comforting to be able to lose myself in the sights, sounds and beauty of the competition.

Earlier in the summer, just prior to the summit, I had attended a breast cancer reconstruction conference held at the wellness community building. During the meeting, I submitted a question to the panel of experts regarding my previous experience with cording. There was an excellent physical therapist on the panel named Barbara Feltman, who specialized in breast cancer and lymphedema.

It was a tremendous relief to discover that she was very familiar with lymphedema and cording. After the conference, I spoke with her personally and she gave me her card and told me to ask my physician to write a referral to be evaluated and treated by her after surgery. This was one of the best things I could have done.

After the operation, it was not long before the cording started to make itself known once again. This time it came back with a vengeance. Barbara worked on the ever-growing subcutaneous network of cords that stretched out from my underarm incision site all the way down to my fingertips. I had weekly appointments to be seen and treated by her. Initially she started to gently stretch and massage the cords, but it became very apparent that the cords were part of me and just as tenacious and stubborn as I was. This was another battle that was just beginning.

The fine cords would snap and pop beneath her skilled hands. Although painful, this yielded almost immediate relief and I instantly regained some range of motion. Unfortunately, there were some other cords that started to become thicker and harder to break, specifically in the axillary (underarm) area. The cords there were very difficult to access and manipulate, therefore, they grew stronger and more resistant. This problem began to seriously affect the range of motion of my arm at the shoulder.

It was at this time that we decided to take more aggressive steps. She began treatment by sharply pulling up on the arm, while I pushed down on the side of my hip to stretch the cords and force them to release. This was extremely painful, but definitely worth it in the long run. I believe that if I had not gone through this painful popping and ripping of the cords, I would not be able to lift my left arm to the extent that I can today.

A month after the incisions healed, I visited Dr. Johnstone and began radiation. They made a mold of my arms positioned over my head so that it would be exactly the same every time I received treatment. This took many hours, lying on the cold steel surface where I was measured, marked then remarked to identify the field that was to be irradiated.

Treatments were scheduled to be twenty-five weekdays. Not knowing what to expect, I didn't realize how tired I would become, or what I would experience. This was another mystery in uncharted territory.

Every day, I reported to the small waiting area, where people sat in unfashionable, scratchy, green hospital gowns, flipping through magazines or playing music on their iPods while they anxiously waited to be called. Once I was called back into the very large, dimly lit room, the staff was kind and accommodating and responded quickly when I asked for a foam wedge to be placed beneath my knees and an additional pillow under my heels on the hard steel table. They did everything they could to make me comfortable. I put in ear buds and listened to a book on tape in an effort to escape and go far, far away from the clicking and whirring of the machine circling around my head. The radiation treatment didn't last as long as expected and I didn't feel a thing at the time. In fact, getting up from the table I thought, "Really? That's all?"

Radiation has a distinct accumulative effect. I didn't feel anything at first, but as the days wore on; the skin where the radiation was focused grew more and more pink, and turned into something that resembled sunburn. The staff gave me creams and ointments to apply to the skin as it became increasingly angry. The crushing fatigue came on quite gradually as well, but there was no cream for that.

On the very last day of treatment, my mother accompanied me. I had become quite close and comfortable with the radiation staff and wanted to show my appreciation for their thoughtful care. Instead of wearing the usual drab hospital gown, I had started to wear my own pink fuzzy bathrobe. They got a kick out of this. I asked my mother to write, with a permanent marker, on the skin where my breasts used to reside, "Bye-bye cancer!" When I removed my robe and laid down on the cold, hard steel table, in the all-too-familiar radiation pose, the radiation technicians noticed my message to them, and to cancer. They found this amusing enough to make sure that Dr. Johnstone came in to see as well. It's important to have a good sense of humor when fighting cancer, for everyone involved.

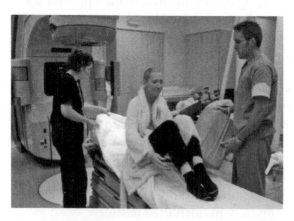

A few days later, I was scheduled for a follow-up exam. It was Halloween and Madison's birthday. My hair had just started to grow back and I had dressed up with a green painted face and pointed ears like an elf. When Dr. Johnstone walked into the exam room, his face lit up at first sight. "I think we have an unexpected side effect of the radiation." I said, as he smiled from ear to ear.

After recovering from surgery and radiation the cording had stopped attempting to take over my body and immobilizing my left arm. With all that behind me, I was increasingly motivated to get the gears turning for our survivor organization.

*   *   *

Cyclists Combating Cancer had become an incredible on-line support group for me. I proposed to the group my idea of taking our talents a few steps further in our efforts to help others. We started having conference calls to brainstorm with some of the CCC movers and shakers. Some of the participants were Bob Sega from Nevada, Ken Youner from New Jersey, Steve Bartolucci from California, Branan Cooper from Delaware, Jeffrey Rowe from Tennessee and Sharon Duncan from Pennsylvania.

We looked at different angles of approach, and my first thought was to try to connect the hometowns of the interested CCC'rs by riding from town to town. However, we had some gaps and not everyone could take the time out of their schedules to ride across the country. So for our first year, we decided to start out small and ride from Indianapolis to Washington, DC, connecting with riders in between. We also had participants in Minnesota, Texas, Rhode Island and New Hampshire who would ride in their home states on the same days we were riding, in an effort to show solidarity and faith in our mission.

One main goal we wanted to achieve was reaching out to patients in treatment and connect them with survivors who had been through the same experience and lived to tell about it. Therefore, we plotted to travel from one cancer center to another. An additional goal was to bring people together who would speak to our lawmakers in DC and present a different perspective of survivorship in an effort to gain support for increased funding for cancer research.

Before making this happen, we needed a name. We decided on "Spokes of Hope." The symbolism of a spoked wheel would reflect our passion for cycling and would also represent people working together, converging on cancer and attacking it from all directions.

The very first Spokes of Hope event was in September of 2009. We started with a group of riders in Indianapolis and began our journey from the IU Simon Cancer Center where I had received treatment. Dr. Robert Goulet, my surgeon, and Dr. Abanour, an oncologist specializing in treating Multiple Myeloma from IU Simon, were among the riders, as well as Bob Harwell, Craig Rice and Lana Richmond, skaters and cyclists that I coached in Indianapolis, Mike Edwards from Regenstrief Institute, CCC'r Jeffrey Rowe from Tennessee and Susan Williams from Northern Indiana.

Ken planned to drive support. Many of the riders were going to either turn around at the state line or had arranged to get a ride back to Indy while many others continued on through Ohio with us. Since we had never orchestrated anything like this before, we had a lot to learn. As we left the city streets of Indianapolis and entered the rolling countryside we found it was difficult to keep the group together. Jay Bodkin volunteered to help support the riders who needed to take a slower pace, so we divided into two groups.

Jay has been our friend for over twenty years. He and Ken had worked at a bike shop together before we were married so we knew this man was in his element whether he was camping, hiking or riding. Anywhere Jay went, he would be self-sufficient. If there was a situation when survival in the wilderness was an issue, he would be the person you wanted on your team. We had a U-Haul trailer that Ken was pulling behind the support van with everything we needed inside.

Ken drove ahead and set up food and water stops. The original idea was that we would all ride out of town together, and then, at the first food stop, break up into relay teams. One group would be on the road while the other rested in the support vehicle. This works very well in theory, but it doesn't work if no one wants to stop riding.

I felt very comfortable with my riders. So much, in fact, that I kicked into coaching mode. I decided that the best way to help manage the group would be to organize them into a rotating paceline. Time and time again it has proven to not only be efficient and safe, but fun. It was even more applicable for the ride on that day as the wind was coming from the East, which meant we had a headwind all day.

During one of the rotations, when I was riding next to Dr. Goulet, he turned to me with a huge grin and, in his enthusiastic New York accent said, "Man, you're bossy!" At which point I leaned over to him, put my arm across his back and replied, "Welcome to _MY_ operating room." We both laughed heartily and pedaled on in celebration of life in the moment.

We stopped a few times to regroup along the way and had a few motorists stop to ask us what we were doing. The response was generally very positive, except for one elderly driver who complained that our yellow jerseys looked too much like the lines on the road from a distance. After he left, we had a good laugh and agreed that there was no way we could please everyone, no matter how hard we tried.

At the state border friends and family met to cheer for us and some were going to drive our returning riders back to Indy. Others chose to stay and travel on into Ohio and beyond. My parents had driven over from Ohio to stay with Madison while we were gone and I was so glad that they would be able to see the great group of riders that shared our adventure.

We stayed overnight at Ken's father's house in Dayton. He had an empty house that was listed for sale, so he allowed us to use it for the night. It had no furniture, which was fine, as we came prepared, because Jay was with us.

While we were setting up camp in the house, Jay made multiple trips to the trailer and came back with bags filled with some interesting piece of furniture or comfort item. He was like Mr. Gadget on wheels. Between Jay and Ken, we were prepared for just about any situation that could occur.

Jeffrey Rowe was our blogger. He set up his laptop and started transmitting the events of the day to the CCC group on-line. The fellowship and camaraderie were very satisfying and we knew we were on the road to adventure. Lana Richmond and Susan Williams were our steady state riders, and worked well together. They were going to stay with us through Columbus, Ohio, then return to Indiana. Lana was also a nurse and one of the speed skaters we coached with IndySpeed. She was an amazing supporter through my treatment, and was there for me when I was throwing up at the Velodrome after chemo. Susan was also a breast cancer survivor and CCC'r. She had battled cancer with a stem cell transplant and knew the struggles of survivorship all too well.

We took a very large banner on our journey and our plan was to collect signatures and messages along the way to present to our lawmakers DC. We wanted to show them that we were not just a bunch of fanatics on bikes; we were representing a large group of real people whose lives had been turned upside down or even ended by cancer. That morning happened to be Phyllis O'Grady's birthday, so we made sure we put her name on the banner along with those of many other CCC'rs who could not be with us.

Ken methodically plotted our course from Xenia to Columbus, using the bike path for our convenience and safety. We appreciated the path, as it was newly paved, flat and sheltered from wind. Everyone was comfortable riding together after the long day of headwinds the day before. Our next stop was the Zangmeister Cancer Center.

The staff cheerfully greeted us at the front door with snacks and water. They were very excited that we were visiting their center and asked us to speak to the patients in the outpatient center along with the medical staff. We collected signatures on our banners and spoke with many of the patients personally after our presentation. The responses were heartfelt and very rewarding. We knew that we were definitely on the right path.

From there we traveled to The James Cancer Center on The Ohio State University campus where the LiveStrong Summit had been held the year before. We rode up to the front entrance, where a guard told us to put our bikes over to the side. I argued with him at first, thinking that he mistook us for students, then he explained that he was assigned to us for security and would be standing guard over our bikes. I felt much better knowing they would be safe. We entered The James, where we were greeted by the media guide who gave us an in depth tour of the hospital.

One highlight of the tour was when we were shown the lab where stem cells and blood products were stored. This was of particular interest to Lana and me, because we were nurses, but even more so for Susan Williams, whose life had been impacted by a stem cell transplant.

We were wearing our cycling clothing, including matching cycling caps, as we walked into the apheresis unit where the cancer patients got infusions of stem cells. As soon as we entered the large room, with multiple beds surrounding the perimeter, one of the young patients, in his twenties, attempted to sit up excitedly as he saw us and yelled, "Cyclists!" and was quickly reminded to stay in bed by the port connecting him to the life restoring sludge that moved slowly into his body through the tubing.

He was a cyclist himself and his eyes sparkled with excitement. You could see the joy of future rides stirring in his very soul. We went to his bedside and talked with him about our mission at first and then about riding. We presented him with a Spokes of Hope cap, which he quickly and joyfully accepted. He knew how to wear it and flipped the bill of the cap up as he placed it on his head. A proud grin stretched across his face as he realized we were all in the fight, and the ride, together.

The nursing staff picked up on the healing powers we stimulated, and began taking us to other patient rooms. We were meeting with frightened and anxious people, sharing our personal cancer stories, and letting them know that we understood what they were going through. Our goal was to leave them with the sense of hope we shared.

We met a thirty-five year old drummer, clad in his classic black, sleeveless rock and roll band T-shirt, who had just been diagnosed with

cancer. He was afraid that he would not live to see his six year old son grow up. Every patient we spoke with had a story, and we listened, and then shared our stories with them. Everyone involved, everyone we met, seemed transformed by the experience, including us.

After Columbus, we traveled to Cleveland, where we met with Jan Frandsen and Dave Mitchell at the Cleveland Clinic Tausigg Cancer Center. Even before we entered the building we were stopping and talking with patients and spreading hope. They escorted us to the area where breast cancer patients were in treatment. We met several metastatic cancer patients and Dave was awesome working with them. Having been a metastatic survivor himself, he understood and shared his optimistic perspective with them. He was in his element.

Pittsburgh was our next destination and we stayed at Dave and Anne Mitchell's home. Their hospitality and warm spirit were very appreciated by all who crossed their threshold. Chris States flew in from San Francisco to join us. I had not seen him since we crossed the finish line together at the Ride for the Roses. Even though we were all very tired from the day's activities, we were like children at a slumber party who didn't want to sleep, for fear they may miss something special. We stayed up much longer than we should have, energized and talking, but like all survivors know, every second counts.

The next morning we went to Gilda's Club, a place where those affected by cancer, can gather and address their concerns regarding survival in an environment of support. It was located in the Strip District on the river and Dave had arranged for a meet and greet session for us called, Bagels and Bikes. We met local survivors and shared our personal stories, talked about bikes, and answered questions as we invited people to sign our banners.

From Gilda's we rode on to the University of Pennsylvania Hospital. There we met patients who were receiving bone marrow transplants and required more intense treatment. In the community room, we met a petite young woman named Michelle who was dressed in pajamas and wore blue hospital slipper socks. We realized that she was in a debilitating stage of her battle as she shuffled into the room, where the hospital staff had arranged our meeting. The scant remnants of her blond hair peeked out the side of her blue bandana.

With a faint, wavering voice, Michelle told us that she had been a hairdresser before her life was interrupted by cancer. She was battling Leukemia and attempting to recover from her recent bone marrow transplant, which was very traumatic and appeared to be taking its toll.

Her curiosity was understandably peaked when she saw us, in our bright Lycra clothing. Her face was pale yellow and her eyes, bright red with blood, where the whites had once been. Her hands and body trembled as if she was very cold; however, her skin was noticeably hot. She may have been frail and soft spoken, but her message was loud and clear. Michelle wanted to live! We were motivated to fight for her and do everything we could to help her regain the life she once had. Her presence helped fuel our drive and passion all the more to convince our lawmakers to fund cancer researchers and give them the tools they need to find a cure. Time is of the essence, especially for fighters like Michelle.

With hands that shook as if she had Parkinson's, Michele signed the banner and appeared to be proud to see her name among the others we had collected. We presented her with a Spokes of Hope cap, to replace her bandana, and she wore it well. She told us about not being able to see her three year old son in four months because she had been in isolation. Jeffery tried to encourage her to take an active role in her recovery, so he told her that getting up and walking might help the body grow stronger more quickly and bring her closer to seeing family again. We then visited with the other patients. Before we left, we saw Michelle shuffling in the hallway, getting one step closer to holding her precious little boy in her arms once more.

We stopped at three hospitals in downtown Pittsburgh that day. At the Children's Hospital, we brought our bikes into a large four story atrium, where we rode around in small circles answering questions from curious pediatric patients and their parents.

After entertaining the children, we went on a bike tour of downtown Pittsburgh with David Mitchell serving as our guide. Dave rode his fixed gear bike and nimbly led us up and down the steep streets of his city. We crossed a bridge spanning over the river, through narrow paths connecting to another path. It felt like threading a needle, one hundred feet in the air, traveling at 15-18 mph. At times I caught myself holding my breath and staying close to his rear wheel, for fear of losing sight of him on one of the quick turns on the path.

At one of the scenic landscape sites, near the Pirates baseball field on the North shore trail by the Allegheny River, we stopped to take pictures at a manmade waterfall. It was very fortunate that we stopped, because we were then joined by Patti, who had arrived late at the event at Gilda's Club that morning. She had been diagnosed with breast cancer a few days earlier and had not yet told her family or started treatment. She brought her bike and was ready to ride and talk with us.

We rode together, side by side, Patti and me. She knew that I was a breast cancer survivor from our gathering that morning at Gilda's and we started talking and couldn't stop. I had so much to share with her, from treatment side effect details like hair and head covering options, to what to expect with various surgical reconstruction procedures. We talked for over four hours. There was no way that I was going to allow her to be taken off guard as I had once been. We made sure that she had all the ammunition we could give her to totally destroy her invader and reclaim her life.

The best news we heard later was that Patti had gone through treatment successfully with a new "Spokes" family on her side. She had approached the experience like a true champion and trained and ridden through her treatment and came out stronger than when she went in. The next year, sporting a new shorter hairstyle regrown after chemo, she joined us in our Spokes of Hope tour and helped reach out and touch others. She proved to be an excellent advocate and a strong cancer ambassador on Capitol Hill.

Meeting Patti and helping her develop some of her battle strategies was confirmation that Spokes of Hope was right on track. We were recognizing that there was a real need for what our mission had to offer. Each one of the people we came in contact with helped shape and determine the direction that our volunteer organization was taking.

It was difficult to say goodbye to Pittsburgh, the hospitality of the Mitchell home and the lives we had met. Dave and Anne gave us a warm send-off breakfast, and we headed out for our next destination, Hershey, Pennsylvania.

Running behind schedule, we arrived later than planned at the Penn State Cancer Center. Sharon Duncan, a dynamic planner and organizer, had meticulously orchestrated our Hershey to Harrisburg spoke. She was a breast cancer survivor herself and had been treated at the very center we were visiting.

The media was there to meet us, as well as the chief medical officer of the cancer center. They welcomed us graciously, considering we were running behind schedule. I learned that organizing large groups of people traveling over a great distance is a challenge of its own. I was very thankful that they understood.

Once we did arrive, we kicked into "SPOKES" mode. We gave interviews, shot video footage and gave speeches to the medical staff that had gathered to greet us. We were so impressed with their open, friendly attitudes that Spokes of Hope has returned to the Hershey Cancer Center every year since that inaugural ride. This center was perfectly configured so that we could go in like bees pollinating flowers, floating from room to room; interacting with patients who seemed planted in their chairs and wired to life-saving infusions, in quiet alcoves waiting for the drips to stop. Our swarm spread out and met them individually and greeted them cheerfully. Armed with attitudes of hope, we made sure we left no patient and/or family without attempting to infuse them with the passion we had to reclaim what cancer had attempted to take away.

We gave each patient a Spokes of Hope cycling cap to wear in honor of their fight and help conceal the loss of hair. The caps are bright yellow in their base color and decorated with cancer ribbons of every color. The ribbon colors symbolized the different types of cancer that we were all fighting together. The caps are soft and conforming to the head with no hole in the back concealing any baldness.

One patient that I had the honor of meeting was Fred, accompanied by his wife Janice. They had been married over forty years and it was obvious from the way they looked into each other's eyes that they were in love and the honeymoon was far from over. I told them that I believed my passion for cycling was something that had really helped me through my cancer battle.

One of the things that I wanted to share with patients was how important it is for everyone to pursue their passion, no matter what it might be. I asked them to identify what their passion was, regardless of what the cancer treatment was putting them through at that moment, and then urged them to continue to fight to keep that passion alive. When I asked Fred, he said, "You mean besides Janice here?" He looked over at her and squeezed her hand as she blushed. "Fishing, I love to go fishing," he declared. Smiling, Janice interjected, "He would be fishing right now if he could." We talked a little about fishing and Ken's brother, Mark, who was an accomplished fly fisherman and the president of *Trout Unlimited*.

Then, as I had done with many other patients that day, I presented him with a Spokes of Hope cap, which he proudly donned. With a gleam in his eye, he looked up from his chemo chair to his bride and kissed her. The three of us posed together for photos. The spark that existed between the two lovers was something I wanted to capture forever.

A few years later, when we finally got our website built, I was looking through the photos of many of the patients that we had met and connected with. The picture of Janice and Fred struck a real chord with me. There was life, energy and hope in the couple, captured in that photograph and I wanted to put it on our website. Since I wanted their permission to use the photo, I sent a message along with the photo to the email address they had given me at the time of our visit.

The following response was unexpected:

"God Bless you for sending this picture. I really appreciate your taking the time from your busy schedule to send this. If you ever get the time I would appreciate any others that you took.

I know that is asking a lot and I apologize for that. Sadly Fred passed away this April 5, 2011. I cannot thank you enough for the caring, hope and the energy you project to others. That is so nice to have our picture on the webpage.

I must tell you that Fred treasured his hat (as the girls at Hershey can attest) and the only place he didn't wear it was to bed. He loved the hat so much that I put it in the casket with him.

God bless you for your work and may God keep you all safe on your journey to visit the hospitals. Janice""

Choked with unexpected emotions as I read her words, I was even more convinced that Spokes of Hope was part of my purpose. You never know how much impact you might have on another person's life, either by a chance meeting or planned one. We had given a gift to Fred and Janice, but they gave us back so much more.

Sharon had arranged to have local riders meet and ride with us from Hershey to the capitol in Harrisburg. We inhaled the scent of chocolate wafting through the air at the beginning of the ride and knew the day would be memorable.

There is something special about getting on the bike. I don't know if it is the wind in your face or the sunshine of the day that reminds us that we are indeed alive. The thrill of your heart beating in your chest matching the rhythm of your legs has a way of energizing your spirit and exciting the soul. I think we all felt it and were bonded together in the experience.

A few of the local riders who initially felt the need to surge off the front were reined in when reminded that we needed to consider the others on the trip who were tired from their long journey. They respectfully slowed their pace and refocused the ride while exchanging stories of bikes, life and cancer along the way.

Another Cyclist Combating Cancer member, Pete Collins, joined us. He was a survivor of cancer as well as military service and a motorcycle accident that left him with a serious injury to his leg. He rode proudly, flying a US flag on an already tall bike frame. Pete referred to himself as "The gimp," but he rode strong enough to lead us through several stretches of the route and reminded us all that we are united in the fight.

At a midpoint, our trek took us from the rolling roads to a 'Rails to Trails' bike path. Some of the most scenic paths in our country were once railroad tracks. We stopped at the trailhead, as our prostate cancer survivor / riders requested a nature break. While we waited for their return, Pete shared stories and cracked jokes.

As we stood enjoying each other's company, three women exited the bike path, stepping out of the shade of the tree lined path into the bright sunshine. The sight of our large group of cyclists wearing matching uniforms generated much curiosity. The women walked up and asked, "So what are you all doing here? What are you all riding for?" Chris States gave them an overview of our mission, including what we had been doing up to that point and how we were on our way to DC to see our lawmakers to support cancer research funding.

One of the women became very animated and her voice rose as she said "Oh my goodness! My best friend, Bonnie, is fighting cancer right now. She is scheduled to have a transplant and is scared to death. She is very tired and alone and feels so isolated. If your group could just stop by her house it would mean the world to her. Bonnie only lives five miles up the bike path and I can go ahead and wait on the path for you and guide you to her house from there." she pleaded. How could we refuse? This was our mission. Then Jeffrey Rowe spoke up and offered that we could sing to her as well. He said this as a joke, but she enthusiastically accepted his offer and we were committed.

Riding through the lush, green, canopy of trees on the trail was a cool respite from the heat of the day. Our hearts were again warmed at the sight of the woman waving frantically with both arms above her head and jumping up and down excitedly as she watched us approach. We stopped where she stood and got off our bikes, leaving the path as she led us out of the valley to Bonnie' house. While we walked with her, she told us that Bonnie had been preparing for a Stem Cell transplant and was really feeling the effects of the total depletion of her immune system.

We all decided to stand with our bikes on the street below the house, while the friend knocked on the door and invited Bonnie to come out onto her porch. As we stood, awaiting her arrival, we tried to decide what we should sing. It had to be something we all knew. Someone suggested, "Happy Birthday?" and we all shook our heads. "Silent Night?" again heads shook. "You are my sunshine," was the song we agreed on. Before Bonnie appeared, her friend had one more request. "After you finish singing, could you please raise your hands with three fingers in the air and shout 'Three!'?" She demonstrated. "This is our sign that means I – love - you." We were delighted to honor their special friendship.

When Bonnie made her entrance onto the stage, we stood below looking up. She peered over her isolation mask, eyes perplexed; face round from the medications used to help suppress her immune system and a shiny hairless crown glistening in the light. We began to sing and to her surprise, she started to smile. We could see even though her mouth was covered, her eyes were smiling. Then, as promised, at the completion of our song, we all raised three fingers to the sky and shouted "Three!"

Visibly moved, she placed her hand on her chest, clearly surprised by this simple gesture. She waved back as we bid goodbye. We wished her the best of luck and life, and then she retreated back into the house. Bonnie's friend was elated. She kept repeating, "I cannot tell you how much that meant to her." Her eyelids could no longer contain the tears that she had held back for so long and she hugged me. I realized in that moment, that this had been her way of expressing how she felt to her friend and our appearance had meant a great deal to her as well. She had been frustrated and was unable to find a way to help and we became the vehicle that enabled her to express her love for the friend who had been separated from her for so long by cancer.

What a long lasting impact that spontaneous moment had on the people who were there. To this day, when corresponding with other members of Spokes of Hope, we often sign off a message with a written "Three," or gesture in a photo that is posted and the meaning is still understood.

Over a year later, when the local Harrisburg newspaper published an article about Sharon Duncan celebrating her tenth year anniversary of cancer survivorship, the photo in the paper was of Sharon standing next to her bike in her Spokes of Hope jersey.

After the story was distributed, Sharon got this e-mail message:

"Dear Sharon,
I received a visit from you and the other bikers in Sept. 2009, a month prior
to my stem cell transplant for Leukemia & Lymphoma. Your group stopped
by my house on the way to Hershey & DC, at the request of a friend volun-
teering for your organization.

You may remember that you sang "You Are My Sunshine" and told me that
you were survivors. It meant so much to me and gave me the hope that I
needed, as I was undergoing intensive chemo and a pending transplant. I
can't thank you enough. Today, I am 15 months out of treatment and my
cancer is in remission. I started biking again last summer, and am feeling
well. I would like to participate in your next event and reach out to other
cancer patients as you did to me.

I want to give hope and support to others like you did for me. I believe that
it was you that sent me a Christmas card that year and I wanted to contact
you, but didn't know how until I saw an article in the Patriot News with
your photo.

Could you please let me know when your next event is and how I can get
involved. I look forward to hearing from you.

Thanks. Bonnie."

Bonnie did indeed join us the next year at our event in Hershey. That was where she had been treated and was now able to go revisit and

 show the nurses just how vibrant and alive she was. This woman was one of us now and able to share the true impact that survivors, reclaiming their lives after the ravages of cancer could have on others. In fact, one of the patients we visited that day was a young man diagnosed with Lymphoma and he was very frightened regarding his upcoming bone marrow

transplant. Bonnie was later able to connect with him. What an amazing circle of life!

* * *

The ride to Harrisburg culminated with an impromptu sprint down the wide boulevard, where street lights, standing like gendarmes guarding the final stage of the Tour de France, lined the street with the capitol building standing at the end like the Arc de Triumph. The path was clear, with rarely a car in sight. With an unspoken desire to race flickering in his eyes, Chris challenged me as he started a long jump that ended in a glorious championship sprint, with no one to see us but the riders clamoring to hold on behind.

Two of the riders that accompanied us were women on a Calfee tandem. In the world of tandems, that was a Ferrari. It is pretty rare to have a woman piloting a tandem, so after we had all stopped for a photo opportunity on the steps of the Pennsylvania Capitol building, I could not resist the opportunity to ask if I could ride on the tandem and see what it was like. I had ridden tandems at Nationals before, once with Ken and once with Gary Schmitt, but never with another woman.

As I climbed on the back, I realized that the fit was perfect. We started out fairly quickly and adapted to riding together seamlessly. When she started to pick up the pace, I answered the call gladly. After all, if you were taking a test drive in a Ferrari, you wouldn't just take it casually around the block. It was a great rush and upon our return to the group, she confessed that she had never ridden the tandem that fast before. That was a real treat.

With our new found friends and teammates, we gathered for a late lunch at Duke's bar and grill, known for their crab pretzels. We sat in the outdoor café basking in the sunshine, discussing our friendship and the events of our trip so far. We wondered aloud "How could it possibly get any better than this?"

* * *

That evening Sharon and Randy Duncan graciously invited us to stay at their home. The relaxed atmosphere was casual and comfortable and just what we needed. But as tired as we all were, the ever present realization of what we were doing seemed to take on a life of its own and made it difficult to surrender to sleep.

The Spokes of Hope tour started out as a bike ride with the goal of stopping at cancer centers and collect signatures on banners along the way, but evolved into so much more. Along with taking the advocacy and awareness issue to DC, we had the opportunity to touch the lives of others going through the battle, simply showing that we cared and that cancer doesn't always win.

When I first told Madison that I had cancer, she shared the story of the girl at school that other kids thought was contagious. Because of Madison's experience with this girl who had cancer and how she was treated by her peers, I realized that there were people out there who still thought cancer was contagious. That thought resonated with me when we were deciding on a message to print on the Spokes of hope banners. "Cancer is not contagious, but HOPE is. Spread the hope." is displayed on our banners, and we began our mission to infect everyone within our reach with hope.

We left Mechanicsburg and drove to Columbia, PA, where we met Sharon's brother-in-law, David Webb, who works for the military; his specialties involve math and statistics. Therefore, when asked to plot out our route to Baltimore, he managed to create the most highly detailed ride/route cheat sheet that I have ever seen. If I ever wanted to plan a cross country ride or a secret foreign invasion, he would be high on my list of logistics experts. At least that is what I thought, until we later discovered how challenging the route turned out to be.

We started near a recreational lake, surrounded by lots of summer cottages and fishing docks, where the roads were flat and scenic. When we moved away from the low lying area, climbing out of the Susquehanna River valley, we encountered the mountains of Pennsylvania and they seemed to be unending.

On one of the long, steep downhills, Jay's front wheel started to shimmy to the point that his bike was becoming dangerously uncontrollable. His eyes widened with terror as he was traveling in excess of 30 mph. His muscular forearms were taught, controlling the beast that was trying to throw him. He tamed the potential disaster and brought the bike to a stop. Breathless and speechless with the blood slowly returning to his face and the adrenaline obviously still shaking his grip, he declared that he was going to take a break. When we discovered that Ken was waiting at the bottom of the descent with the support vehicle, Jay relinquished his bike to the trailer and decided to ride in the vehicle for a while.

We later envied Jay's decision, because the climbs grew steeper and their length increased. There was one time in particular where we were forced to climb standing out of the saddle, pushing the gears with all our might, longing for the crest of the climb to come or another gear on the bike to bring relief. Approaching what appeared it could be the top of the climb, the road turned and we could see through the cover of trees that it was continuing on. Another daunting wall to climb revealed itself with no rest in sight. It was then that I heard Branan's voice behind me mutter, "Oh Sh*t!" which made me feel much better, because that was exactly what I was thinking, but didn't have the energy to say.

With mountainous terrain to overcome, fatigue started to set in quickly. There was a timeframe we needed to follow to reach Baltimore, where we were scheduled to see patients at the Greenebaum Cancer Center. Along the way we had also planned to meet Brock Yetso from the Ulman Young Adults Cancer Foundation. Our route came upon a 7-Eleven and we stopped briefly to down frozen Slurpee's without encountering brain freeze. The sugar and cold, icy liquid seemed to replenish our strength and spirit.

During one segment of the ride we discovered seemingly endless fields of bright yellow sunflowers. The heads of the flowers were in full bloom and the view looked like something you might see along the route during the Tour de France. The picturesque field screamed at us to stop and take in the magic of the moment, so we stopped, hoisted our bikes into the air and posed for pictures.

We connected with Brock and found him to be a very smooth, accomplished rider, and he fit in well with our group. As we entered the city streets of Baltimore we heard a loud bang, much like a gunshot; it was Brock's rear tire. This was the only flat on the entire trip, but we were prepared. Jeffrey pulled out his spare tire and Jay launched into mechanic mode and the tire was changed in record time. Brock then led us through the traffic to other routes along the river, but the cancer center was bedded snugly in the center of some very busy downtown traffic. This was not a problem for me, as I was accustomed to commuting to work in traffic, but some of our riders were on the edge of their comfort zones.

The Greenebaum Cancer Center had arranged a tent with snacks and refreshments waiting for us, as well as media to welcome our arrival. Their hospitality was very much appreciated. The Ulman Young Adults Cancer Foundation people were also in attendance and presented us with their team jerseys. We happily donned the jerseys and joined the hospital staff on a tour of their facility.

We were introduced to a nurse practitioner, who was also a triathlete, working in the cancer center. She was a strong and energetic health care provider who was passionate about her patients. She shared with us stories of cancer's impact on her and introduced us to patients that she thought would most benefit from our visit. There was a patient in isolation who was a school teacher. Her lack of hair in no way reflected her inner spirit, as she was vivacious, outgoing and ready to be done with cancer. She seemed to be energized when surrounded by like-minded people.

We were directed to another young woman, Dawn, who had been recently diagnosed and was just starting treatment. Her mother was in the room as we shared stories and listened to her plans regarding how she was going to get her life back. The following year we returned to the Greenbaum Center and discovered that Dawn was one of the patients still in the hospital in isolation. It was difficult to recognize her from the year before, she had lost a lot of weight and hair, but she still had the same twinkle in her eyes and her mother was again at her bedside. I could not help recalling how my mother stood by me in all of my hospital visits and like Dawn, it was about the same time of year. Cancer had once again managed to strike with a cruel sense of humor and timing.

The people of the Greenebaum Cancer Center were very gracious hosts. They understood our mission and did everything they could to help

further it, as well as help their patients benefit from what we had to offer. I was very impressed by their staff and facility and how well they were treating their patients.

Our next destination was Bethesda, Maryland. While we were riding from Indianapolis to DC, there were other Spokes events in other cities that were riding at the same time. Bob Sega was riding with John Owens and other CCC warriors in Minneapolis, Scott Joy was riding with Mark Knight along with a group from New Hampshire to Rhode Island, where Kathy Robinson picked up the ride with Marcia Dana and rode across Rhode Island. Ken Youner organized a ride from a hospital in New Jersey to New York, where he had been treated. And Chris Hornbeek and Dennis DeAtly were leading a Spokes ride in Texas. It felt amazing, knowing that my CCC brothers and sisters were all out riding at the same time, with the same message for cancer: We were not going to just roll over and take it, but were on a rampage to roll over cancer and crush it.

Riding into Bethesda, we somehow got off course and found ourselves on a winding, undulating wooded bike path near a breathtaking Mormon temple that overlooked the park. Since it was such a technical and narrow path, we were riding single file. All my life, I seem to have had my own personal radio playing in my head. Some may say I have a song in my heart, but really, it is playing in the background of my brain all the time. Sometimes it plays louder than others. Usually there are words or thoughts that trigger the song, and many times I will let the song out and just start singing, usually when I am in the car alone or when I am comfortable on my bike. As we were riding through the lush greenway, and I was riding with some of the most wonderful people I could ever want to know, my heart was full and giddy songs kept popping up in my head with each turn.

We had been on the path for a while and were wondering if we were ever going to find the road again, when suddenly the song *"Hit the road Jack"* popped into my head and I started singing it joyfully. When I came to the words, "And don't you come back no more," the memory of my uncle Jack hit me like lightening. He had hated that song, and then it struck me that Jack had died just a few months before, from lung cancer and he wasn't coming back. Suddenly I couldn't sing anymore. I started gasping for air as my throat tightened and tears poured down beneath my sunglasses. My uncle used to sing to me when I was little and I wasn't ever going to see him or hear his voice again. I never got to say goodbye and it was cancer, most likely caused by a lifetime of smoking, that took his life away. I had never really had the opportunity to deal with my feelings until that moment in the woods, and it hit me hard.

Chris States was the closest rider to me and I thought he must have been completely confused by the way I quickly changed from joyfully joking and singing to suddenly gasping for air and choking on tears. I couldn't ride any further and he stopped with me. I tried to explain that the song had brought full force the fact that I had lost my uncle to cancer, but had never had a chance to grieve. He didn't question or judge, he understood, as he had also lost a very close friend recently. His friend left Chris the bike that he was now riding in his honor.

We finally arrived at our destination where Ken Youner and David Margules joined us in Bethesda at Steve Freidman's house. Steve was a CCC'r and he graciously opened his home to us. He lived close to the National Cancer Institute (NCI) and near a bike path that was a direct route to the National Mall. We set up camp in his basement and after five days on the road, we all had been tired enough that we should have been all talked out and ready to just fall into bed. With new members added to the party, we were once again energized. It was like a slumber party and we had difficulty not cracking jokes and giggling through the night.

We had an appointment in the morning to give a presentation at the National Cancer Institute and I stayed up till 3:00 a.m. working on my speech. I found out later that Jay was up at the same time creating the PowerPoint slide show of photos of our trip to add to the presentation.

We rode to the National Cancer Institute and after going through all the security checkpoints with our bikes, we were met by our escort. She took us on a mini tour and then to the meeting room where we prepared for our presentation. Jay's PowerPoint was very well received and we met with Dr. Julia Rowland, who was the director of the Office of Cancer Sur-

National Institutes of Health

vivorship. She was a skilled speaker and gave a speech after we finished our tour.

That evening we decided to take a ride down the Chesapeake & Ohio towpath that was a 1% grade, sloping down to the heart of DC. Commuter bike traffic was thick and almost constant on the trail. We stayed together in a single pace line and took full advantage of the downhill effect, passing other riders as if we were a train.

The path abruptly opened up and leveled off when we reached the Potomac River. At one point, Jeffrey signaled us all to pause, as he had just reached the one thousand mile mark on his bike computer. We stopped and recorded his moment of pride and achievement, so happy that Jeffrey had joined us and we had been able to share that with him. He had been a pediatric brain cancer survivor diagnosed at age seventeen, still affected by his experience twenty years later.

We traveled across a cement bridge where two large stone lions stood guard, not far from Jeffrey's landmark mile. This was the threshold to the Lincoln and Washington monuments and the lions were the sentinels. As my eyes sent confirmation to my brain that we had arrived, my heart sent back the realization that we had indeed made a difference in many lives. What we had been planning for so long was no longer a dream. An unexpected surge of emotion caused me to stop for a moment and let it all sink in. Elated, I wanted to hug each and every one of my team of survivors and supporters, but I didn't want my wave of emotion to interrupt whatever joy they might have been feeling at that moment.

I suppressed the gasps that hovered so close to the surface, and resisted the tears trying to make an appearance. It was joy combined with sorrow and all the emotions in between that had been building inside me for so long. Realizing we had gone many miles and touched so many lives to reach this point made this my monumental moment.

We approached the steps, leading up to the figure of the great man, watching over a country he helped build and reunite. We posed for pictures at the Lincoln Monument. Like kids on a field trip, we visited the war memorials, looking at and exploring the ones that we hadn't seen before and paid our respects to all the military forces that fought and sacrificed to keep us free.

The following day it would be our turn to fight for those we might never meet, a fight to keep them free of cancer. We reflected on the battles that had been waged on our behalf and were now willing to fight for the freedom of people to live without fear of the terrorist that haunted them from within. Cancer was our terrorist and we needed the support of our lawmakers to stage an all-out war and win.

Morning arrived and the excitement was over the top. Having received a letter from the Sergeant at Arms granting us permission to enter the Capitol Building they limited us to only bringing three bikes inside with us. With this restriction, we couldn't ride our bikes to the Capitol building so we crammed everyone into the support van like clowns in a clown car to travel to the final destination with three bikes on the back. Before we embarked upon this endeavor, Branan had asked if he should bring a suit and tie to wear to meet with our lawmakers. My response was "Why? Our cycling uniforms are our business suits."

We went through the first security gate to get the van in the parking area of the Capitol Building, then unloaded, rider after rider, in our matching black and yellow Lycra suits and our representative three bikes. One of the bikes selected belonged to Ken Youner. Although Ken was

close to 70, he seemed to be the biggest kid there. It seemed to be less than a second after we had unloaded until he was on it riding in front of the Capitol, yelling in his New Jersey accent, "David! Take my picture!" with a mischievous grin.

Going through security at the entrance to the capitol was very interesting. We had to convince the guards that the banners we had in our hands were not protest banners, but contained signatures from citizens affected by cancer. Security dogs sniffed the bikes and they were then wiped down with special explosives detecting wipes. Assured that we were not a security risk, they cleared us to enter.

As we walked through the granite halls, the "tic, tic, tic" of the bike chains freewheeling on the cogs, echoed off the smooth limestone walls and shiny granite floors. The long yellow arrow of cyclists sliced through the dark sea of cold, stone faces held up by stiff black suits. It was amusing to watch eyes flicker as people tried not to look at us, but were unable to resist, breaking all their business focus. We were definitely not something they saw every day, especially not in this environment.

We set up the bikes and the banners to display before the presentation. As members of the House arrived, we answered questions and directed their attention to the banners. As the leader of Spokes of Hope, I gave the opening and closing speeches and each member of the team had an opportunity to speak. Their stories were presented with such passion, that I could see from the faces of some of the people in the audience, how much they were touched.

Chris States spoke about prevention and told his story of battling two different cancers. Jeffrey spoke about his encounter with Michelle in Pittsburgh and Ken Youner spoke powerfully about the health care initiative and the loss of his beloved Cecile. Sharon recounted her personal battle and emphasized the need for appropriations. None of their speeches were rehearsed, coordinated or assigned but like a perfect rotating pace line, they all worked together in synchronization. I was so proud of my Spokes team's performance on Capitol Hill.

Later we posed for photos with our different representatives. Sharon got to pose with her Pennsylvania Representative as she presented him with the Penn State Cancer Center banner. We met with Senator Richard Lugar of Indiana, who was gracious enough to sign our banner.

After meeting with individual lawmakers, we ventured across the street from the Capitol building to a popular restaurant that had been on the Food Network. We sat down to eat and reviewed the events of the trip that touched us. The common thread was the amazing realization of what we had done. We had spread the word, met with hospital staff and survivors, met with the National Cancer Institute, and talked about research needs with our lawmakers. It was even more impactful than anyone had imagined that it would be.

When it was all over, we felt a strange let down feeling. "That's it? Are we done? Now we go home?" were the thoughts swirling through all our heads. It was hard to acknowledge that we would have to leave and return to our normal lives and jobs after such an experience, but it was time to say goodbye and head home.

The evolution of Spokes of Hope was influenced by the spirit of the riders and the needs of the patients. We had a foundation to build upon. This was magic and not something one could just say happened. We realized that there was a real need that could be filled with Spokes of Hope and now that we knew what was possible, it was time to start planning for the future.

In the years to follow, we expanded our mission to visit more Cancer Support communities, like Gilda's Club and other centers. We started speaking at Middle Schools about cycling and cancer in an effort to promote lifetime exercise and open discussions about what cancer really is. We explained that it was not contagious, outlined steps to prevent it, and provided information about how they could deal with cancer when it affects them or someone they know or love.

The teachers cringed and the students giggled when I told them that they had to know every inch of their bodies and realize what it felt like when something wasn't right. As I emphasized that they were not supposed to start exploring this while at school or in public, I heard more giggles. My focus was intended for the age range for testicular cancer, normally found in men and boys ages 15-26 and breast cancer which can also occur in women at an early age.

We changed the format of our bike rides so they would no longer be point to point, but decided to engage the local communities by driving to the different cities and riding with local people on their roads, in an effort to reach more people. By using what we had learned from years of racing and coaching, we created bicycle clinics for breast cancer survivors and called our organization "Pink Pedal Power." Instead of giving one large presentation to lawmakers in DC, we started visiting them in their offices, still dressed in our "business suits" of Lycra.

Working with support from Bicycling magazine and the Valley Preferred Cycling Velodrome, Spokes of Hope began honoring pediatric cancer survivors in a very special event. The first year, we were able to honor an 8 year old boy, who was the cousin of Jay Bodkin. Jay had been involved in cycling and skating with us for many years. When we started

Spokes of Hope, he was one of the first to support us. Now we wanted to support him and his family.

His cousin, Jack, had been fighting brain tumors, called medulloblastoma, since the age of four. In the process of his battle, he ended up having three strokes. Jack was a fighter and it really helped that he had Jay on his side. Jay built a specially adapted bike so Jack could ride and control it with his good arm. The bike was not only providing him with a means of freedom, it helped him get stronger. Pedaling helped his affected side build muscle and improved his range of motion.

Spokes of Hope arranged to come to the velodrome for the last race of the year. At the season's grand finale, there were over three thousand spectators either in the stands or surrounding the track. Cancer survivors from around the country would be joining us. We were going to take "Victory laps" around the track during intermission. The velodrome gave us some time before the event so that I could conduct a mini-clinic to make sure everyone would be able to safely ride on the banked track and know the rules of riding in that environment.

The intermission was choreographed, with riders lined up in the tunnel under the spectator's stands, awaiting our cue to take the track. Jack led us onto the track when the music "Vox Populi" started and people began cheering loudly. We could feel the joy and see the elation on the faces of the riders as we rode in a moment of glory, high fiving outstretched hands, with hearts beating to the rhythm of the spectators pounding on the boards surrounding the track. The faces and colors were all a blur, but the memory was absolutely spectacular.

We exited the track, rode into the infield, and waited for Jack to finish his final stretch. When he came into view, he was pedaling his bike with his guide dog running alongside. We gathered as a team to envelop him as the roar of the crowd escalated, then escorted him to the winner's podium and presented him with a Spokes of Hope shirt and cap, just as though he was the winner of a professional stage race.

He stood strong on the podium and was then joined by his proud, supportive family, which included his younger sister, brother, parents and grandfather. He was shining with hope and the joy of survivorship, which outweighed pity or fear. The celebration was electric.

Shortly after our return from DC in 2009, Special Olympics International contacted me about conducting a coach's cycling clinic in Hiroshima, Japan. I told them that Ken and I were an experienced coaching team and wanted to know if he could come as well. My strengths were the physical and psychological components and his strengths covered the mechanical/engineering areas of the sport.

We were told that Japan had only budgeted for one coach, so I contacted the person in Hiroshima who was coordinating the clinic, Frank Thornton. He lived in Hiroshima with his wife and teenage sons, one of whom was autistic while the other was a rising competitive cyclist.

Frank had created a cycling team of Special Olympians, which he named, "Team Panthaka," in honor of a Buddhist fable about a brother who was mentally slow but physically very strong. Hiroshima had many potential coaches with experience working with the intellectually disabled, but they needed training in the sport.

When I first contacted Frank, he asked how long I needed to conduct the clinic. My first thought was of our bike camp format, which would cover all aspects of racing and give them hands on experience with riders. This would take a minimum of four days, but they apparently thought it would all be covered in one afternoon. So we compromised and agreed upon a two day clinic. I asked if it would be acceptable if I brought Ken and Madison with me to Japan, if we paid for their travel expenses. He agreed and said we could stay with his family instead of a hotel. That was more than a financial bonus, as I much prefer learning about the culture first hand.

We had to really dig deep to figure out how we could afford the trip, so we decided not to tell Madison that we were going to take her with us until we were certain it would happen financially. She had always been unhappy that Ken and I got to go on international adventures with Special Olympics while she had to stay behind with Nana. She didn't seem to grasp the fact that these trips were actually work, not play, and that we would be unable to spend any time with her or even see her during a competition. I had some major travel site searching to do to make this possible and include Madison.

237

The opportunity was unique due to the hospitality of our hosts, but we still had some bills left over from chemotherapy and it was difficult to find international airfare that was within our meager budget. For a while it appeared impossible to come up with the money to bring Madison with us. Then my parents decided that they would pay for Madison's flight as a combination birthday and early Christmas present for the whole family.

Her birthday had always been a costumed Halloween extravaganza. The basement was transformed from our exercise area to a scare fest with black and orange streamers draped from the rafters, rubber spiders with faux cobwebs in every corner, bursts of fog billowing out from the fog machine and eerie monster sounds from the boom box that could barely be heard over the squeals related to eating gory candy worms and drinking green slime punch. After her costumed friends had given her their gifts, we handed her an envelope. She took it with a quizzical look, and then opened it as we watched her expression change from confusion to disbelief, then excitement when she realized it was an electronic airline ticket to Hiroshima and HER name was on it. The best part was listening to her voice change with realization. "I'm going to Japan?" She asked. We nodded. "I'm going to Japan?" She asked once more, rising to her feet. "I'M GOING TO JAPAN!" she shouted to the friends around her as she jumped up and down in excitement.

The flight was long but well worth it. We flew into Tokyo and then took a commuter plane to Hiroshima. The hour of our arrival was late in Hiroshima. Frank Thornton picked us up at the airport. His English was perfect, as he had been born in Hawaii and taught English as a second language from his home in Hiroshima.

Madison was doing everything she could to keep her travel weary eyes open. Even though she was dealing with the time change after an international flight, she didn't want to miss a thing. On the way to his home, Frank stopped to get gas at a 7-Eleven, so we decided to see what a Japanese 7-11 looked like. We were delighted to find steamed buns that were sold right beside the cash register. It was love at first bite and Madison readily devoured the delectable warm meat surprise enveloped by the pale steamed bun.

Upon arrival at our destination Frank's beautiful wife, Masami and his sons, Mike and Duke, greeted us. They showed us to the room that would be our home for the week. A traditional tatami mat floor, where shoes were removed and large puffy white mattresses, covered in thick down comforters, awaited us.

In the morning, Frank went to work and the boys to school. When we collected in the kitchen, Masami asked if we would like a western breakfast. We unanimously chimed in that we would like to eat as much traditional Japanese food as possible, so she served a breakfast consisting of dried whole fish, beans with very sticky white strands like melted marshmallow connecting the beans to the spoon, and miso soup and rice. I was very proud of Madison for trying all the food without complaint. She embraced the experience with bravery and willingness to try almost anything and even followed Masami's suggestion to eat the fish, head first. What a unique experience that was.

Masami drove us into Hiroshima, where we toured the Peace Museum, which stood on the site that had been ground zero for the nuclear bomb that the United States dropped over their city during World War II. We gazed at beautiful statues, with long strands of origami folded paper cranes hanging from them, at the entrance to the park. Inside the museum we learned the story of the folded cranes.

It was the story of a thirteen year old girl who was exposed to the radiation from of the bomb and was slowly dying of Leukemia as a result. She had heard a legend that if a person folded 1000 cranes out of paper, a miracle would be granted. She started folding cranes out of every piece of paper she could find. As people learned of her quest to use the paper cranes to help survive Leukemia, they too started to fold cranes and sent them to her. Soon people from around the world began to do the same. Unfortunately, she did not get the miracle she wished for, but her story was able to live on, immortalized in the elegantly folded, graceful paper birds of hope.

Normally I am very proud to wear my Team USA coat, but on that day, after seeing the devastation of all those innocent lives, I was tempted to take it off in respect for the lives lost due to the bomb the United States dropped. The people memorialized in the Peace Museum were not soldiers, but the children, mothers and fathers that were going about their daily lives. You could still see outlines of bodies on the stone steps, etched where the blinding light hit and melted them in place. We were extremely moved by the museum and impressed by the wall of letters written and sent by every Mayor of Hiroshima since that horrible day, to any country in the world testing nuclear devices designed to end lives, like those lost in Hiroshima.

After touring the museum, Masami took us to one of her favorite restaurants, located on the corner of the street across from the Peace Park. A friendly wait staff welcomed us and the smell of something wonderful and warm drew us in. Escorted to a booth, we slid across smooth, wooden benches covered with mat cushions facing a large shiny metal cooktop table.

Masami ordered Okonomiyaki; a Japanese pancake with seafood and pasta inside, and egg and pork on top, sprinkled with flakes of seaweed, delicate dried fish shavings called Benito flakes and Okonomiyaki sauce. Masami described the sauce as Japanese Steak sauce. The pancakes were to be eaten with spatulas, not chopsticks. We devoured this fun and intriguing meal, and it quickly became Madison's new favorite food.

Later we went shopping in downtown Hiroshima where I saw a sign advertising a very low price for eyeglasses and a full eye exam that could be done in thirty minutes. I remembered that Madison needed a new pair of glasses so we stopped. It was entertaining to watch Madison, who resisted learning Japanese before we arrived, in a situation where she was forced to learn how to count to two in Japanese. As the optician switched the strength of the lenses back and forth, she would say, "Ichi? Ni? Ichi" (one) then switch to the other power, "Ni" (two).

Our trip did not correspond with any regularly scheduled vacation time from Madison's school, so before leaving for Japan we did a little research into school policy. We discovered that any day she spent in school, even if the school was half way around the world, would qualify as a day in class and she would not be marked absent as long as we had documentation of her attendance. Madison was not at all thrilled with the possibility that she would have to attend school while she was in Japan and made it clear that we were mean parents forcing her to do so.

Frank's oldest son, Mike, was one year older than Madison. His parents spoke to his school and got permission for her to shadow him for a day while we were visiting. Japanese students wear uniforms to school, so we improvised with a blazer, skirt and knee socks to resemble the proper uniform for a Japanese school girl. The one thing that we had not known and were not quite prepared for was the fact that Mike went to an all-boys private school.

That morning, Frank drove us all to Mike's school, which sat on a hill and was much farther away than I had imagined. We passed many boys in uniform walking and pushing their bikes up the very steep incline. Mike usually rode his bike all the way up to the school. It was no wonder he was such a strong competitive racer.

Madison was very nervous about going, but I felt in my heart that it would be a great experience. All day I thought about her, envious of what she might see and what new things she might experience. I could hardly wait for her to return and tell us all about her new adventure. After school they took the train back to the house and the moment she entered our room, she exploded with all that had happened. She was bubbling over; telling me story after story in rapid succession and my heart soared with a combination of relief and elation.

She told us that her adventure began as soon as we dropped her off. She was greeted at the entrance by the principal who spoke very little English. When she started to walk into the school, she forgot to remove

240   CINDI HART

her shoes, so he asked what size shoe she wore and gave her an oversized pair of pink slippers. Shuffling forward, she was directed up a few flights of stairs where her focus was on the slippers and trying to keep them on her feet. They finally entered a large room filled with teachers working at desks. The Principal told her to stand beside his desk at the front of the room as he made an announcement in Japanese. All eyes focused on her as she introduced herself.

An Australian teacher who taught English asked Madison to help with his English classes. The corridors leading to the classrooms were lined with glass walls and the students sitting in the rooms could see anyone passing through the hallways. As she walked along, heads were turning quickly in her direction. A teenage girl in an all-boys school was enough to get everyone's attention.

When she entered the English class she was shocked to be met with enthusiastic applause. Mike ushered her to a seat at his desk. Instantly she was approached by several boys. One in particular knew more English than the others. He boldly stepped up and said, "Hey! I'm Ken. What's your name?" To which she replied, "My name is Madison and my father's name is Ken." He replied, "That's cool, see you later." She was impressed because she had not met anyone else in the school who spoke American slang.

She described how an upper-class boy came running up to the classroom, opened a sliding door, shoved a camera phone into the room and took her picture. The photo, she later learned, was sent to the whole school within minutes.

The teacher stood up and told both Mike and Madison to come to the front of the class where she was to introduce herself. "Hello. My Name is Hart, Madison and I am from the United States. I live in a state called Indiana." This information was greeted by a chorus of, "Ooooooooo!" The teacher gave her a piece of chalk and instructed her to write her name on the board She asked if anyone in the class would like to ask a question, but they all just stared at her and remained totally silent.

The teacher also gave her some work sheets with dialogue and asked her to read aloud to the class. When she finished speaking, they again surprised her with applause. When she walked into the next class, there was even more applause and cheering. She was instructed to stand on a wooden podium before the class and introduce herself. "My name is Hart, Madison and I am from Indianapolis, Indiana which is known for growing corn and racing cars. We don't have any mountains or oceans near where I live."

The English teacher then gave the students a comprehension quiz over what she had just said. He asked the class where she was from and they answered, "India." She giggled and told them, "Close enough."

After the question session was over, they were to work in pairs with some strictly English conversation written on their worksheet. One boy didn't have a partner so she was paired with him. When approached, he lowered his eyes and sank down in his seat. The other boys began shouting in Japanese. The teacher told her, "They are complaining because they all wanted to be the one chosen to work with you."

Madison recounted that in the next class, the primary question was, "Do you have a boyfriend?" The boy that asked had poufy hair due to creative use of hair styling gel. She answered, "Yes" and the entire class groaned. After that, they asked many similar questions, such as "Who in here do you find most attractive?" Her answer was, "You would all be more attractive if you asked productive questions." Then about five more hands went up. "What do you want in a Japanese boy?" She answered, "Someone who talks more than all of you and less than him!" as she pointed to the poufy haired boy who then lowered his head to his desk.

Changing the subject slightly, she was asked, "What do you want to do in life?" and she replied, "I plan to be a surgeon." There was a collective, "Oooo! House MD!" Apparently the TV show *House* was quite popular in Japan. A boy sitting in front of her asked about CSI Miami and Grey's Anatomy. When asked if she liked football, she started talking about the Indianapolis Colts, only to find that they were referring to soccer.

When the class was nearly over, she asked to have a picture taken with the teacher, but ended up with a picture of the teacher and the entire class. She learned much more than she ever expected that day and I relished listening to every detail.

That evening we went to a sushi bar with a conveyer belt that paraded plates of freshly prepared sushi by each table. Since I had experienced this while in Matsumoto, I wanted Ken and Madison to try it too. There was no sushi menu. If a person saw something they wanted they just picked it up from the procession of plates cruising by the table. When the meal was finished, the collection of empty plates are counted to determine the amount of the bill. It was an interesting and delightful treat.

The following day was the start of the coaching clinic. Frank took us to the Chou Shining Park. It was the perfect location for bike racing, since it had been developed as the cycling venue for the Asian Games. The start/finish line had an official's building with timing equipment and a PA system. This beautiful venue would work very well for our clinic.

As the coaches and athletes arrived, we became concerned that the heavy clouds that hung low in the sky could possibly rain, making outside demonstrations of cycling drills very difficult. Our class room lectures were to be held in a large wooden structure with high arched ceilings. We organized seating to leave space around the perimeter of the room, to allow us to demonstrate skills should it rain. Ken and I took turns lecturing and Frank stood by steadfastly interpreting everything we said. The people were very attentive, interested and engaged. It was a pleasure to share our love and experience regarding cycling, with people so interested in learning.

While we lectured, Madison sat at a table at the edge of the room listening to music with her new Downs Syndrome friend. With headphones connecting them as they listened to the same iPod, I felt she was acting as a teenaged ambassador should. She was comfortable with Special Olympians and the fact that she was a redheaded girl didn't hurt her ambassadorship at all.

As the lecture progressed, I noticed that Madison had disappeared. My thought was that she must have still been adjusting to the change in time zones and having heard our lectures so many times before, she had likely gone somewhere quiet to take a nap. When we took a break, everyone left the building to go to the restroom or get something to drink, but I stayed behind to work on the notes for the next part of the lecture. I was startled when Frank breathlessly appeared in the door of the lecture area. "Cindi, you have got to come out and see this!" he invited. My curiosity was peaked and I was sure by the twinkle in Frank's eyes, that it had something to do with Madison. My first thought was that she had found it difficult to adapt to the time change and was napping in a golf cart somewhere.

I exited the lecture hall and discovered that the rain had stopped and the sun had returned, peering through the clouds. All the participants in the clinic had gathered just outside the door and were joined by many of the wives or mothers of the attendees of the clinic. Everyone gathered in a large cluster like bees, excitedly moving toward the center of their group. When my arrival was noticed, smiling faces turned to greet me with obvious anticipation in their eyes.

They began to step back as I walked forward, parting, wordlessly guiding me to the center of their interest. I was drawn down the corridor of people, as they stepped back and revealed Madison. She was a vision of beauty, dressed from head to toe in a beautiful traditional Kimono. Her red hair was braided, adorned and swept up with pearly hairpins. The bright pink Kimono had a stiff midsection belt embroidered with flowers. She was stunning in their traditional attire, all the way to her toes covered by white stockings and sandals. What an extraordinary gift they had given her, and us. The vision of her standing there, waiting for us to discover her, will remain with me for many years to come.

It seemed that "Team Panthaka's" women's auxiliary had kidnapped Madison during the lecture and taken her to an area in the next building where women were prepared for formal photo sessions in the garden. She later revealed that five women had worked together, wrapping and dressing her as well as styling her hair. I was so moved by their kind hearted generosity and elated by the results. This was an experience of a lifetime for our whole family.

I was very impressed by how well all the attendees responded to the clinic and pleased to see them applying what they had learned at the final time trial. It gave me confidence that Team Panthaka would be very successful. I felt that we were creating a legacy that would have an effect on many lives in the future.

The following day, Masami took us to Miyajima, which is a historical Japanese holy place with a Buddhist and a Shinto shrine. Since it was located on an island off the coast of Hiroshima, we had to take a ferry. During the out time on the ferry, Masami cautioned us. "I had a deer eat my map before. Be careful with the deer," she said. Coming from Indiana, we were very familiar with the deer and were not at all afraid of them; therefore we assumed that this behavior was most likely a strange and isolated incident.

Even though the day's weather was overcast and it was misting rain, the sight of the huge orange gate, seemingly floating over the water, was still breathtaking. The dock where the ferry landed emptied out onto a small walking street lined with shops.

We were lured down the street by the smell of maple cakes and chicken on a stick. Having found some freshly steamed buns, we were walking toward the shrine while eating them and discovered a small, dog sized deer, which appeared to be stalking us. Masami gave the deer a fierce look and before we knew it, we were being pursued. In fact, the animal was chasing me down the street. As I picked up my pace it grabbed the tail of my coat with its teeth! I have never before seen such aggressive deer and understood that Masami's earlier caution was certainly warranted.

We loved everything about our experience in Japan, including touring the local bike shop and visiting the Keirin race track. As a cultural exchange, we brought an example of an American treat to share with the Thornton family. They were delighted to see the S'mores and marveled at just how much the boys enjoyed them. We held marshmallows skewered on chopsticks over an open flame in the middle of the table and taught the boys how to let them ignite, then blow out the flames and press the caramelized sugar between two pieces of graham cracker and a bit of chocolate bar. Although he seemed to enjoy the taste, the Thornton's younger son, Duke, was not so happy with the sticky marshmallow on his fingers. As a result, we helped him with his marshmallows when he asked for more. Duke was autistic and very quiet, but very dignified and proper. He was extremely sensitive to texture, which is not at all an unusual trait for autistic individuals.

The most difficult part of our trip was having to say goodbye to our new family. Just before taking us to the airport, Frank and Masami presented us with our own Okonomiyaki spatulas to remind us of our stay. To this day, I continue to make Okonomiyaki for Madison, but it will never taste as good as it did when we shared that afternoon with Masami at the Peace Park.

*   *   *

Over the winter, the Cyclists Combating Cancer group lost some very strong members. Bob Sega and Kathleen Carrico, both metastatic cancer veterans, left us with a big hole in our hearts in January of 2010. They were both huge fans of a cycling event that took place in Iowa called RAGBRAI. This ride takes place every year during the last week in July, and Bob had been trying to talk me into riding it for several years. Now that he was gone, I decided to ride it, as a tribute to him.

RAGBRAI stands for "The Register's Annual Great Bike Ride across Iowa" and starts at the Missouri River and ends at the Mississippi River, covering over 400 miles in seven days on bikes. Riders camp in host towns every night and over twenty thousand people come from all around the world to participate. It really is a rolling party across the state.

It was CCC'r, Mark Kargol who successfully talked me into participating in July of 2010. I didn't think I would be able to go since there is a lottery to get an entry, and I had missed that deadline. He messaged me on Facebook and told me that there was a forum online where people were selling their entries when, for some reason, they found themselves unable to go. I went on the website and found many weeklong entries for sale.

James Higden, one of the people who had posted a ticket for sale on the site, explained that his brother was unable to go that year. I purchased it and he transferred it into my name and told me that for a bit more money, I would be able to join their team and they would take care of transporting my baggage from town to town and establishing a campsite for us each evening. This sounded very reasonable, so I joined the "Clean Team," so named because Jim looked like Mr. Clean.

Jim lived in Iowa City, where the team collected and piled into the team vehicle, heading west toward the Missouri River. It felt odd to be on my own, on a team that I would not be coaching or having to take care of. I could just ride and eat my way across Iowa with twenty thousand other people in Lycra. It was CRAZY FUN!

Bob was right; I should have joined him long ago. We rode on smooth country roads lined on both sides by corn and soybean fields. Occasionally we would pedal past a poultry or pig farm, but usually it was corn for as far as the eye could see. The line of riders seemed to be endless. Every 10 miles or so, we came upon a small farming town, completely overrun by a plague of cyclists looking for food, water and restrooms. Whenever we came to a town, we were forced off our bikes due to the sheer number of cyclists walking in front of us. Side by side, wheel to wheel, and handlebar to handlebar we clip clopped through in our cleated shoes.

In anticipation, the entire town shuts down for the day. The towns-people appeared to be overjoyed to have us in their community. They brought out bands and cheerleaders for our entertainment. The local fire departments, Boy Scout and church groups set out food for sale: home-made pies, smoothies, pancakes, and cookies were available in every place we stopped. Bars were open at 9am and it was not unusual to see lines forming to buy Bloody Marys. Ragbrai was a major fundraising opportunity for everyone along the route.

Anyone who thinks that Iowa is flat has obviously never ridden a bike through the state. My experience has proven that the roads are one large rolling hill after another and they seem to never end. The heat was unbearable whenever we got off the bike and walked, so we headed to anything water related we could find, from slip-n-slides to fire hydrants turned into fountains.

I stopped at every Casey's General Store I encountered and loaded my water bottle with ice. We broke camp early each morning to be on the road before 7am. Jay had loaned me his tent and sleeping bag and I rolled everything up and put it in my assigned tub and shoved it into the trailer each day.

At first dawn we often found a low lying fog hanging in the air and a rainbow of colorful jerseys could be seen riding through the white mist. Riders spread all the way across the lanes, filling the breadth of the road, because there was no motor traffic on the routes. Etiquette dictated that the slower riders were to stay on the right, so the faster riders could pass on the left.

I had a fantastic time riding and meeting people and had no prob-lem finding temporary team mates to draft for the day. I met two brothers from Minnesota on the first morning and kept running into them throughout the week. There was another man from Germany who was training to ride across the United States and I found him to be a smooth and strong rider who didn't mind my sitting closely behind him, taking advantage of his hospitality. He told me that his wife back home was currently fighting breast cancer and I promised that I would send a Spokes of Hope package to her if he would send me their address.

I was usually the first one from our team to arrive at camp after completing the ride, finishing between noon and 1pm, in the heat of the day. Since showers cost around five dollars and admission to the swimming pool that had unlimited showers was about six dollars, I opted to hang out at the pool all afternoon. By dinner time it was full of riders, just standing, laughing, talking and judging the lifeguards on their diving performance.

Dinners were in the towns where we were staying for the night. Most every church in the town opened their doors and had meals for sale. We had our pick of a spaghetti dinner, baked potato bar or chicken and noodles, depending on the church, and they always had pie. The price for dinner was capped at eight dollars and the line to get in to eat frequently wrapped around the block until they ran out of food.

There were some food venders that traveled along with the ride and placed signs on the road, giving the riders notice of the number of miles remaining till they would reach the food stop. Signs weren't always necessary. We could see and smell the smoke for nearly a mile before we got to "Mr. Pork Chop." The iconic pink pig themed bus was loaded with pork chops that were over an inch thick and as big around as my hand. In front of the bus, they slow roasted them over smoking corn stalks. The flavor was intoxicating and the size was more than I could handle in one meal. Anticipating that not all riders could finish their large offering, they supplied me with a zip lock bag to put in my back pocket and I was able to finish eating it later.

If it was old fashioned ice cream that you wanted, there was Beekman's ice cream, churned on the spot with steam powered engines. We heard the "Shh, chunk, chunk, shh, chunk, chunk" of pistons and gears turning, and saw an array of bikes scattered in all directions that looked like an explosion of bikes, abandoned on lawns, while riders stood in long lines waiting for the frozen treat in the hot summer sun. The taste and grainy texture made it well worth the wait.

The journey across the Iowa culminated Saturday afternoon with another long line of cyclists waiting to ceremonially dip the front wheel of their bikes into the Mississippi river and pose for photos. This carefree week motivated me to find a way to share the experience with others. We immediately started planning to form a Spokes of Hope team, and have had wonderful RAGBRAI adventures with them every year since.

For first time riders at RAGBRAI, it is customary to write "Virgin" on the back of their calves with a black marker to let everyone know to be nice to them. On Spokes of Hope's first RAGBRAI, we had 12 virgins and I'm sure that has to be a record. Getting to share the joy of the experience with close friends made the adventure even better. I felt like it was a summer camp for grownups, where we were isolated from the outside world and it was an unconditional love. It didn't matter how fast or slow you were - what counted was that you were there!

As an experienced coach and mechanic, Ken adapted to the role of SAG driver with great ease. When we rode into camp after sixty to seventy miles of hills and wind, he had already marked the route to our campsite, set up chairs and refreshments with many other comforts of home. I felt guilty that we were having all the fun, riding and eating and seeing all the sights, but he appeared to be very content making us happy and comfortable. This was Ken being "Ken," a giving and caring person and all the more reason to love him.

Tim Wozniak, another rider from Indianapolis, joined our team. He was lean, strong and smooth on the bike and volunteered to be my "Domestique" across Iowa. A Domestique is a racer who rides for the benefit of the team. That is actually a very good description of Tim in general, as he is one of those silent heroes that never asks for anything for himself, but is always giving.

Sitting in his draft was very comfortable. He rode with a steady confidence that let riders around him know that they were in good company and could trust him with their life. He would lead me out for miles, passing riders by the thousands, easily before the day was done. He rode in front to break the wind so my ride would be easier and I could go faster for a longer period of time. I felt very fortunate and hoped that I wasn't holding him back too much. As we snaked our way through the throngs of cyclists, I would honk my bike horn to let people know that we were passing. Riding for sixty miles yelling, "On your left!" gets a little tiring after a while. I thought it was the least I could do for our team.

It was very nice to be able to have someone to share the experiences found in the pass- through towns, as well as share an occasional snow cone or Danish pastry. When I got a flat tire, I felt guilty when he insisted on changing it for me. "It's my job." He said, "It's what Domestiques do." And a grin spread across his face, as he skillfully changed my tire on the side of the road.

When I rode RAGBRAI with Tim in 2012, it was an extremely hot, dry summer and mid-week the temperature soared over 100 degrees before noon. There was no shade to be found riding through corn field countryside, and there appeared to be no clouds anywhere to disperse the hot sun above us. As the day grew hotter, I started asking Tim to stop every chance we had to put ice in my sleeves and soak my head under water, and he never complained. We were riding into Des Moines that day, and it was one of the longest distances of the week. Around mile 90, I began stopping every couple of miles as the temperature reached well over 110 degrees.

Ken had arranged for us to stay in a hotel that night instead of camping, which was a welcome promise of air conditioning, soft beds and showers. To get to the hotel, we had to ride through the hills to the other side of town. Nearing our destination, we saw a bank sign that flashed the temperature on its digital display. "114 degrees." It flashed, across the street from a Dairy Queen that beckoned to us from the top of a steep driveway. "Tim, let's stop here. My treat!" I said. "Ok" was his response. When we opened the doors, the chill of the air-conditioning was almost a shock. As we entered the establishment with faces bright red and shiny from the combination of heat, sweat and sunscreen, wearing Lycra cycling clothing and clomping in our stiff cycling shoes, all eyes of the patrons and staff looked our way. We looked as if we had just crossed the desert without a camel and had finally found an oasis. That's what it felt like too. We sat and soaked in as much cold as we could, both internally and externally. The ice cream was very appreciated and we lingered with each spoon full, watching the temperature on the sign across the street continue to go up.

Having someone to share adventures with, not only enriches the experience, but helps make the moments even more powerful and long lasting. Years later, when you recall an experience and wonder, "Was it really that good?" or "Was it really that hot?" it helps to have someone who validates your recollections and says, "Yes, it was, and maybe even better." It always helps to have friends to reminisce and savor memories from the past.

*   *   *

A month before the ride across Iowa, we participated in a charity fundraising ride to benefit the cancer center where I had been treated. The event was held on a 3.5 mile loop around the Butler University campus. I was excited and truly impressed when Dr. Goulet joined my team, and even more impressed by how dedicated he was to riding every lap he could during the 24 hours. David Fritz, a tall, thin, dark haired fifteen year old boy that I had been coaching in speed skating and cycling, joined our team as well. He was determined that he would complete his first century there. His riding skills improved with every lap. He kept me company and sat in my draft so well that I couldn't tell he was even there at times.

Also joining our team was John Lind, a stage four, head and neck cancer survivor who was a year out of treatment at that time. I first met John when he contacted me after he purchased a Spokes of Hope jersey on-line. He stood six feet, two inches tall with sparkling blue eyes and a white mustache that wiggled when he laughed, which was often. He had a wit indicative of his education as a physicist and could make an endless number of highly irrational jokes about Pi. John started riding after his diagnosis to reclaim his life from cancer and we introduced him to riding on the velodrome, where he blossomed. He purchased a track bike and rode two hundred miles during the 24 hour event. That was quite an impressive accomplishment in itself, but then when you add the fact that he was 60 years old and on a fixed gear bike, where he was unable to coast a single pedal stroke for 200 miles, it was even more remarkable. Only two years earlier, he had questioned if he would live to see the next 200 days, let alone ride a bike for 200 miles.

After riding the course for five hours, I had pain in my left hand that was very similar to the pain I had felt with the cording. My hand felt tight and restricted. As time went on, my fingers began to look like sausages sticking out of my glove. Torn between wanting to ride through the 24 hours and stopping to get relief from the pressure, I did everything I could to reduce the swelling. By the time I stopped to eat, the swelling had grown to the point that I had difficulty bending my fingers. I knew that riding was making it worse, but I was the leader of the Spokes of Hope team and felt that I couldn't stop while everyone else continued on. It just didn't seem right.

By 2am, most of the cheering spectators around the course began retiring for the evening, leaving only the diehard supporters and the police officers guarding the intersections. The posse of riders grew ever thinner as the night continued to deepen. As a growing teenager, David needed his sleep and took a break to nap at our campsite. I remained, riding solo, in the still air where all I could hear was the buzz of my tires on the pavement and an occasional shifting gear.

It was absolutely peaceful, almost meditative. The heat of the day had dissipated, and I felt as though I was riding through a tunnel of light, forged through the darkness with the headlight on the front of my bike. I would occasionally pass other riders, seeing their hypnotic red flashing tail lights as I approached. It was in these laps that I felt the most alive. My pedaling became so smooth and effortless that it felt as if there was no chain on the bike. I had heard references to being "in the zone" before, and if this is what it felt like, I wanted to live in there for a very long time.

I felt no fatigue and was numb to any effort. My mind wandered back to how I had come to be there, to thoughts of good friends lost to cancer and how cancer had changed my life and the lives of my family. I thought of Madison as being my hope for the future after I was gone. She has no idea just how much she is loved and how I hope that one day she will be able to look back and smile, remembering her goofy mother, and know that I was so very proud of her. In that way, I would not die, because I could live on in her and her memories.

Indianapolis had been experiencing a drought for many months prior to the event. Not a drop of rain had fallen anywhere and the corn crops were in danger of withering but at 3 am during the 24 hour charity ride, a huge storm came out of nowhere and swept through campus with tornado like winds and torrential rain. We were removed from the course and told to take shelter.

Although I was sorry to stop riding, I was relieved to be able to elevate my hand and rest. It was difficult to remove my cycling glove because the edema was severe at this point. My hand didn't look like my hand at all. It reminded me of my brother's large hands. The swelling dissipated somewhat, but did not go away completely. I began massaging and wrapping my hand with bandages to try to make the edema go away with pressure and time. It was indeed lymphedema, and I HATED the fact that there was something else from cancer that continued to torture me. It was an ever present reminder that I was still fighting its effects.

When I had surgery to remove the lymph nodes in my left arm, I had been cautioned to watch for any signs of swelling, otherwise known as "Lymphedema." The doctor warned me to wear gloves while gardening and avoid getting cuts of any kind on my left hand, as well as no longer having my blood pressure checked on that side. There would to be no blood drawn or shots given in that arm as well. Taking trips to areas with high altitude or traveling in an airplane were also risky because of the change in air pressure.

I had seen breast cancer survivors with large, swollen arms covered by compression sleeves, and thought that perhaps they had more lymph node involvement than I did. It was always in the back of my mind and I'm sure that my family thought I was obsessive, trying to avoid any injury to my left hand. I had been quite fortunate all the times I had flown to Colorado, traveled to Copper Mountain, and flown to Japan, China and Korea for Special Olympics, that I had experienced no problems with my arm or hand. Still, I had that constant concern in the back of my mind.

There was only one time that I can think of that I let my guard slip. And once is all it takes, I suppose. Since I visit clinical areas for my job, I am required to get a TB test every year. Two months earlier, I was due to get my annual TB test. Since most people are right handed the injections are commonly given in the left forearm. For over 30 years I had been getting shots in that arm. I was engrossed in conversation with my co-worker, who was administering the shot, and I forgot to alert her about my arm and she forgot to ask. The needle went in the left forearm and I didn't realize what I had allowed until later.

I made an appointment with Barbara Feltman, the physical therapist who specialized in breast cancer treatment and had helped me with my cording when no one else could. She confirmed that it was Lymphedema and taught me how to wrap my hand and arm to control the swelling until I could get a fitted glove. As the glove was custom made, it took weeks to get, and was very expensive.

Going to work was also a reminder that was hard to avoid. Since I saw different people almost every day and interacted with them on a personal level, they noticed my bandaged hand and invariably asked, "What have you done to yourself?" I know they were just being concerned and caring friends, but this started to annoy me after a while. It was not the people that annoyed me, but the fact that it was so apparent and I could not conceal it.

I would explain, "Its lymphedema, a side effect of my breast cancer treatment. When the lymph nodes in my left arm were removed, it removed the pumps that move the lymph fluid out of the hand and arm. I now have swelling with nothing to help move the fluid out of my hand and arm. The glove is used for pressure to keep it from blowing up like a balloon." The usual response is, "Oh."

*   *   *

After my experience conducting the coaching clinic in Japan, I realized that being a technical delegate could possibly be a way to build a legacy even greater than one- on- one coaching. Special Olympics International had asked me in 2007 if I would be interested in that role for speed skating world games. The technical delegate is responsible for ensuring that all aspects of competition meet the requirements and expectations of a world class event, while taking the needs of Special Olympians into full consideration. The responsibilities include everything from: venue selection, temperature of the ice, athlete compliance with safety requirements, conducting meetings with head coaches and officials, enforcing rules, overseeing the protest and complaint process, approving final results, and accommodating VIPs.

At that time I told them that I was not interested, because I found coaching Team USA very rewarding. For selfish reasons, I was not ready to give that up. And in 2009 I returned as coach for Team USA at World Games.

In 2011, I was asked again to be a technical delegate, and after much thought, realized that I would be coaching all the head coaches at the games and would have a greater impact on the athletes, although it would be indirectly. The World Winter Games in 2013 were to be held in South Korea. As technical delegates, we were required to travel to the proposed competition locations, on multiple occasions, to meet with the games organizing committee and work out the details.

Once an understanding and agreement had been made regarding the venues, a trial competition, referred to as the pre-games, was held in 2012. Pre-games are a smaller version of the World Games, with the purpose of testing the venue and shaking out any bugs before the actual event a year later. This gave the organizing committee enough time to resolve any issues discovered by the Technical Delegates. The Special Olympics Winter World Games would serve as the pre-games for the regular Winter Olympic Games to be held at the same venue in 2018.

Ursula Jankowska had been the Speed skating technical delegate, previously in Nagano and Boise for the last two Special Olympics World Games and she was ready to step down from that position. As Head Coach, I had enjoyed working with her and now we would be working side by side. Ursula, from Poland, was on the Olympic Committee for her country and had worked very closely with the International Olympic Committee. She spoke English very well and had an infectious accent. Every time I came home from a trip with Ursula, I would find myself speaking with her accent for the first few days. She stood about five feet, two inches tall, had green eyes that flashed behind her glasses and reddish blonde shoulder length hair. She was older than I, but still had a youthful adventurous spirit. We went on a few shopping and sightseeing trips together in downtown Seoul before the games were to begin.

We made a great team due to her experience working with the officials, as well as the details of timing and scheduling. My experience as a coach helped me address issues from the coaches and athletes perspectives.

During the games, Ken was on the coaching staff for Team USA. Even though we were both there, in the same venue, we very rarely had the opportunity to see or speak with one another. It was still comforting to know he was there. I did get to catch glimpses of him from across the rink a few times, and felt that, even though we were separated, we were still working together to make this the best experience possible for the skaters, who were living what might be the brightest moments of their lives.

Speedskating was to have a spotlight exhibition event that drew celebrity and media attention. I was to select a race that would be focused on for that event. I chose the relay for speedskating's spotlight. A relay is a team race with four skaters on each team. VIPs were designated to participate with the athletes on the teams. In a relay the racers can either exchange skaters with a push or a tap.

Relays are very exciting to watch, but also very complicated. I wanted to make sure that the skaters understood how the relays were conducted and had an opportunity to practice before the actual race. The day before the relay we held a clinic for the Special Olympians and their coaches and by the end of the clinic we were confident that all of them had the knowledge and skills they needed to race safely.

As an exhibition, the teams of four were to be composed of two Special Olympians with two celebrities. Most of the celebrities were Olympic speed skating gold medalists from various countries, including Dan Jansen and Apolo Ohno, from the United States, Catriona Le May Doan from Canada, along with Ko GI-Hyun, who was also the Sport Manager and my friend and partner in the execution of the games. Since the games were held in Korea, there were many other South Korean Olympic gold medalists in attendance as well. Other celebrities volunteered to participate on teams. I was assured that they had backgrounds in skating, just not speed skating. Some of them had never seen a relay, let alone participate in one; therefore I was a bit concerned and gave them instructions in the ready room before the event. Recognizing that there was still some uncertainty, I asked, "Would you like me to come out on the ice with you and run through a few of the exchanges before the race?" This proposal got a resounding, "Yes, please!"

We took the warm-up time to run through and practice a few exchanges. I was pleased that most of the VIPs who were not speedskaters were picking it up very well. There was one dignitary from an eastern bloc country, however, who did not appear at the warm-up session and this concerned me. An assistant informed me that they were still attempting to find skates for her. Once she appeared, I could see the terror in her eyes as she stepped onto the ice. The door to the rink opened and she took her first step onto the ice and immediately fell hard. When I tried to assist her, she turned and refused to go any further and clamored to get off the ice. For a brief moment I was stunned. What were we going to do? The team would be short one team member. In a flash the resolution occurred to me and I asked a volunteer to retrieve the VIP's helmet and I took her place on the relay team. I was not planning to skate in the event and had not warmed up or participated in a relay in quite a few years. Gi-Hyun was on the team, which eased some of my concerns and once again my years of training paid off. When I returned to the official's area, the look in my assistant's eyes said it all. "I didn't know you could skate fast!" she said. I laughed and told her, "That is all part of my job as TD, being ready to do anything at any time to get the job done."

Working in this role had its share of challenges and rewards, but for me personally, the biggest reward came on the last day of competition. Before the races were to start, I looked out the door of my office to see the skaters from the Netherlands team warming up before competition. When I realized that there was no coach with them and they were coaching each other I was impressed. A few of the more advanced skaters were helping their teammate's stretch and practice technique drills.

As I went out to compliment them, I was once again surprised when I saw the Canadian team jogging down the hallway warming up; they too were without a coach and were well organized and supportive of one another. To top it off, the two teams, from different countries, stopped and greeted each other with genuine friendship. Although they were competitors who didn't speak the same language, their blossoming pride, skill, confidence, independence and humanitarian spirit served as a fine example for us all to follow. It was a testimony of the spirit and success of the games.

*   *   *

On a bright sunny day in June of 2013, I found myself sitting patiently in quiet anticipation in an institutional folding chair. The expansive convention center room was crowded with parents and families milling about, finding seats and settling in. Words that had fortified me throughout my cancer treatment echoed loudly in my mind. Almost exactly nine years earlier during my very first appointment to see Dr. Miller, she had said, "If you want to live to see your daughter graduate from high school, you will undergo chemotherapy." I sat with Ken, my mother, my brother and his wife in quiet anticipation, as names of Madison's classmates were called to receive their diplomas.

Dr. Miller's words were even more poignant, since the day before I had been sitting in a hospital gown in quiet anticipation, waiting to see Dr. Miller. She had discovered that my cancer spread during an annual oncology exam five years earlier. Dr. Miller walked in and sat across from me as we casually talked about the new electronic medical record system she was now using.

She initiated my physical exam by deftly sliding her smooth, cool fingers around my neck, searching for any changes in lymph nodes. She listened to my lungs and asked if I had any trouble breathing or bone pain. I told her "No." as she continued to explore my underarms looking for any other possible signs of invasion by evil cancer cells. Finding nothing unusual, she told me that I would be given a prescription for another year of hormone suppression and she would see me again in a year.

I challenged her, "Can't I stop the hormone suppression now? It's been five years since my last recurrence." "Current research leads us to believe that 10 years on this medication will help you live a lot longer," she returned. "Can I have any testing to see if the tumors have spread anywhere else?" "No." she replied, "Now we just *watch and learn.*" Again, my father's words impacting my life.

*   *   *

Madison's name was announced and we watched, on the edge of our seats as she proudly and confidently sailed across the stage, with a red graduation gown flowing over her white dress, to receive her diploma with high honors. She had blossomed into such an incredible young woman and I had been there to see it happen. There is no wealth greater; no pride more deeply felt, no gold medal podium more glorious, no love more heartfelt than to be able to see your child grow into a confident and happy adult. To think that I could have missed that moment, even missed the last five years of my life, inspires me to be grateful and DETERMINED to make a change for others and even angrier that the threat of cancer exists at all.

After announcing the graduates of the class of 2013, air was filled with flying red caps, and everyone struggled to find their loved ones. Madison and her friends and classmates were all buzzing around, sharing hugs and mugging for the cameras. Of course I fulfilled my motherly duty, snapping photos as she posed with friends she had known since kindergarten. It was a bittersweet moment of celebration and realization that she may never see many of her friends again. I was pleased to see that she did not miss the opportunity to celebrate with Mauren, one of the special needs friends that Madison had known since elementary school and had helped mentor through photography class over the past year.

So many thoughts darted through my mind; so many emotions stirred in my heart. When you learn that you are expecting, there are hundreds of books available that are filled with advice and direction, as well as an endless supply of anecdotes and suggestions from friends and family. Labor typically lasts less than a day, and at the end you have beautiful velvet skinned baby in your arms with an unbelievably addictive "new baby" smell.

Through the infant and toddler years there are books to read about feeding, teaching, molding and shaping your children until they get to school. There are no books, no clear cut guidelines or real advice on how to give birth to an adult. The labor is nearly 17 years long and can sometimes be painful. Some mothers experience a feeling of depression after giving birth, called postpartum depression, but I did not. What do you call it when you realize that your baby will never again run and jump into your arms and give you a full body hug as if you were the only person on earth or when they no longer depend on you for just about everything and only need you for tuition and gas money? There is no book, no advice, just an empty hole in your heart, longing for another genuine hug wrapped in the exuberant joy of childhood. You would return that hug with the knowledge that you would die for them in a heartbeat if need be.

As I watched Madison buzz like a bee from friend to friend in the hive of the convention center, that hole in my heart was momentarily filled with the knowledge and understanding that this was the way life was supposed to be. Our goal for Madison was to get her to this point. My goal for chemo was to get me to this point. The realization that we had both arrived was enough to make me feel weak in the knees, yet full in my heart and light in the head.

When Madison was asked by friends and relatives what course of study she was going to pursue, she told them, without a glimmer of hesitation or doubt, "I am going to be a surgeon and do for others what my mom's doctors did for her." She wanted to be a surgeon, like Dr. Sood and Dr. Goulet, and was determined to do everything she could to make that happen. She had shadowed them both and witnessed the dignity of life they helped restore for many who were dealt the disfiguring breast cancer card. After shadowing Dr. Goulet in surgery, she was even more confident, that was what she would do.

When you live life as a goal oriented person, as I have, you place many aspirations and goals on the horizon and do everything you can to arrive at the point of crossing that finish line. Madison's graduation from high school was one of those landmarks that I was very grateful to be able to attain and to celebrate with my family. I look forward to being there for Madison as she crosses over into every new stage of her life's race.

I have been fortunate enough to have seen my daughter grow up and my parents grow old. Now, looking over at Ken and seeing his hair streaked with silver, I feel honored and look forward to being able to witness and participate in our original dream that was once threatened; growing old together. One day I hope that we will be able to look back over our lives and say, "That was a race well run."

*   *   *

The more difficulties one has to encounter, within and without, the more significant and the higher in inspiration his life will be.

Horace Bushnell

Acknowledgements:

Writing a book is not an isolated endeavor. It takes teamwork. Crossing the finish line could not have happened without help from my team.

The race to completion would never have begun if it hadn't been for the persistence of my daughter, Madison Hart, insisting, "Mom. Just write the book," and Sandy Poremba who gave me the encouragement, drive and support to get things down on paper and invested her time and energy in making it happen. Their faith in my story and the need to share it with others is why this book is here. Thank you for entering me into the race.

Thank you, Ken Hart, for sacrificing and understanding the many dinners I didn't cook, and general housekeeping and attention that I would have given you had I not been immersed in getting this done.

Thank you to Joy Fowler, for early edits and mentoring. Your patient grace in leading me through discovering my voice is greatly appreciated.

Additional thanks to the other members of my team:

JJ Kaplan - Color my World studio for her photographic skill and talent in the book cover.

Brian Wind - Graphics and content editing

Tim Wozniak- Analytical eye and steady wheel

Jay Bodkin and Julie Wind - Helping me stay on track and acting as my sounding board through the trials of the writing process

Anna Dorner - Fresh editing eyes

Cyclists Combating Cancer (ww.ridetolive.org)

Spokes of Hope (www.spokesofhope.org)

IndySpeed Sports Club (www.indyspeed.org)

Special Olympics (www.specialolympics.org

CPSIA information can be obtained at www.ICGtesting.com
Printed in the USA
LVOW04s0813081014

407587LV00010B/1/P